IMAGES
of America

ANTELOPE COUNTY

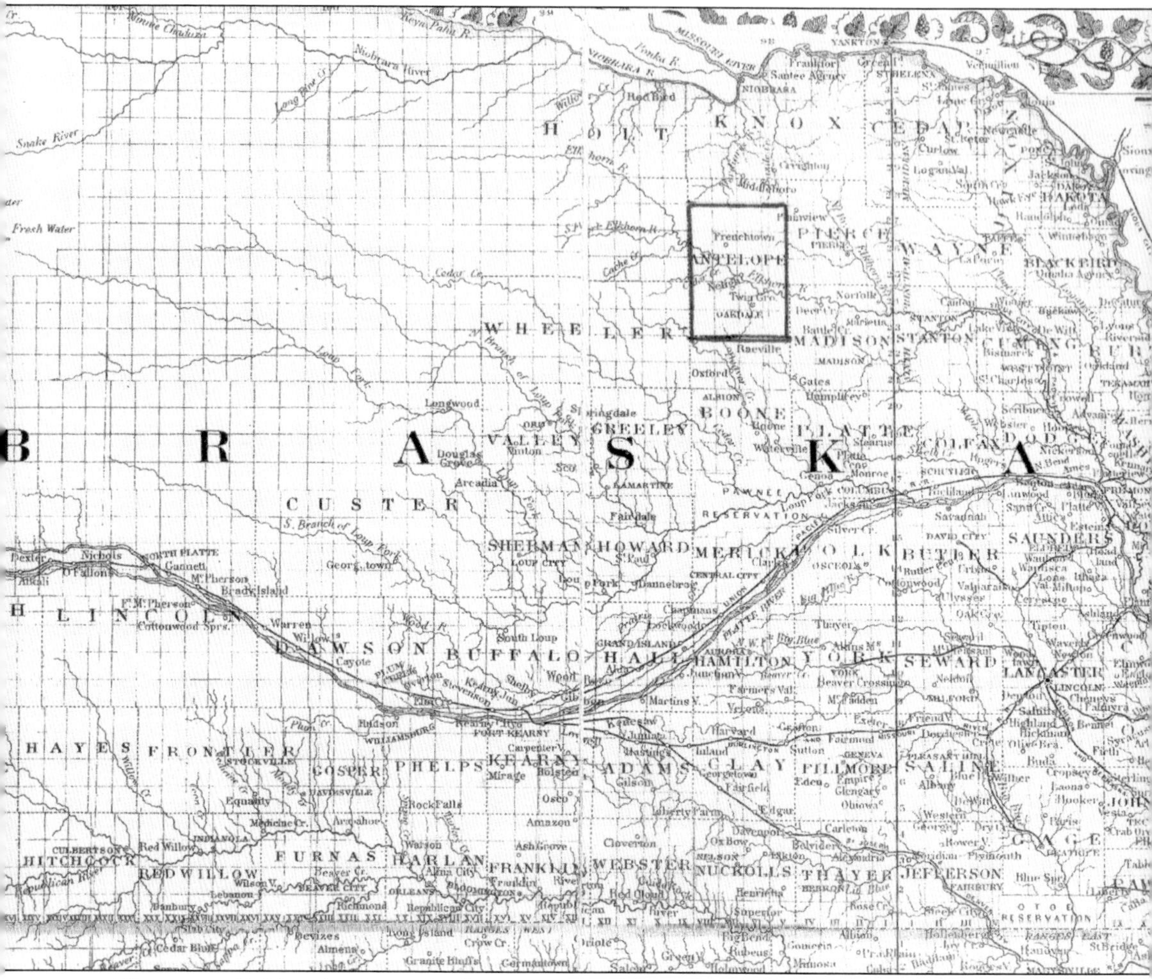

This map of Nebraska shows the location of Antelope County in the northeastern part of the state. Prior to the county's founding in 1871, buffalo fed on the area's lush prairie grasses and were hunted by Native Americans. Fur traders named the river running diagonally through the area the Elkhorn because its branches resembled the horns of an elk. (Courtesy of Kenneth Krohn.)

On the Cover: Stacking hay was a hot and dusty summer activity on Antelope County farms. This unidentified farmer sits on a horse-powered hay sweep. After the sweep gathered the hay, a stacker lifted it onto the growing haystack. Horse-drawn wagons transported the hay to farmyards and barn hay mows to feed livestock in the winter. (Courtesy of the Antelope County Historical Society.)

IMAGES
of America

ANTELOPE COUNTY

Marie Krohn

ARCADIA
PUBLISHING

ISBN 978-0-7385-9887-1

Published by Arcadia Publishing
Charleston, South Carolina

Printed in the United States of America

Library of Congress Control Number: 2012952345

For all general information, please contact Arcadia Publishing:
Telephone 843-853-2070
Fax 843-853-0044
E-mail sales@arcadiapublishing.com
For customer service and orders:
Toll-Free 1-888-313-2665

Visit us on the Internet at www.arcadiapublishing.com

To the residents of Antelope County

Contents

ACKNOWLEDGMENTS

The Antelope County Historical Society Archives supplied many of the photographs used in this book, which are credited as "ACHS." The archives also contain town histories that I referred to when writing introductions for each community. I thank Pat Kenaston of the Antelope County Jail Museum for loaning me the histories during the past year. I also thank Jennifer Norton of the Neligh Public Library for allowing me to check out town histories for an extended period of time.

Several individuals responded to my requests for additional images and loaned photographs from their personal files. I thank the following people for allowing use of their photographs: Lois Johnson, who supplied many of the Oakdale images; Dr. George Strassler, who loaned additional photographs; Arlene Hofmann, who supplied Tilden images from her personal collection; Walter Patras, who loaned photographs for the Clearwater section from his extensive collection; Robert Busteed and Marie Vanderheiden, who added photographs to the Elgin chapter; the Orchard Historical Society, which sent four photographs; and Duard Dempster, who shared additional Orchard photographs from his family albums. Prior to his death, Eldon Marsh of Brunswick donated the Rose photograph collection to the Antelope County Historical Society, and that collection made up the majority of Brunswick photographs. Author and historian Dick Haskin also allowed the use of Haskin family photographs for the Royal area, and Patty Rader Eucker's photographs added to the Royal section. Vanita M. Thomsen supplied photographs of the former Rundquist store in Royal.

For helping me request photographs from individuals and for scanning them according to Arcadia's specifications, I thank my husband, Kenneth Krohn. I am also grateful for his encouraging words and for reading and identifying mistakes in the manuscript. Local computer technician Walt Storey kept our computers running and helped with scanning. Our daughter Alison Krohn and son-in-law Rob McEntarffer also helped solve technical problems.

My Arcadia editors, Jill Nunn and Winnie Timmons, have been cheerful guides throughout the writing and publication process and deserve a special thank-you.

INTRODUCTION

Named for the frisky and elusive animals that bounded across the prairie, Antelope County is located in the center of Nebraska's northeastern corner. Stretching 36 miles long and 24 miles wide, the county's gently rolling slopes are bisected by the Elkhorn River Valley.

An Indian Office map from 1797 and the Lewis and Clark composite map of 1814 were the first to show the Elkhorn River flowing through the future county. French Canadian fur traders named the river. Because its branches resemble an elk's horn, the traders called the river Corn-de-Cerf, or "horn of the elk."

In addition to the fur traders' activity in the area, transient Indians camped on land in the vicinity of present-day Neligh. The Pawnee tribe claimed large amounts of land in the region, and the Lakota Sioux, Cheyenne, and Arapahoe tribes periodically hunted in the territory. After the Lewis and Clark expedition of 1804–1806 proved the possibility of overland travel to the Pacific coast, adventure-seeking individuals soon began trekking westward. Although reports from the 1806 expedition of Lt. Zebulon Pike and the 1819 excursion of Maj. Stephen Long declared the Great Plains useless for human habitation due to the sparse amount of timber and surface water, more perceptive travelers noted that the abundant grasses growing on the plains supported herds of bison. Bluestem, wild oats, red top, and buffalo grasses were among several varieties that grew in the county and were considered a natural resource.

With the passage of the Homestead Act in 1862 and the end of the Civil War in 1865, the lure of starting a new life on unclaimed land west of the Mississippi River was an irresistible force, similar to the magnetic pull of the 1848 gold discovery that drew prospectors to California. This time, the prize was land ownership rather than gold.

In 1867, Michael J. Hughes was the first temporary settler in the Antelope County region. He resided on the north side of the Elkhorn River, but excessive visits from Native Americans caused him to move to West Point, Nebraska. Early in 1868, George St. Clair built a cabin beside a creek near present-day Tilden. He had trapped on the Elkhorn River and knew the country well before taking his homestead, which contained the finest oak timber in the county. Although he abandoned his claim, St. Clair Creek still bears his name. Allan Hopkins filed the next recorded claim, and his settlement was permanent.

The Nebraska Legislature approved an act to form the county on March 1, 1871, four years after Nebraska's statehood had been established. Stories vary about the selection of the county name, but they all involve Leander Gerard, a member of the Nebraska Legislature in 1871. One story reports that he suggested the name because he shot an antelope for food while he and his companions were on the trail of Indians near Columbus, Nebraska. A second version claims that Gerard was accompanying a group searching for a homestead in northeastern Nebraska when he shot the antelope to supplement their dwindling food supply.

When the Civil War ended, railroads expanded their lines farther west, penetrating the Great Plains. The description of the area was transformed from "the Great American Desert" to the statement that "rain follows the plow." Other railroad advertisements touted smooth soil that was easy to till as well as a healthy climate and picturesque scenery.

After emigrants from New England and the Midwest rode the ferry across the Missouri River, they discovered that the Nebraska land surrounding the river had already been claimed. Often, they were advised to travel farther west to the fertile soil of the Elkhorn Valley. When the newcomers arrived, they tended to claim land in places that reminded them of their home states, and the treed area along the river valley was soon occupied. Those coming later were forced to settle farther from the river, and they discovered that the upland soil was just as fertile as the river valley land.

The first towns in the county, Oakdale, established in 1872, and Neligh, founded in 1873, engaged in a 10-year feud over which would be the county seat. When the election to organize the county was held in October 1871, Oakdale settlers overlooked the designation of a county seat because they did not have a copy of the State Statutes of Nebraska, which stipulated that a county seat should be named at the election. Before a second election took place in October 1872, John Neligh completed a petition for Neligh to become the county seat and sent a young man to deliver it. Unfortunately, the messenger lost his way and arrived after the submission deadline. Oakdale was subsequently named the county seat. Several elections took place in the following years to determine whether Oakdale or Neligh should house county government, and Neligh won the final vote in 1883.

By December 1, 1879, the railroad reached the Antelope County line. A week later, it arrived in Oakdale, and in July 1880 it made its way to Neligh. Clearwater Station was established in the fall of 1880. After the Fremont, Elkhorn & Missouri Valley Railroad erected a depot on the line dividing Madison and Antelope Counties in 1879, the town of Tilden was organized in 1880. Orchard, originally named Pacific Townsite, was one of several towns founded after the Chicago, Burlington & Quincy Railroad built a line from Sioux City, Iowa, to O'Neill, Nebraska. Brunswick, founded in 1890, was on the same route. Royal was also organized in 1890 along the Sioux City-to-O'Neill line. Elgin, created in 1887, changed the direction of its Main Street to correspond with the direction of the railroad.

Trains contributed to the county's growth, bringing settlers to claim government land. In 1877, the population was 1,036, and by 1883 it had grown to 6,407. In addition to carrying passengers, trains transported agricultural products and delivered cattle and hogs to market. The Neligh and Oakdale mills used the railroad to import additional grains, grind them into flour, and then ship it to other areas of the country.

Gristmills played a vital role in the rural economies of the late 1800s and early 1900s. Farmers delivered their grain to the nearest mill, exchanging it for flour or selling it to a miller directly. The price paid for grain varied with the seasons and with the national economy. Invariably, the winter months brought the highest prices. Gradually, large corporations dominated the milling industry, and small town mills were forced to shut down.

Since the county's founding in 1871, nearly a century and a half has passed, and the passage of time has brought inevitable changes. The most significant change has been the loss of people. The population, which peaked in 1920 with a count of 15,243, has declined in each succeeding decade. The 2010 census reported a total of 6,685 people.

Patterns of land usage have also changed. At the beginning of county settlement, farms averaged 160 acres, while today's farms often cover 1,000 acres. With advances in farming technology, fewer people are needed to grow and harvest crops. Today, only 27 percent of the county residents are engaged in agriculture.

Faced with the demographic changes of the past century, Antelope County residents have responded with the characteristic resourcefulness of their pioneering ancestors. Whatever the future holds, Antelope County residents will continue to adapt to the changes in unique and appropriate ways.

One

Beginnings
Early Settlement

When Crandall Hopkins rode across the Missouri River from Council Bluffs to Omaha in 1869, he asked the ferryman where he might find the best government land. The pilot advised Hopkins that the Elkhorn River Valley had the most fertile soil and the healthiest climate. Heeding the ferryman's advice, Hopkins traveled with his family to the Elkhorn Valley.

After Antelope County was founded in 1871, other settlers began trickling into the valley. Early county historian A.J. Leach stated that many early pioneers were skeptical about the possibility of making a living on the grassy land; nevertheless, newcomers took their chances and began taming the prairie into productive farmland. By June 15, 1871, county officials were elected to hold office until the general election in October 1871. The officers had little to do since they lacked books in which to keep records and because they did not collect taxes. The county superintendent was the only official who kept a log. In the back of his private account book, he recorded the organization of seven school districts.

The years spanning 1869 to 1873 produced sufficient garden vegetables and grain crops to encourage settlers to remain, and they established the first church in 1873. By 1874, drought and grasshoppers drove many pioneers from their claims; some returned, but many fled back to their home states. When the grasshopper plagues ended, the remaining farmers began growing and harvesting grain crops. They delivered their grain to the gristmills in Oakdale and Neligh for processing into flour. After the railroad came to the area, six more towns sprang up along the train lines, and the county prospered.

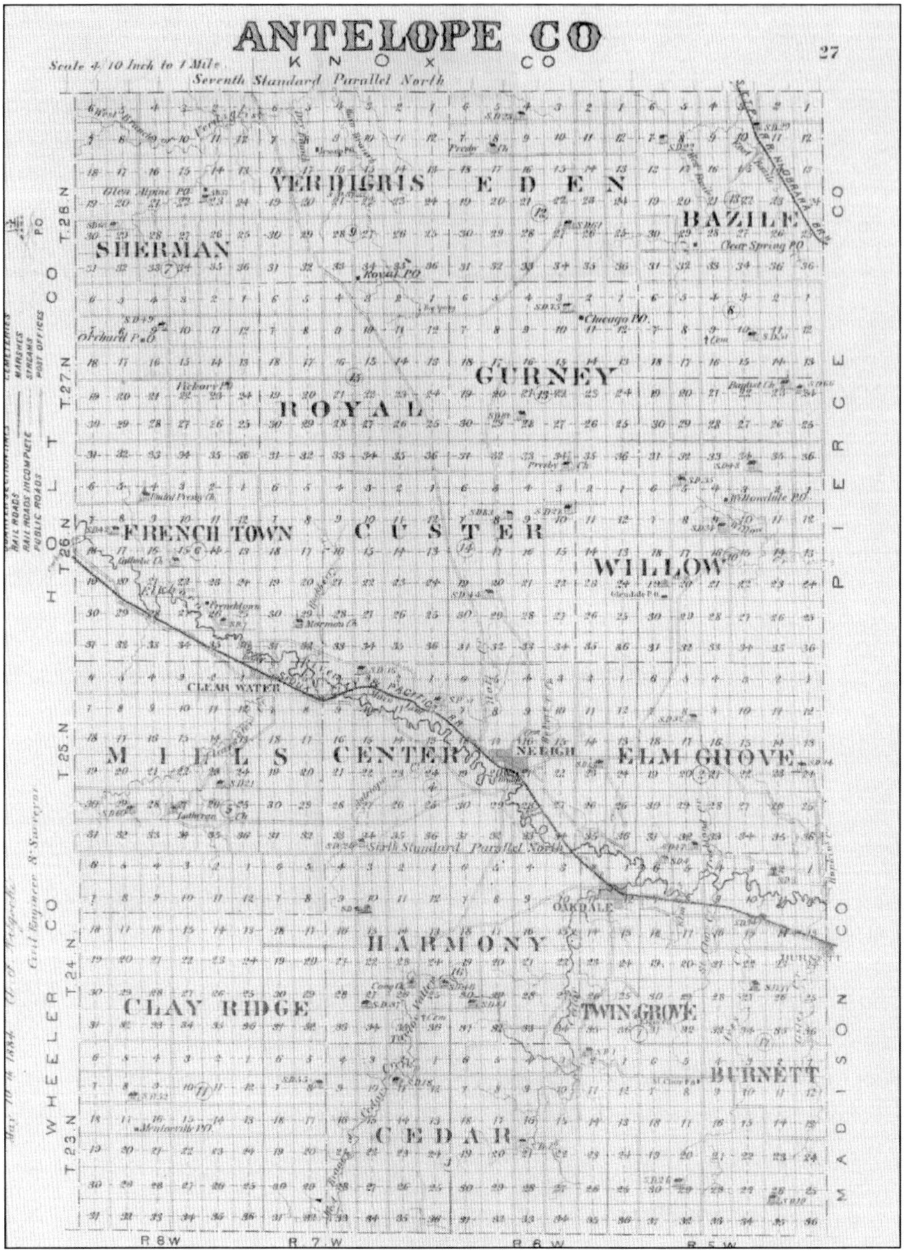

Antelope County is 36 miles long and 24 miles wide, creating a proportion of three to two. The county contains 8,064 square miles, or 552,960 acres. If the state of Nebraska is divided into four equal parts with a horizontal line across the middle, east to west, and a vertical line through the middle, north to south, Antelope County is in the exact center of the northeastern quarter of the state. The Elkhorn River bisects the county. Located in the river valley, Neligh has an elevation of 1,761 feet. The uplands on either side of the valley are 50 to 250 feet higher than the valley. Only the towns that the railroad connected are shown on this map: Burnett (Tilden), Oakdale, Neligh, and the newly formed Clearwater. Jessup is listed as a post office. Elgin, Brunswick, and Orchard were not yet towns. The county population at this time, in 1884, was about 5,000 people, or six people per square mile. (Courtesy of Kenneth Krohn.)

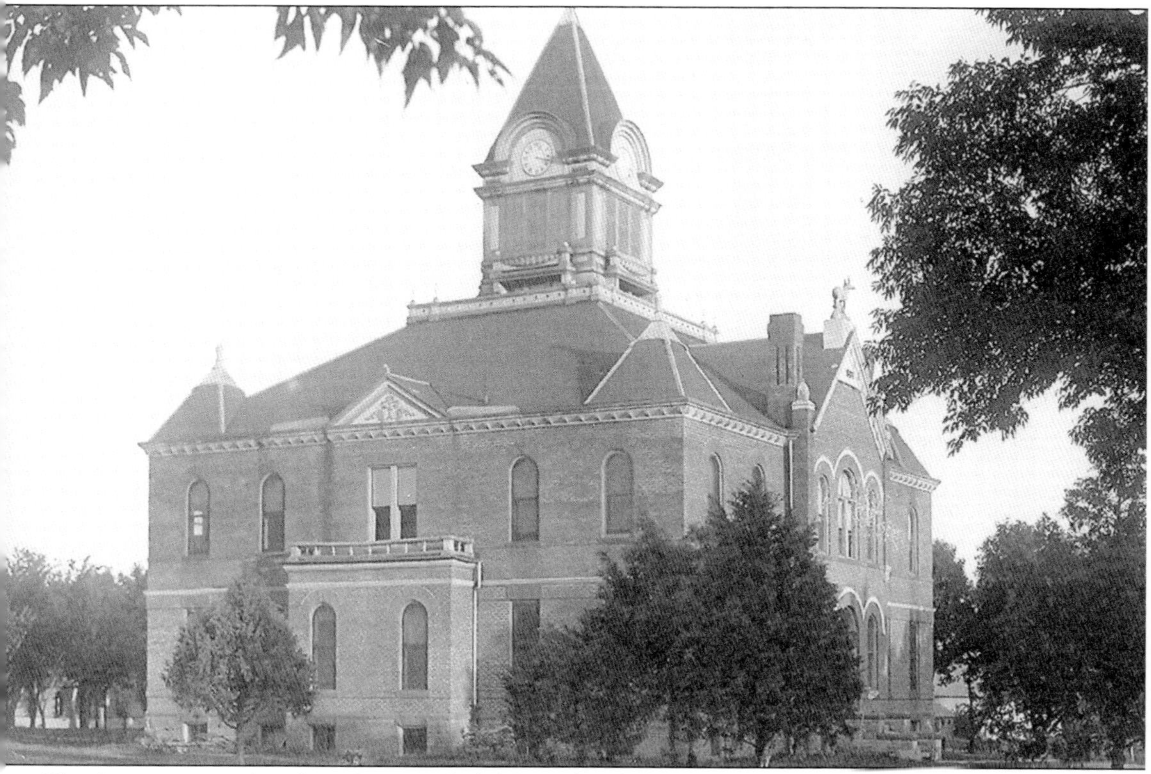

The first towns in Antelope County, Oakdale and Neligh, engaged in a 10-year feud over the location of the county seat. In 1871, Oakdale settlers failed to stipulate a county seat during an election for the county's organization, while John Neligh's messenger carrying the petition to name Neligh as the county seat lost his way en route. In 1872, state officials declared Oakdale the county seat. Neligh challenged their choice in four elections and won the final vote in October 1883. Neligh began serving as the government center on January 1, 1884. Because of controversy over the financing of the construction of a new courthouse, government offices were located in a temporary building. After a mill levy passed, work began on the official structure, with the total cost not to exceed $1,500. Fred Thornton was the architect, and T.H. Benton supplied bricks from his Neligh brickyard. The building was dedicated on January 8, 1885. (ACHS.)

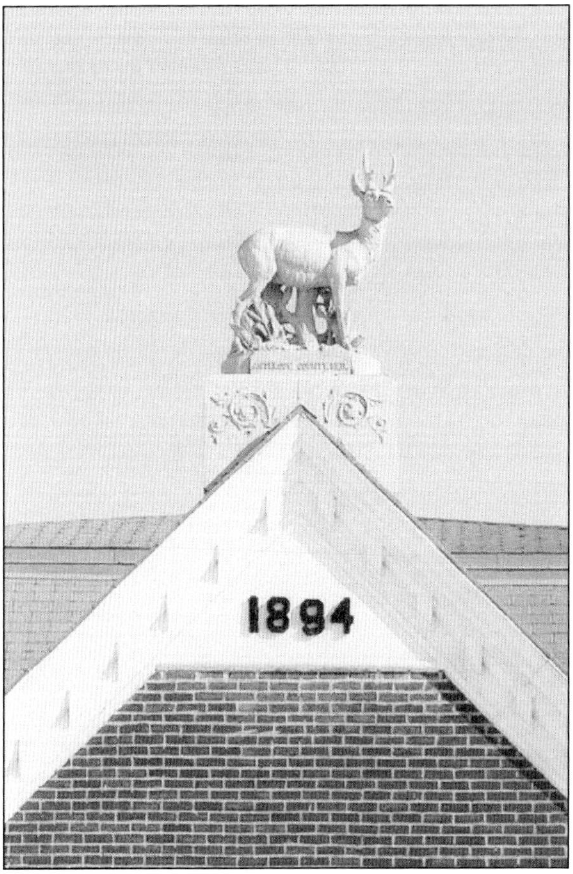

The women of the county decided that the courthouse needed to display the county symbol, and they took action to buy an antelope statue, financing the purchase through the sale of commemorative plates. The completed antelope statue traveled to the 1893 World's Fair in Chicago for display before returning to Neligh. It was placed on the west side of the courthouse, where it remains today. (ACHS.)

In 1868, Crandall Hopkins (left) and his wife, Thankful (right), along with their 12 children, arrived in Antelope County. Their oldest son, Allen, claimed the first homestead recorded in the county, on September 9, 1868. Crandall entered as an Antelope County homesteader on October 22, 1868. The family built a log house on Allen's claim. It was the first house erected within the county limits. (ACHS.)

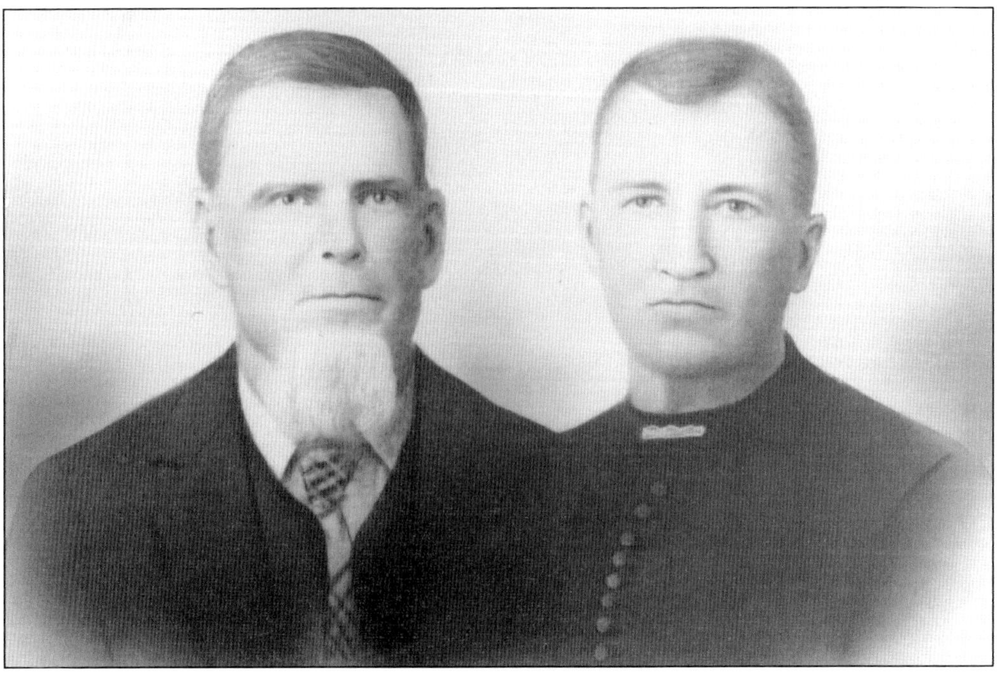

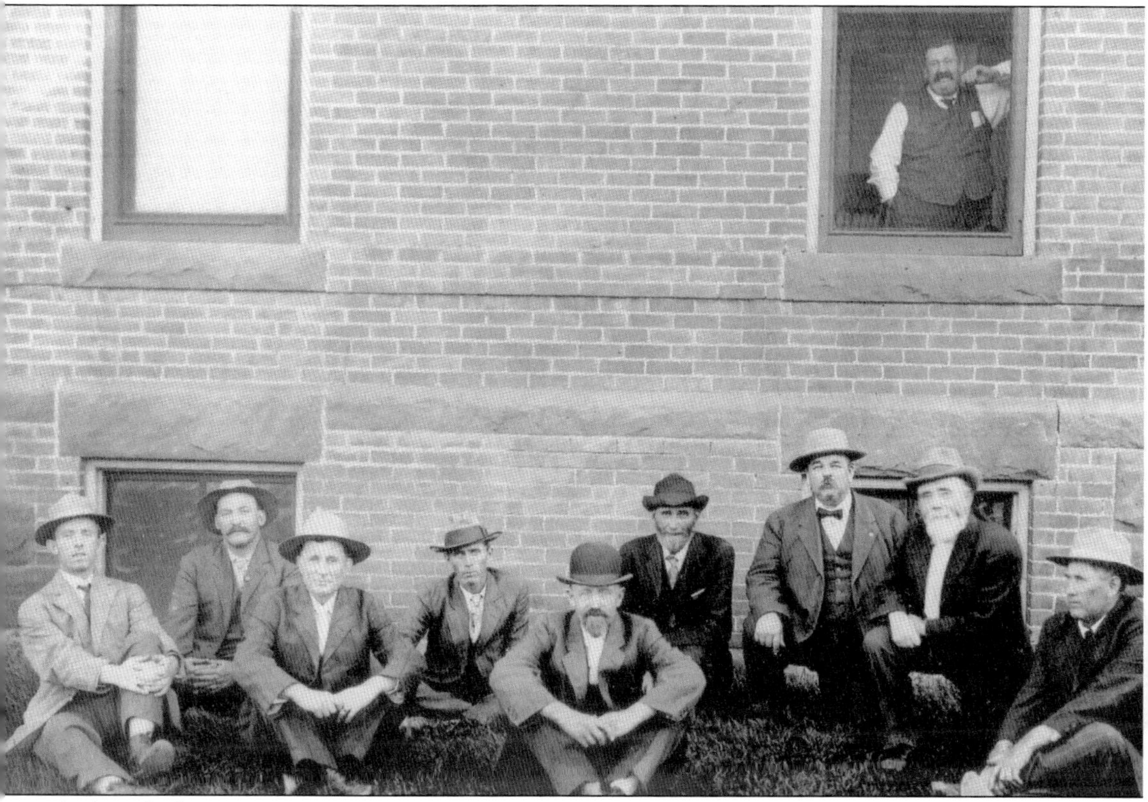

The board of commissioners governed Antelope County from 1871 until 1888, when the board membership changed from commissioners to supervisors. In 1915, the county supervisors and officers posed for this informal photograph outside the courthouse in Neligh. Standing in the window is George Fletcher, the treasurer. Seated from left to right are John Lamson, M.M. Mitchell, George Sweet, Lorenz Thomsen, George McGee, unidentified, Henry Reutzel, T. Everson, and P.W. Payne. (ACHS.)

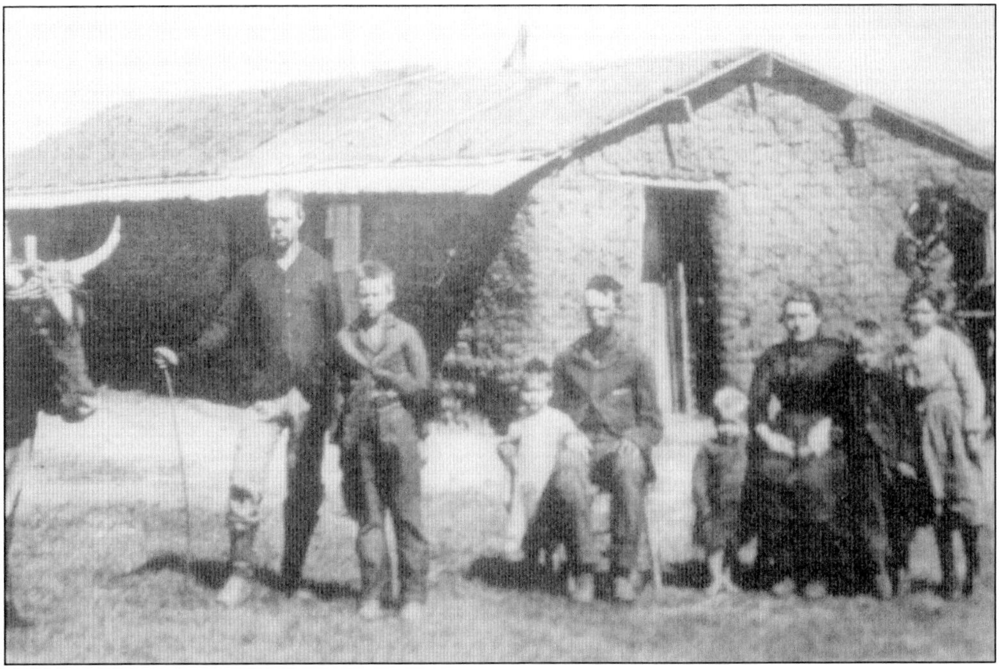

There were several sawmills in the Burnett/Tilden vicinity, and early settlers constructed log houses, frame houses, or dugouts. After the native timber was exhausted, pioneers began building sod houses. Many settlers claimed that sod houses were more comfortable because they were cool in summer and warm in winter. This early family stands in front of their sod house around 1885. (Courtesy of Arlene Hofmann.)

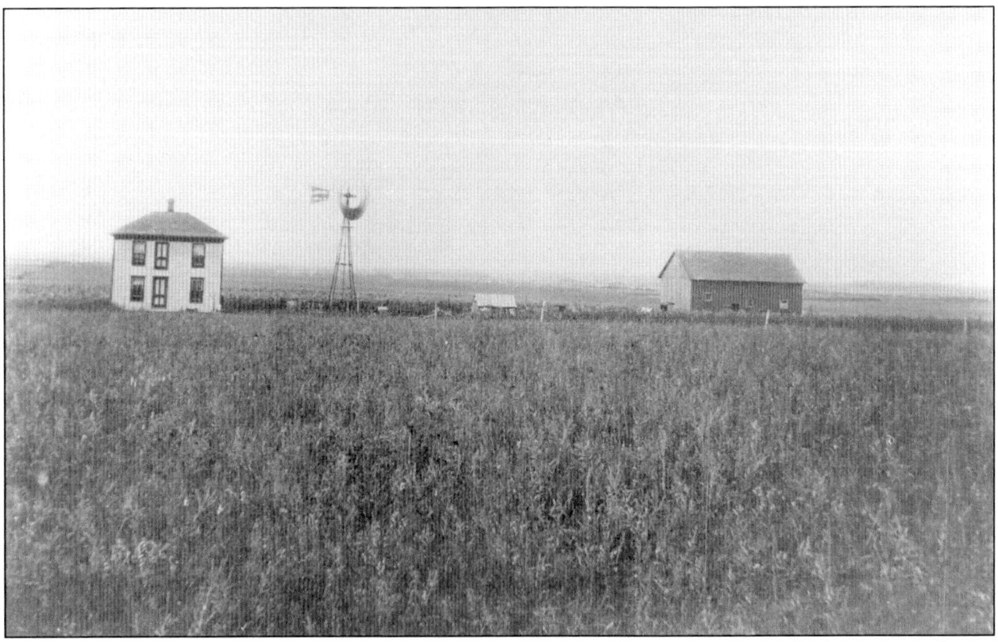

This typical homestead in the Oakdale vicinity, seen around 1890, consists of a foursquare frame house, a windmill, a hog pen, and a barn. A crop of small grain is growing in the field, and there are no trees in sight. (Courtesy of Lois Johnson.)

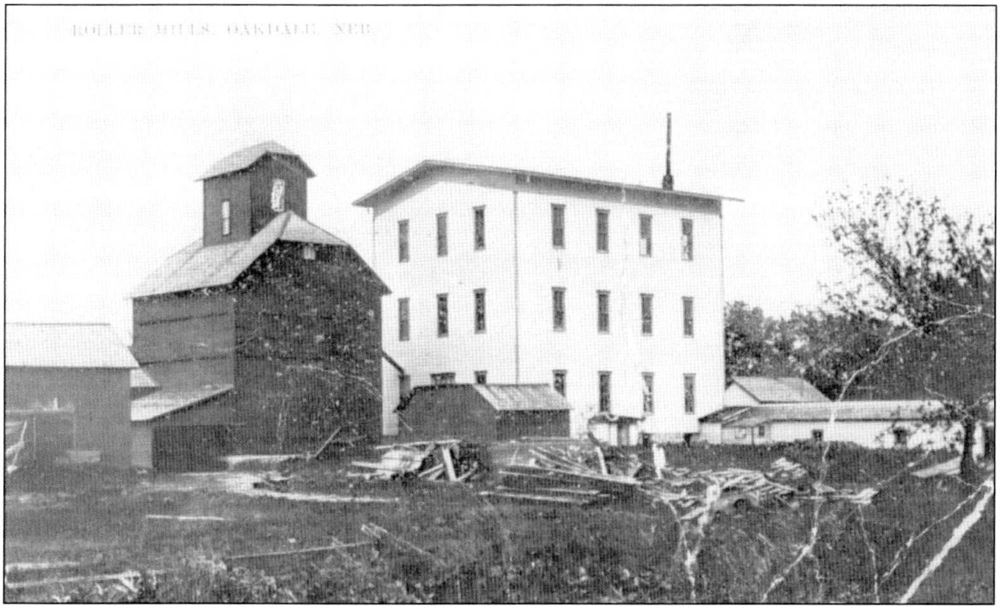

R.G. King built Antelope County's first water-powered mill in Oakdale at a cost of $1,800. Located on Cedar Creek, it began production in November 1873. After King, owners of the mill included O.P. Hurford, Galloway Brothers, and Burdette Boyes. It produced My-Kind, Sno-ball, and Queen Flour until 1944, when the facilities were converted to elevator storage space. (Courtesy of Lois Johnson.)

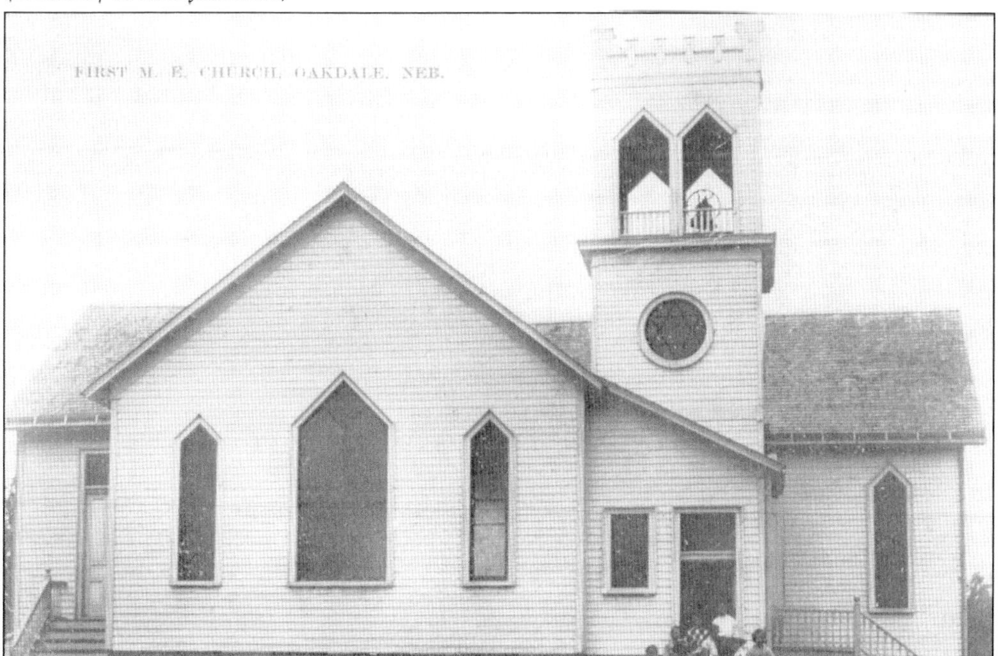

The first Protestant church in Antelope County was organized in 1872 by circuit rider George H. Wehn, who started a class of nine members at Judge John A. Snider's home in Twin Groves. After the group met in homes and schools, the first church building, seen here, was erected and dedicated in 1881. (ACHS.)

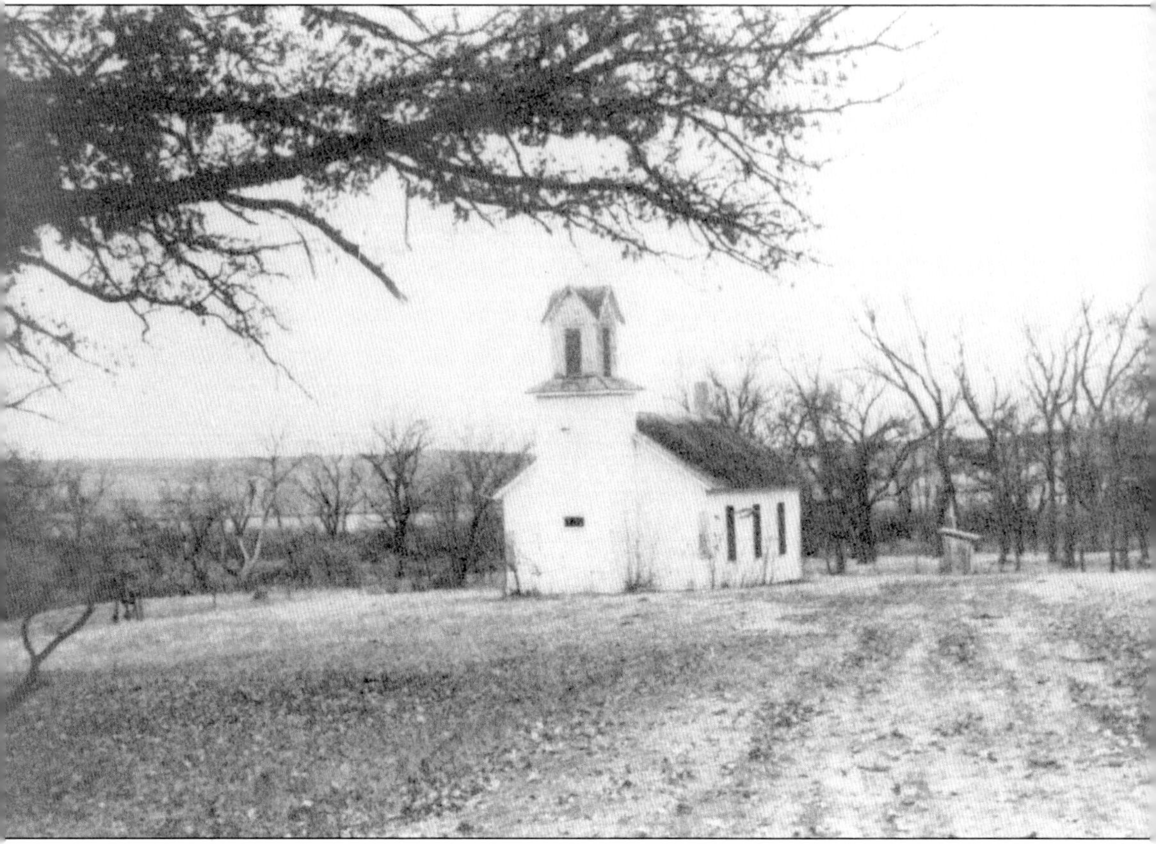

A.J. Leach, the first Antelope County school superintendent, organized the settled portions of the county into school districts from 1871 to 1873. Using oxen for his farm work, Leach did not own a horse and visited areas on foot. In addition to organizing districts, he examined teachers and visited the schoolhouse sites. Since the county treasury was empty, he received no payment for his services. Fortunately, residents of the districts he visited supplied him with food and a bed at no charge. The first schoolhouses were erected in districts four, six, and eight, but the first schools were taught in districts one, three, five, six, and eight. In 1872, there were 16 districts. By 1883, eighty-one districts had been established. The first schools were sod houses with two windows, one door, and an earth floor, and students' desks were handmade. Through the decades, improvements in country schools continued until most resembled the schoolhouse seen here. These schools continued to have one teacher instructing grades one through eight. Rural schools functioned throughout the county until 2006. (ACHS.)

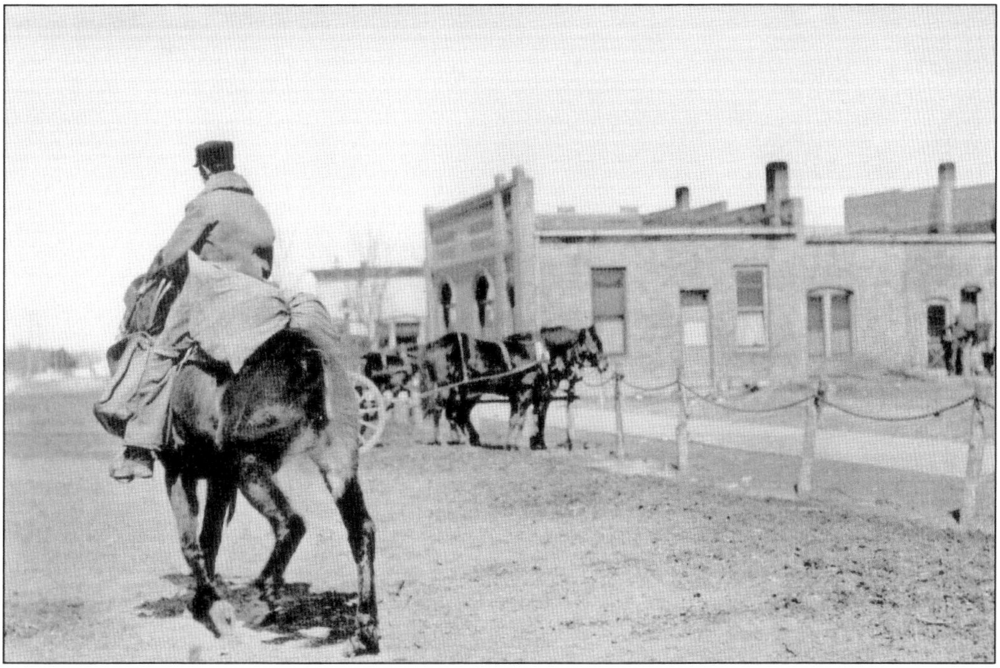

The bundle behind this horseback rider holds mail that was delivered to Brunswick and the area's rural residents around 1900. The mailman is riding north on Franklin Street behind the buildings that face Second Street. Before rural free delivery was introduced in 1897, rural citizens went to the nearest post office to pick up their mail. (ACHS.)

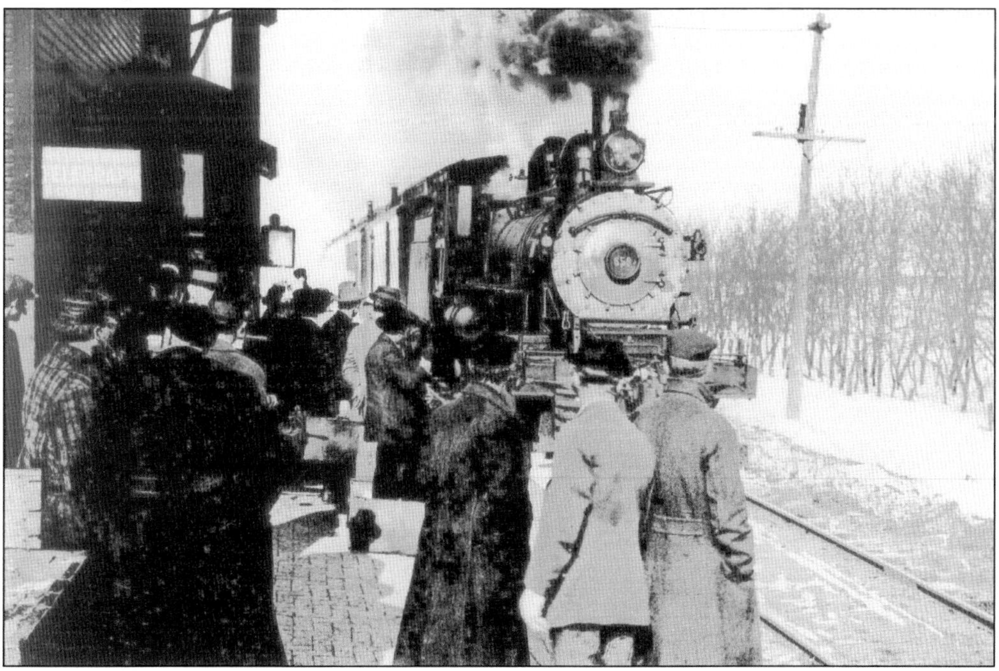

Several people wait to board the train or to greet arriving passengers at the Brunswick railroad station around 1910. The Chicago, Burlington & Quincy train featured a Pacific-style locomotive and was likely westbound. The Western Union telegraph and cable office is on the left. (ACHS.)

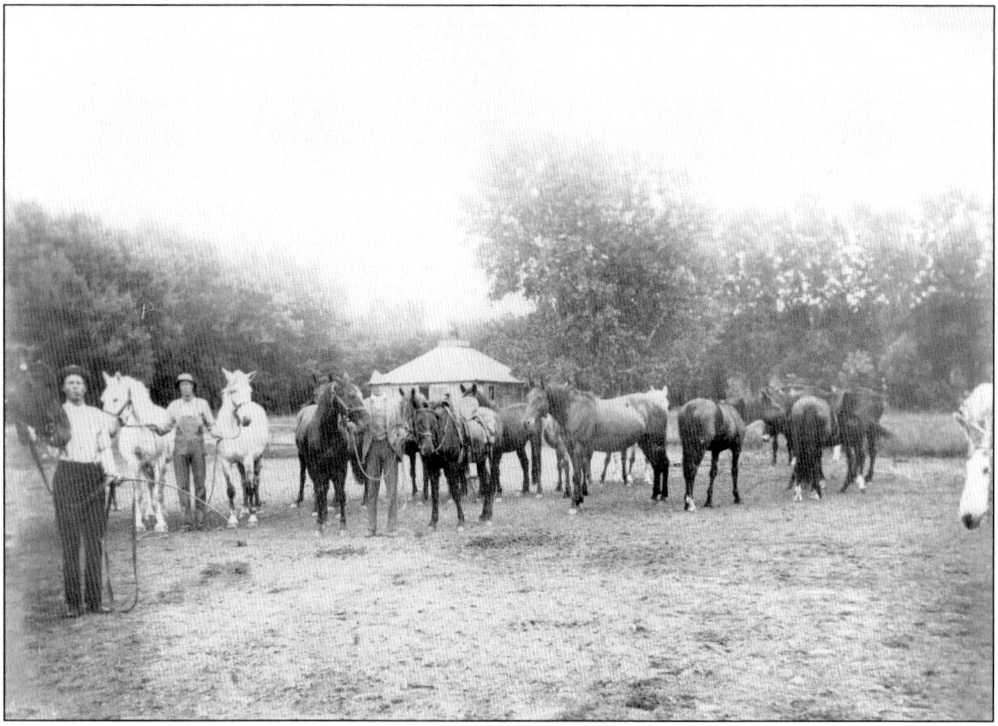

Before tractors became dependable machines for farming, horses pulled plows and planters and cultivated the crops. After harvesting a crop, they pulled the wagons containing the harvest to barns. Here, the Johnson brothers of Oakdale—Bill, August, and Charlie—pose respectively with their horses around 1900. (Courtesy of Lois Johnson.)

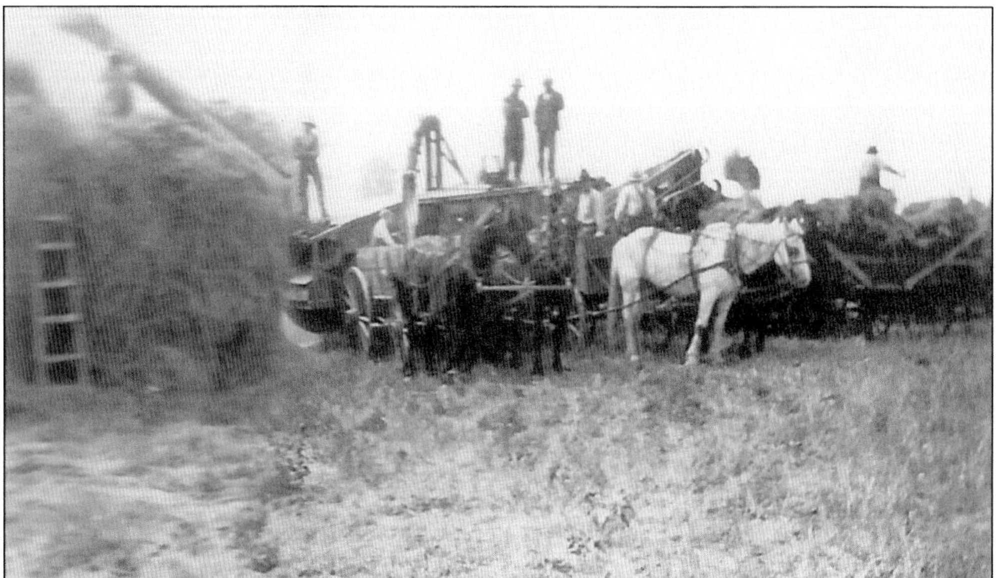

Horses operated the first threshing machines, which also required a larger crew of men than later devices. Band cutting and feeding the cylinder were done by hand. Straw was swept away from the machine using horses because the blower lacked a separator. (Courtesy of Robert Busteed.)

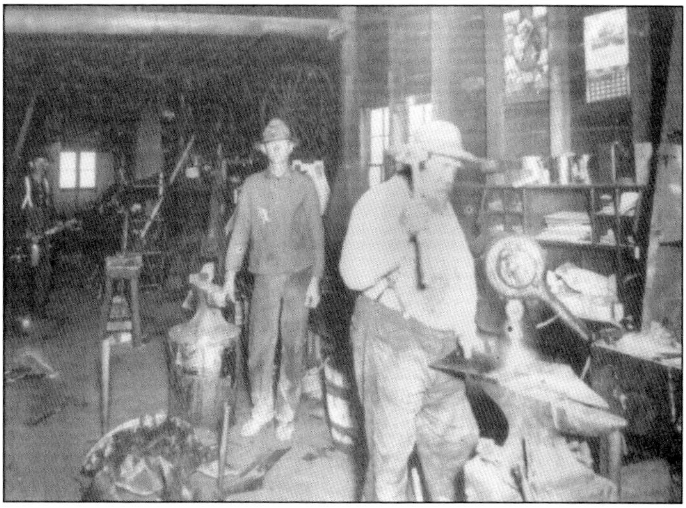

Charlie Schrant opened the first blacksmith shop in Tilden in 1880. This later shop, seen here around 1910, held the equipment the blacksmith used to make tools for farmers and iron rims for wheelwrights. The blacksmith also produced and repaired horseshoes. Here, two blacksmiths are at work, with a small anvil on the left and a larger one on the right. The blower and forge are on the right. (Courtesy of Arlene Hofmann.)

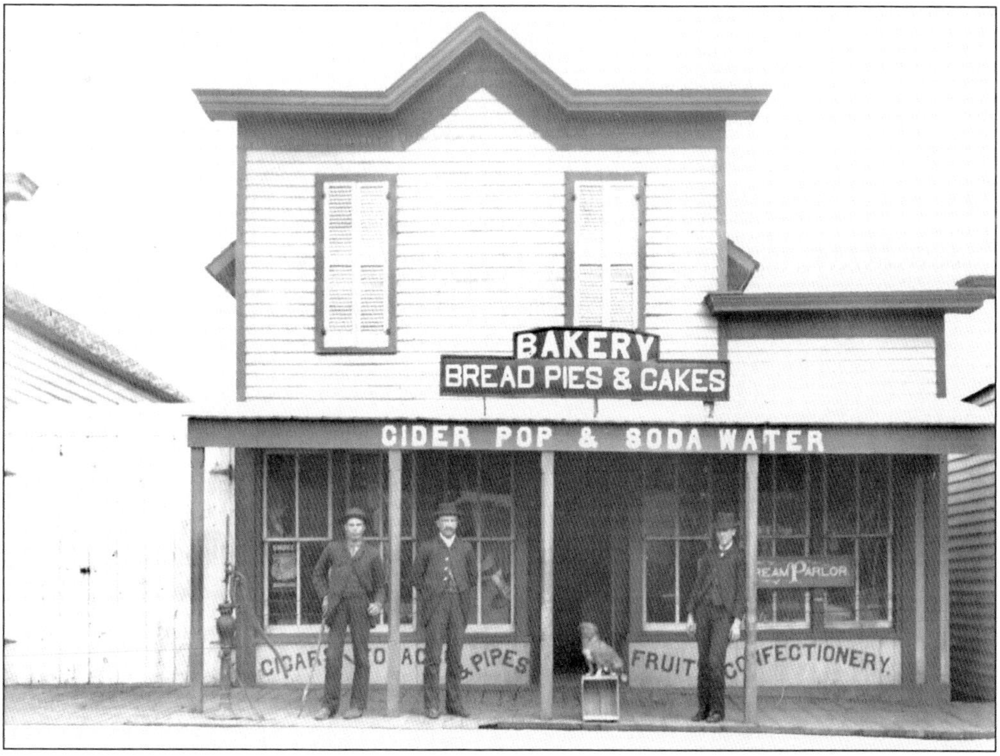

This Neligh confectionery store, seen around 1900, advertised a variety of products on its storefront. It sold baked goods, cider, pop, and soda water, and customers could sit down in the ice cream parlor for refreshing treats. The three men standing in front may have been replenishing their supplies of cigars or tobacco. Note the dog perched on the wooden box. (Courtesy of Kenneth Krohn.)

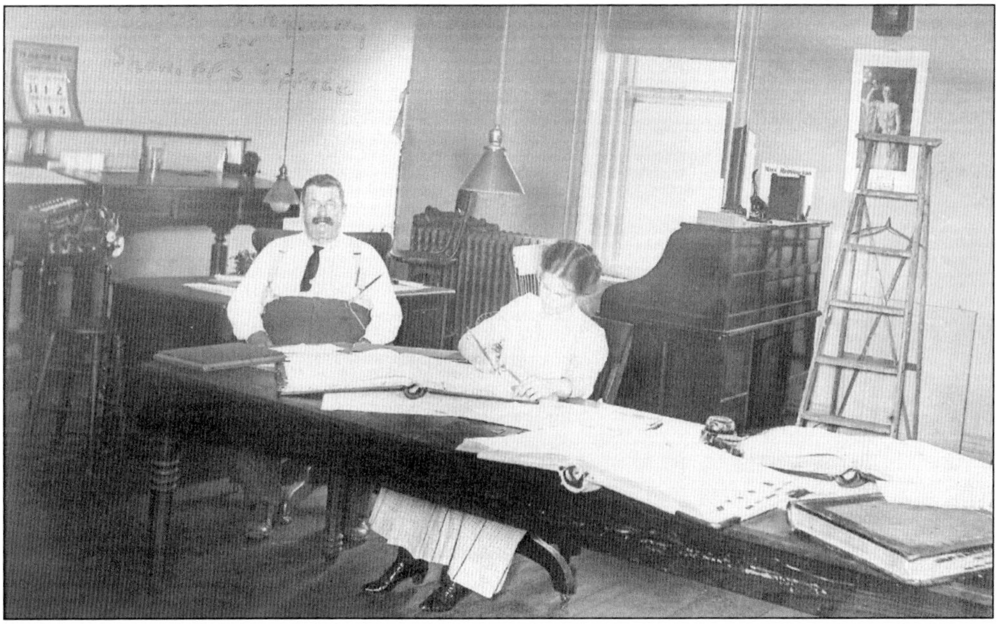

Following the sudden death of county sheriff J.H. Stevenson in 1897, John Mayberry (left) was appointed as the new sheriff. The county sheriff's department provides total law enforcement in the area. A few of the many services they provide include operating county jails, serving court papers, assisting emergency rescues, and providing contract law enforcement for any city or village that requires it. (ACHS.)

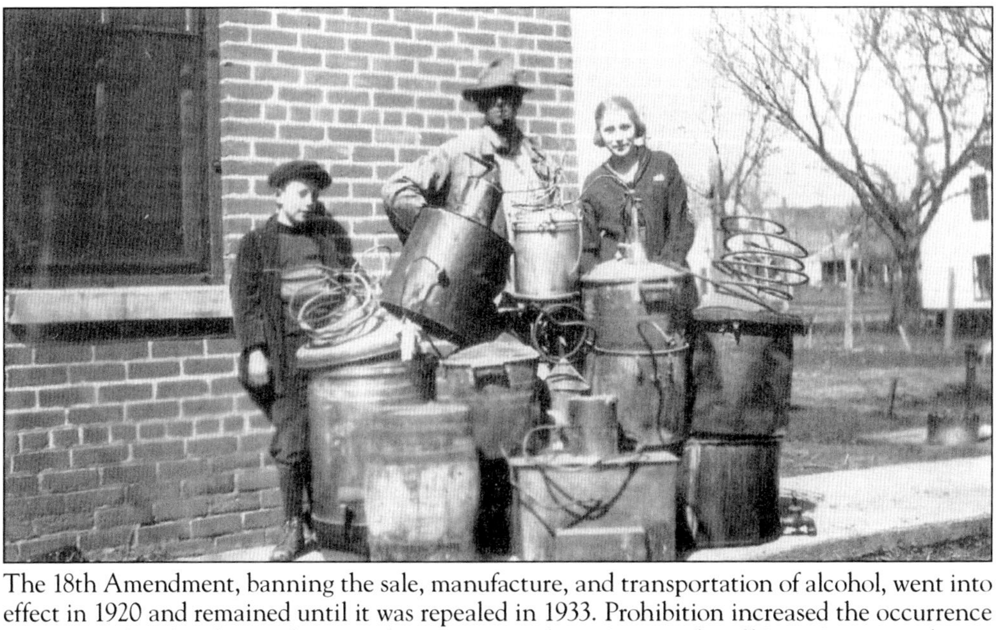

The 18th Amendment, banning the sale, manufacture, and transportation of alcohol, went into effect in 1920 and remained until it was repealed in 1933. Prohibition increased the occurrence of organized and widespread criminal activity. Antelope County sheriff Jesse Sutton and state agents confiscated 34 stills during one series of raids. Sutton (center), who served as sheriff from 1923 to 1930, is seen here with Albert and Ruth Sutton. (ACHS.)

In June 1889, Nick Foley, a hard-drinking fellow, became angry because his employer, Pomeroy Clark, discouraged Foley's attentions to Effie Riggs, the sister of Clark's wife, Ada. Venting his anger, Foley shot Clark and his wife, who lived near Elgin. The Antelope County sheriff arrested Foley but failed to save him from four men who rushed him to a bridge south of Palmer's farm and hung him in June 1889. (ACHS.)

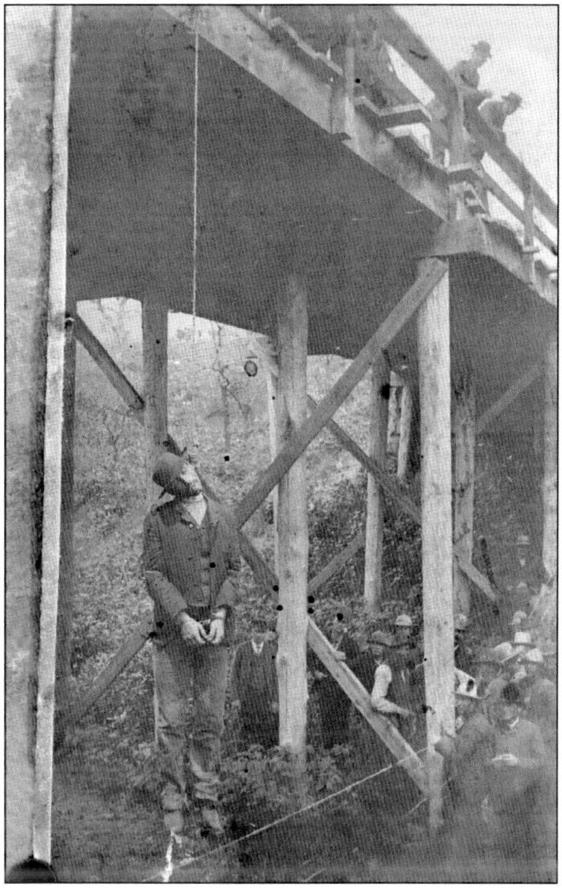

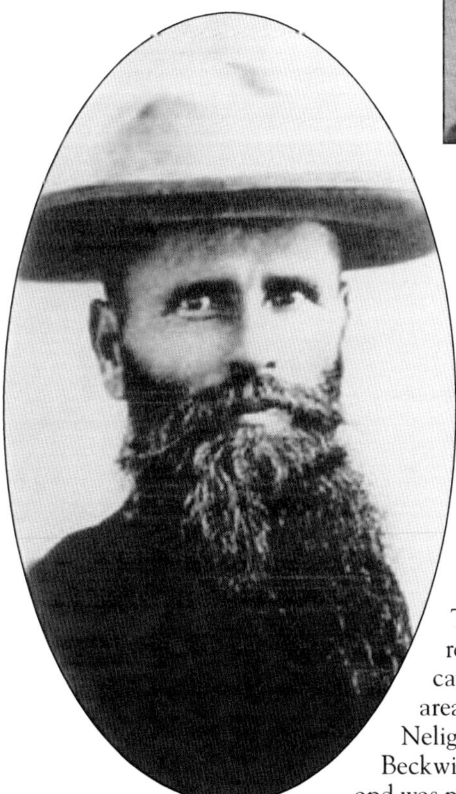

Texan James M. Riley, known as "Doc Middleton," roamed through Antelope County stealing horses and cattle in 1878 and 1879. Middleton's interactions in the area included marrying local Irene "Rene" Richardson in Neligh as well as asking for and receiving food from D.E. Beckwith. Edella Forsell also cooked a meal for Middleton and was paid with a $5 gold piece. (ACHS.)

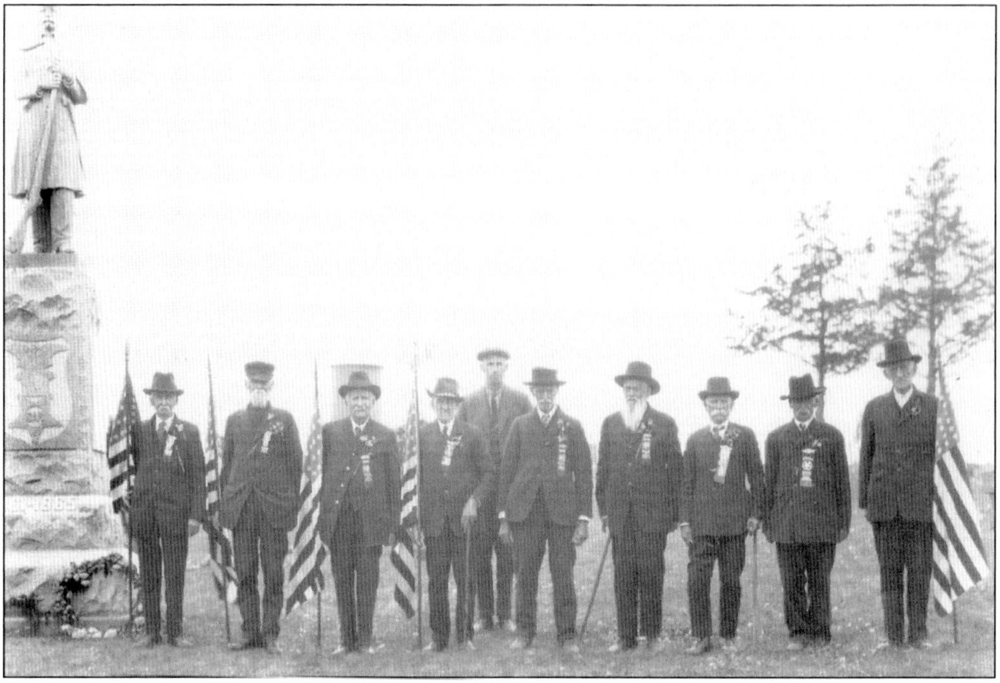

The Grand Army of the Republic (GAR) was composed of Civil War veterans of the Union army. Founded in 1866, it dissolved in 1956. In 1912, Antelope County members gathered at Laurel Hill Cemetery in Neligh for the dedication of the Civil War Veteran statue. The statue cost $500. These GAR members posing for a photograph at the ceremony are, from left to right, unidentified, ? Statten, ? Dewey, unidentified, Jack Sutton, B.J. Minor, ? Fried, ? Gilbert, unidentified, and ? Coe. (ACHS.)

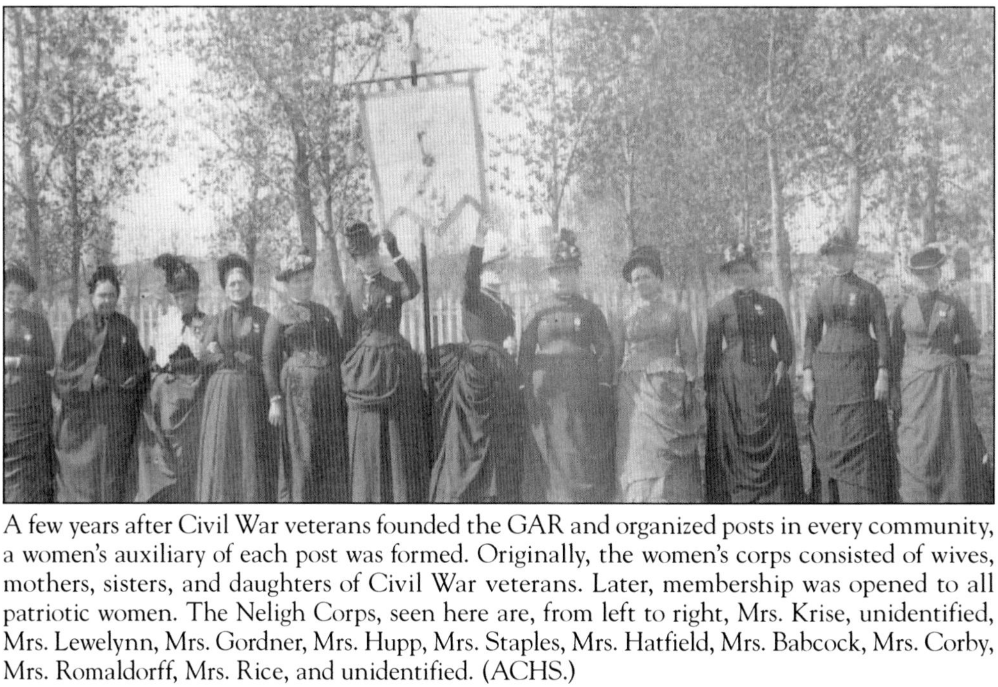

A few years after Civil War veterans founded the GAR and organized posts in every community, a women's auxiliary of each post was formed. Originally, the women's corps consisted of wives, mothers, sisters, and daughters of Civil War veterans. Later, membership was opened to all patriotic women. The Neligh Corps, seen here are, from left to right, Mrs. Krise, unidentified, Mrs. Lewelynn, Mrs. Gordner, Mrs. Hupp, Mrs. Staples, Mrs. Hatfield, Mrs. Babcock, Mrs. Corby, Mrs. Romaldorff, Mrs. Rice, and unidentified. (ACHS.)

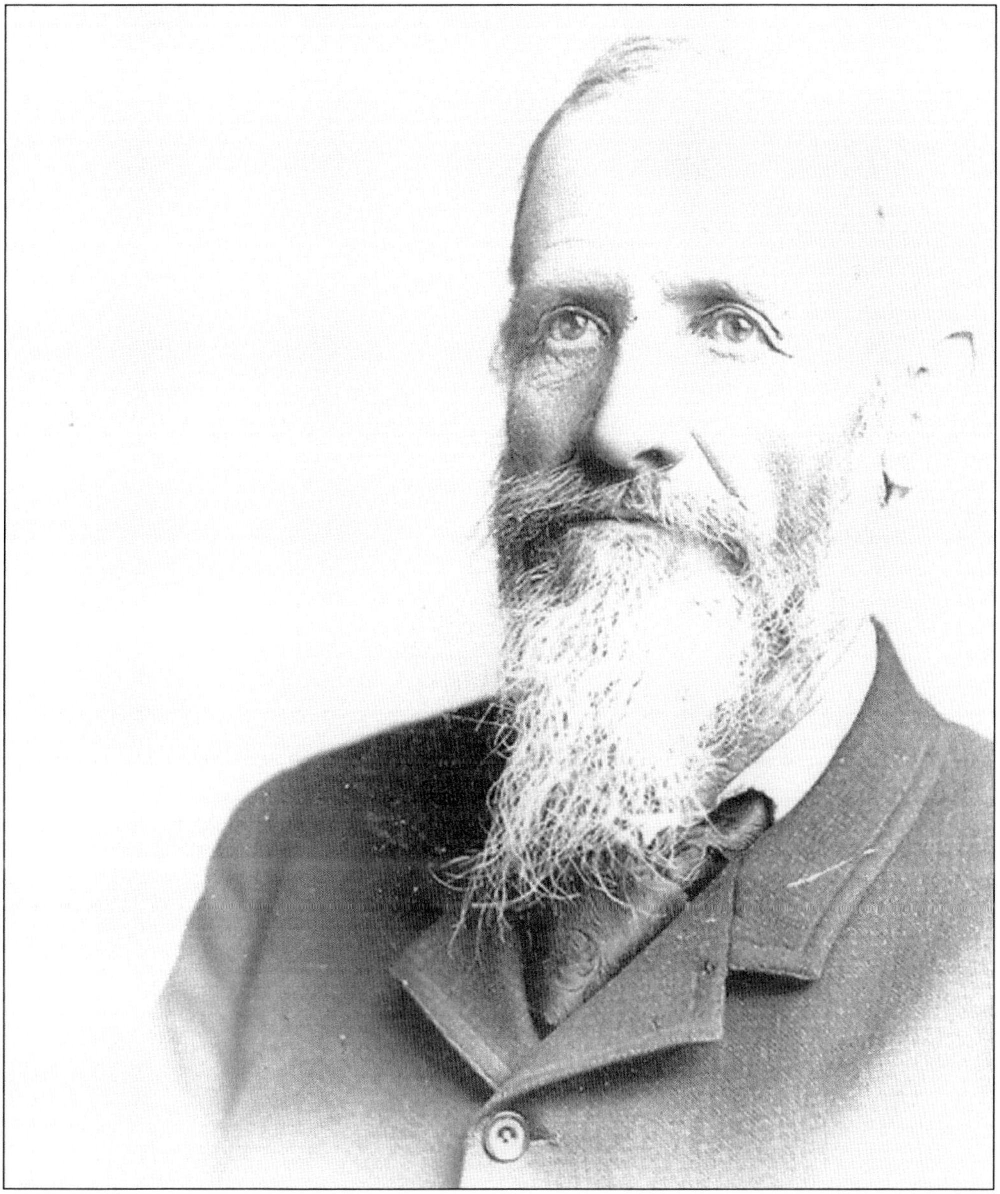

From the time of his arrival in Antelope County in 1869, A.J. Leach served the area as an officeholder and historian. As the first school superintendent, he served two consecutive terms and organized 16 schools. Later, he served as county surveyor and county treasurer. After accepting a position as a land appraiser with the Burlington & Missouri Railroad in 1885, Leach and his wife, Esther E. Hill, moved to Oakdale from their homestead near Cedar Creek. In 1908, Leach began writing a history of Antelope County. Covering the years 1868 to 1883, the work was published serially in eight newspapers. In 1909, R.R. Donelley & Sons published *The History of Antelope County*. Leach wrote a second book, *Early Day Stories*, published in 1916, describing his trip to Oregon at age 18. He organized and served as president of the Oakdale Cemetery Association and was a founding member of the Antelope County Pioneers Association, the forerunner of the present-day Antelope County Historical Society. His obituary stated that he was the "most active spirit in the Antelope County Pioneers Association." (Courtesy of Lois Johnson.)

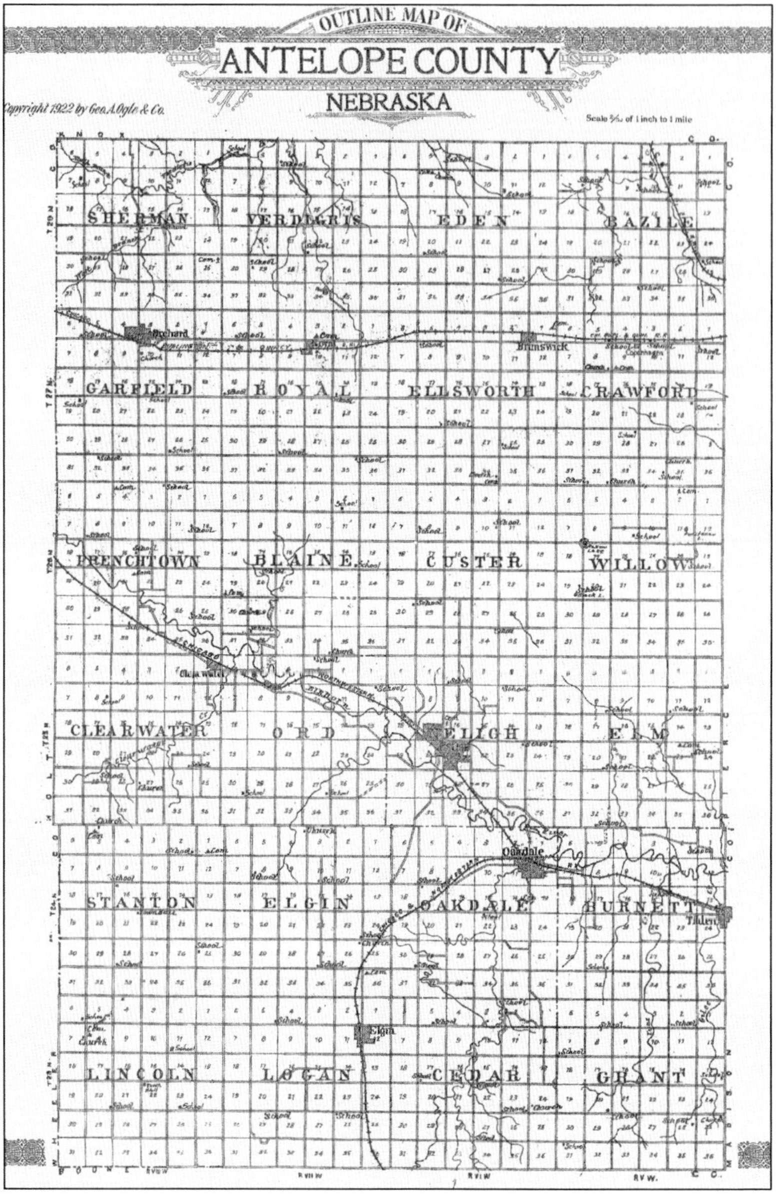

By 1922, Antelope County reached its fully developed state, with 22 townships. Since then, some township names have changed and others have been added. The Chicago, Burlington & Quincy Railroad came to the county in 1890, connecting O'Neill with Sioux City. The expanding railroad resulted in the establishment of Orchard and Brunswick. When the Scribner-Oakdale branch was completed in 1897, Elgin was founded. By 1904, there were 24 townships. In the northern tier of this map, the 1884 as well as the 1922 townships included Sherman, Verdigre, Eden, and Bazille. The second tier included Royal and Gerney in 1884. By 1922, the Garfield, Ellsworth, and Crawford Townships were added. The third tier consisted of Frenchtown, Custer, and Willow in 1884, and Blaine was added by 1922. The fifth tier contained Clay Ridge, Harmony, Twin Grove, and Burnett in 1884, and Stanton, Elgin, and Oakdale Townships were added by 1922. In 1884, the sixth (southern) tier held the township of Cedar, and by 1922 the townships of Lincoln, Logan, and Grant had been added. (Courtesy of Kenneth Krohn.)

Two

Oakdale
Leading the Way

An area known as Twin Groves, northeast of present-day Oakdale, was the center of early settler activity and the scene of several county firsts. The first wedding occurred on August 14, 1869; the first white child was born in May 1870; the first death was recorded on October 6, 1870; and the first church services (Methodist Episcopal) were held in 1871. Also, in 1871, Twin Groves held the first Fourth of July celebration in the county. By 1872, the first businesses were established. A sawmill began operating, and H.P. Elwood opened a general store. Twin Groves began to fade after the Nebraska Legislature granted the Omaha & Northwestern Railroad 32,000 acres of Antelope County land.

Five men purchased property from the railroad and organized the town of Oakdale. Named for the large number of oak trees in the vicinity, Oakdale soon replaced Twin Groves as the settlers' hub of activity. In October 1872, Oakdale was declared the county seat. By November 1873, the Oakdale mill had opened at Cedar Creek, and it remained in operation until 1944, with the exception of a three-year, county-wide agricultural depression from 1925 to 1928. The town received a boost with the arrival of the Fremont, Elkhorn & Missouri Valley Railroad in 1880. Although the county seat was moved to Neligh in 1883, Oakdale continued to prosper until the 1920s, when the town's population peaked at 707. It gradually declined in the following decades, and the 2010 census reported 322 residents.

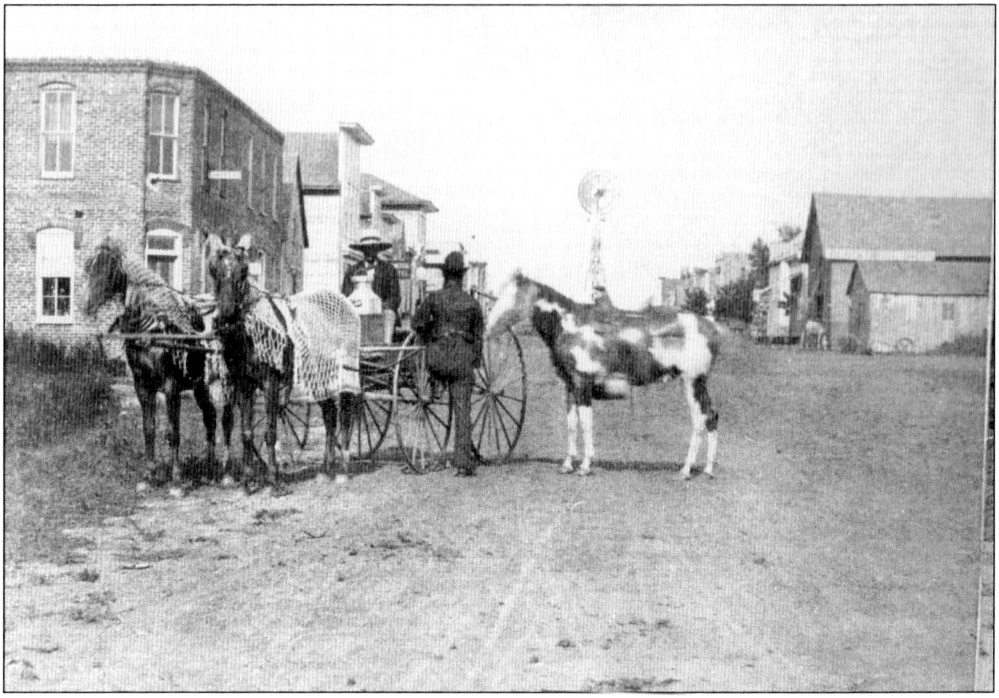

When the village of Oakdale was incorporated in 1882, Main Street was a dirt road, and storefronts still did not have board sidewalks. A windmill stood at the end of the street, and people came to town in their horse-drawn buggies. Here, Samuel Fairchilds is in the buggy, while Alonzo Snider stands in front of it. (Courtesy of Lois Johnson.)

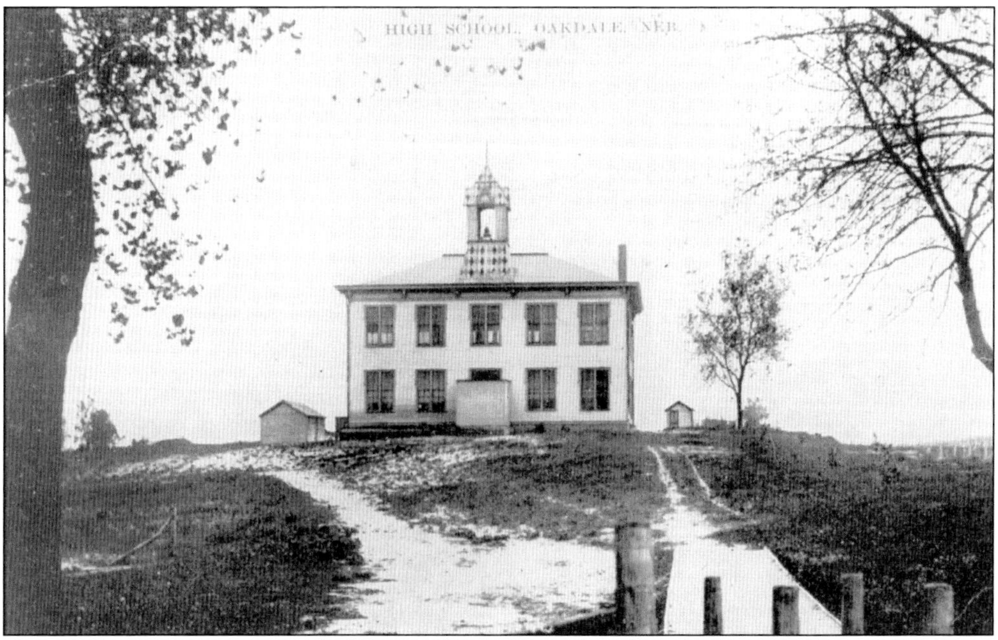

The first school, built in 1874, was replaced with an up-to-date, two-story building in 1886, seen here. The 1886 structure was used until 1912. The first high school graduation occurred in 1891, with two graduates: Ola Launt and Nial Brainard. (Courtesy of Lois Johnson.)

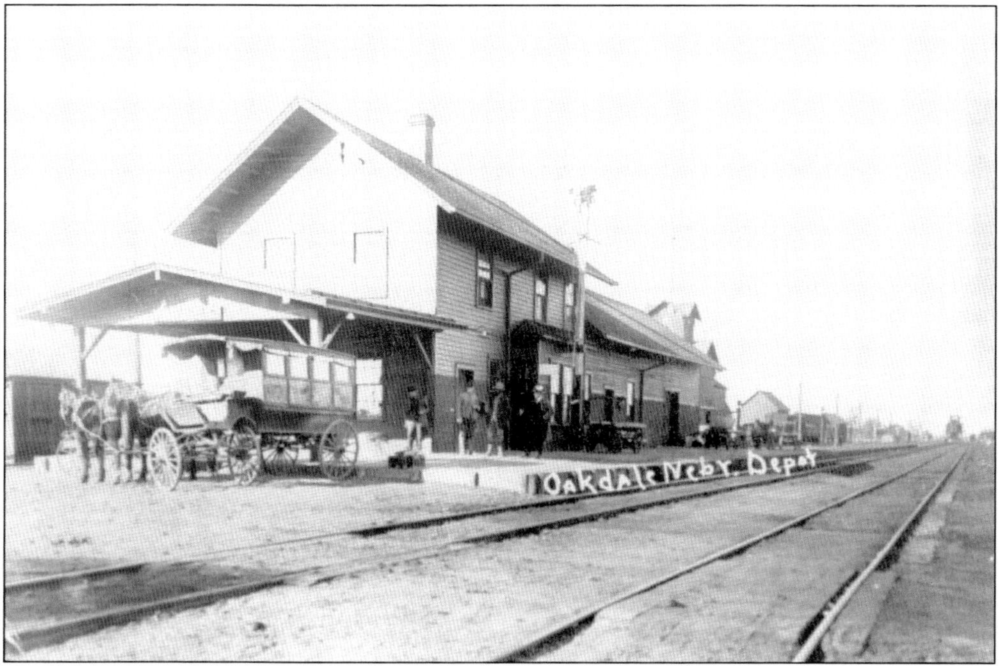

The Fremont, Elkhorn & Missouri Valley Railroad had finished building a track to Oakdale by December 7, 1879. A branch line was completed between Scribner and Oakdale in 1887. In the early 1900s, a stage stood outside the depot, providing transportation to local destinations. (Courtesy of Lois Johnson.)

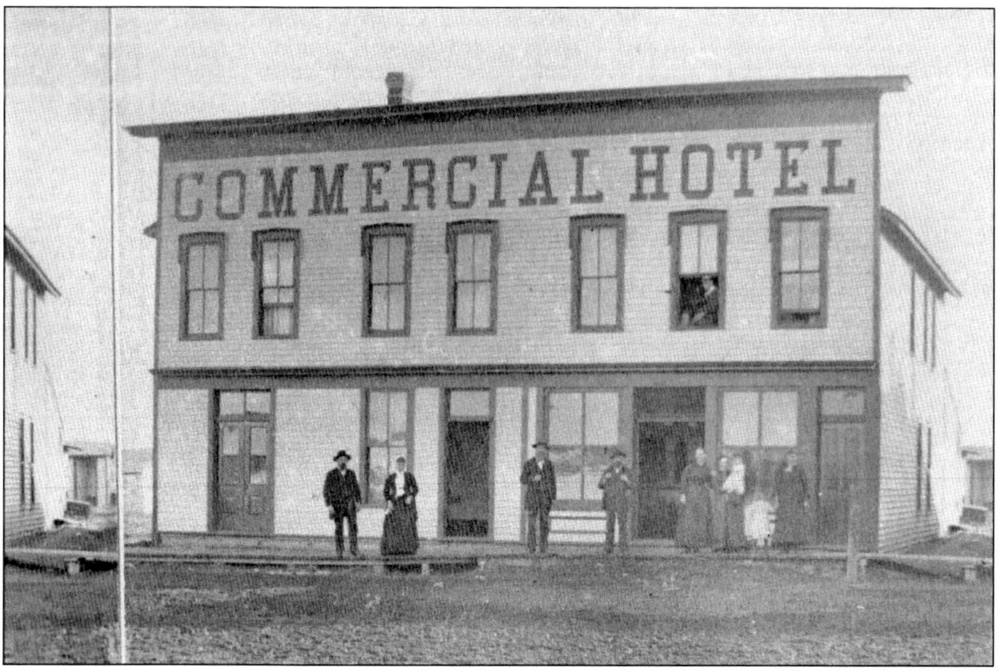

Early travelers pose on a board sidewalk outside the Commercial Hotel around 1900. Note the gentleman leaning out of the second-story window, anxious to be in the photograph. The first hotel in Oakdale was the Elwood House, built in the 1880s. (ACHS.)

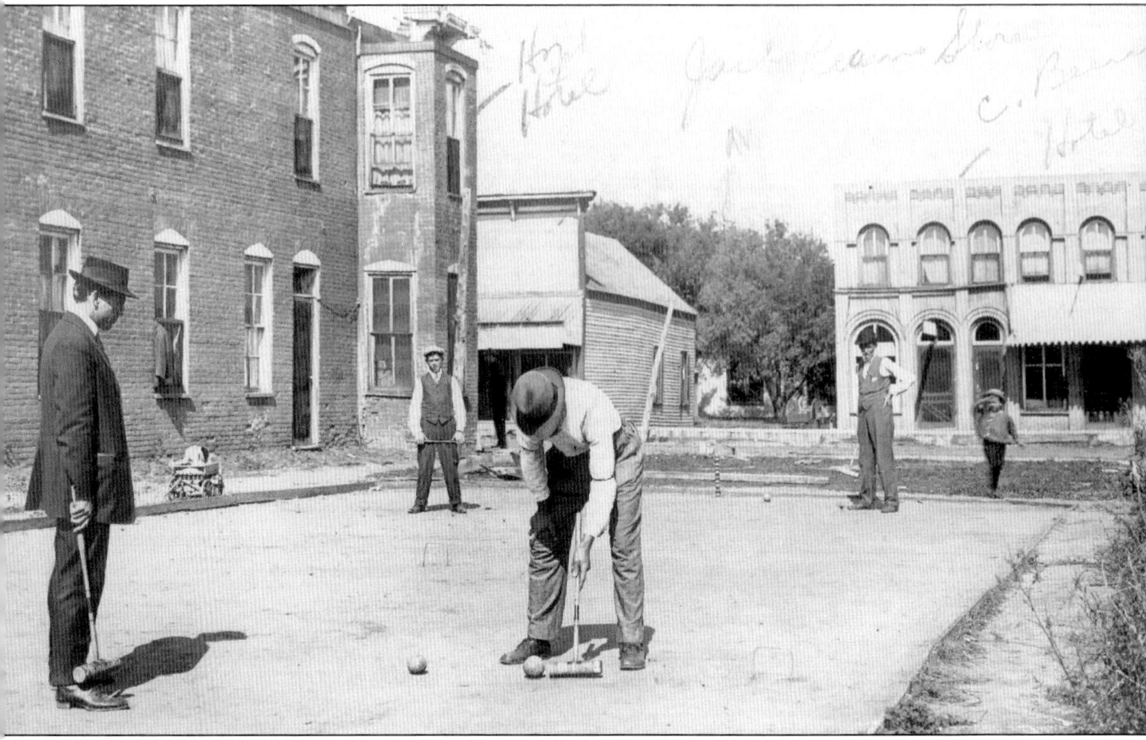

Four men play croquet on the street outside a couple of Oakdale hotels in 1878. An unidentified hotel is on the left, with the Jack Reaves store behind it. C. Beer's Hotel is on the right. (Courtesy of Lois Johnson.)

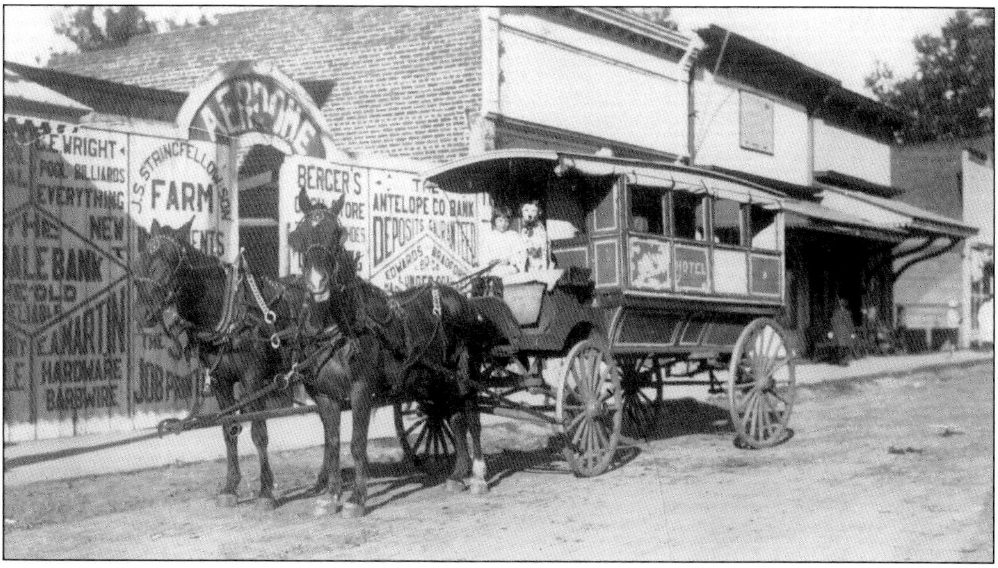

In the early 1900s, this horse-drawn stagecoach transported train passengers from the depot to downtown Oakdale, where the hotels were located. Here, the stage is stopped outside the Aerodrome, which is covered with advertising posters. (Courtesy of Lois Johnson.)

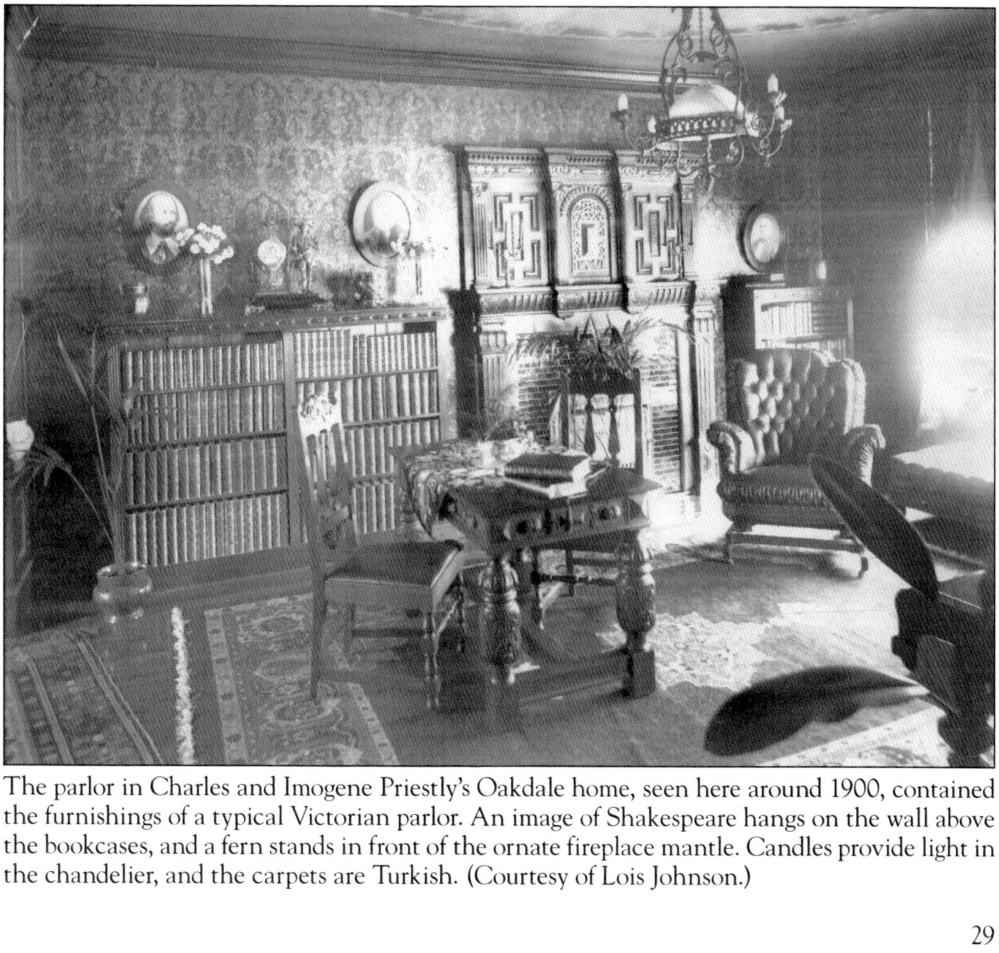

The parlor in Charles and Imogene Priestly's Oakdale home, seen here around 1900, contained the furnishings of a typical Victorian parlor. An image of Shakespeare hangs on the wall above the bookcases, and a fern stands in front of the ornate fireplace mantle. Candles provide light in the chandelier, and the carpets are Turkish. (Courtesy of Lois Johnson.)

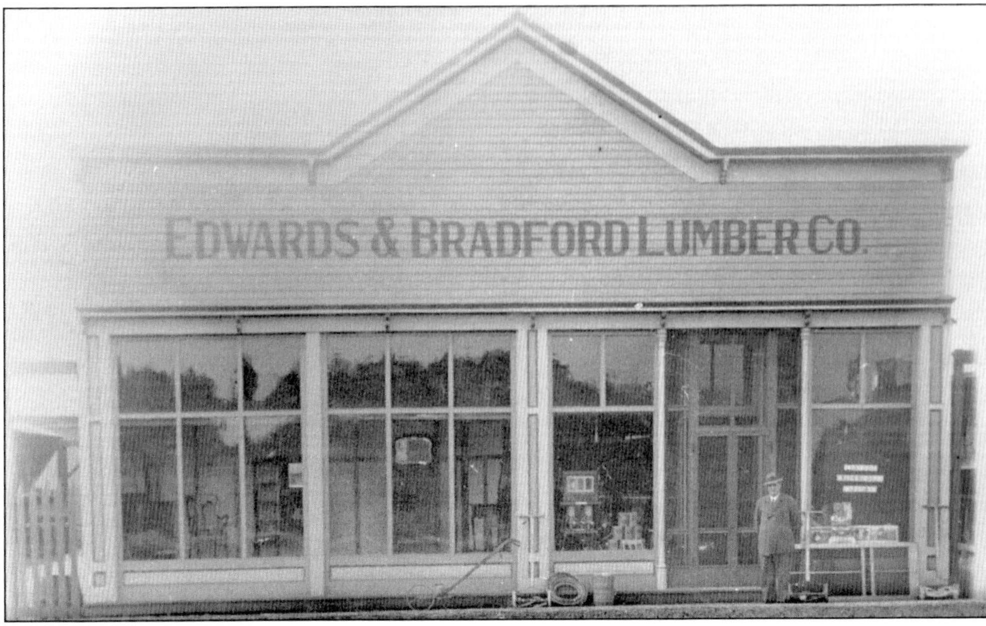

Edwards & Bradford Lumber Company provided hardware and lumber to Oakdale residents in 1900, and the men established a second hardware and lumber store in Elgin. C.H. Brainard managed the business from 1894 until 1915, when he organized it into a corporation known as the C.H. Brainard Lumber Company. In 1962, Ralph Kinnan bought the business and kept the Brainard name. (ACHS.)

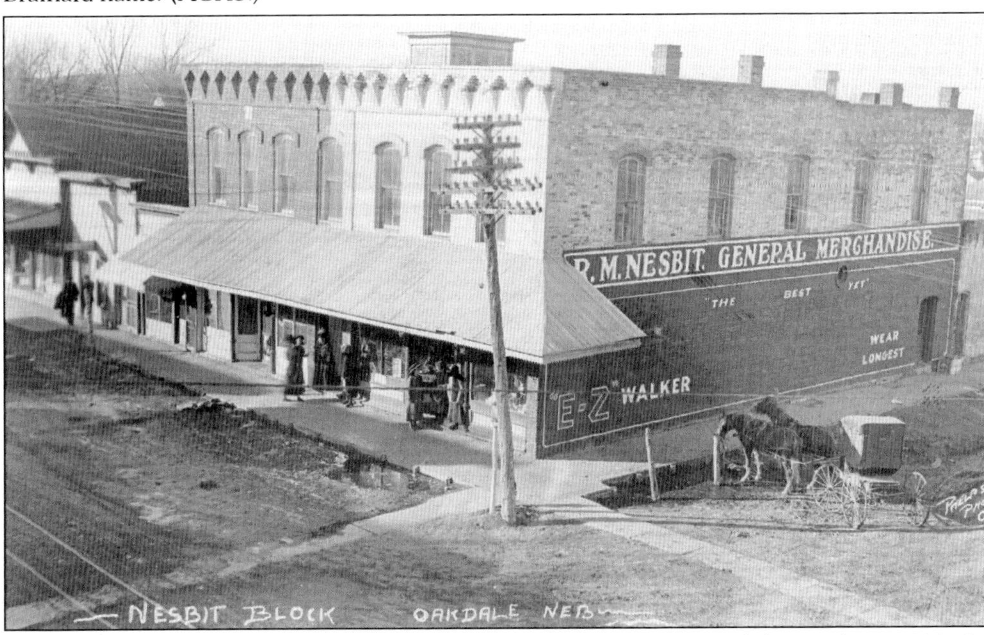

Robert M. Nesbit opened this general store, which carried groceries and dry goods, in 1898. On Saturday nights, people came to town to trade and to attend a movie. Nesbit kept the store open until the movie ended, and people returned to the store to pick up their groceries. The store closed in the late 1920s, when the economy faltered and people could no longer pay their bills. (Courtesy of Lois Johnson.)

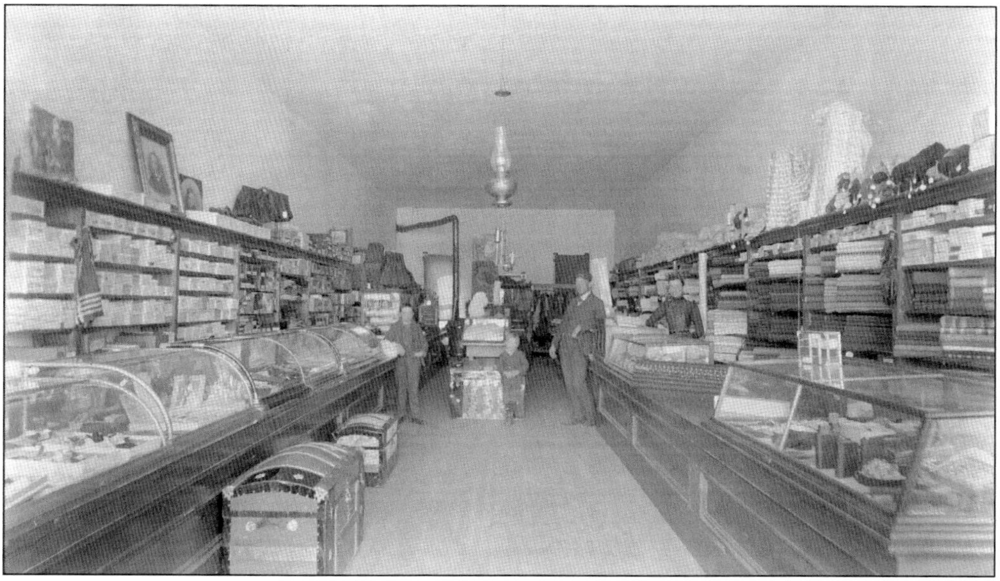

The Wolfe brothers of Neligh opened this store in Oakdale, and Lettie Cooper, the daughter of Frank and Ella Cooper, managed the store for 18 years. When she retired, the Wolfe brothers closed it. Note the gaslight fixture, the trunks, and the large amount of dry goods in the store. (ACHS.)

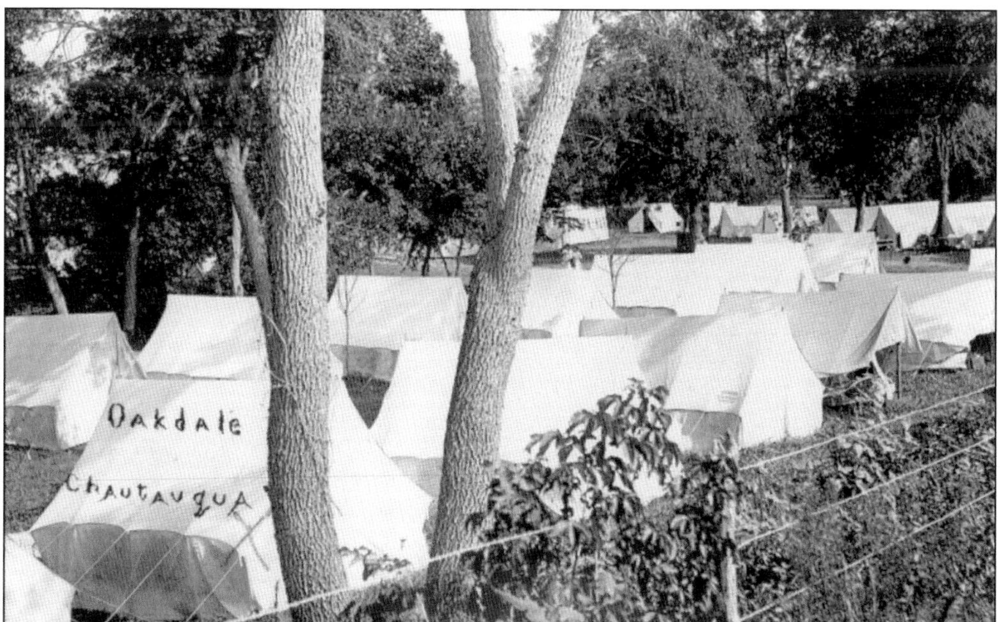

Oakdale bustled with energy in the early 1900s. The Oakdale Booster Club sponsored a Chautauqua in 1911. These small family tents were pitched in Johnson's Park for the duration of the first Chautauqua programs. The tents could be rented for $2. (Courtesy of Lois Johnson.)

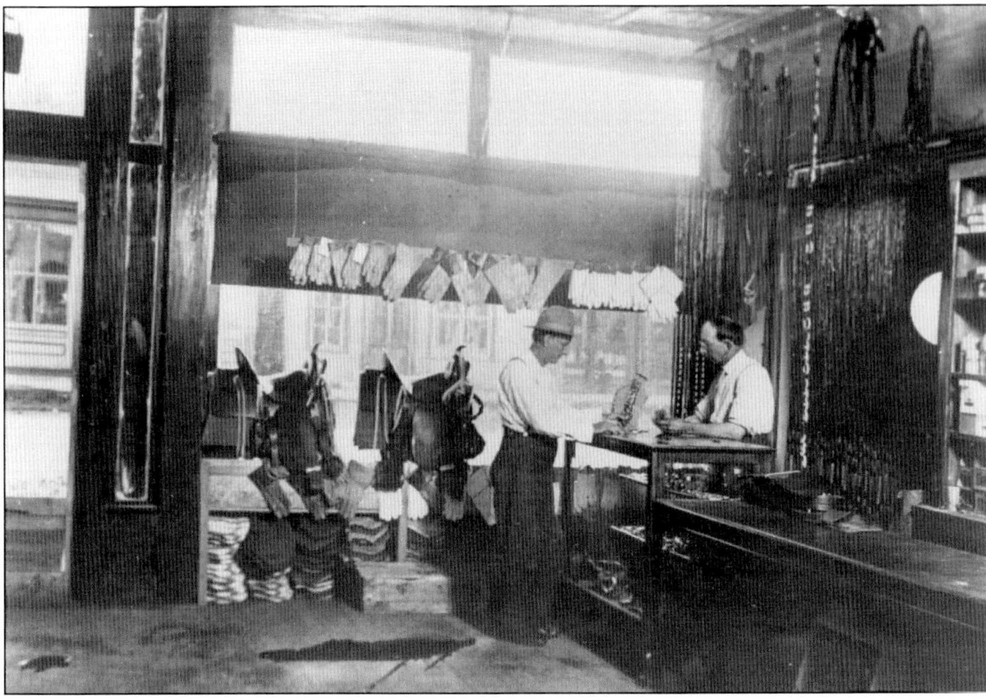

In 1916, Waterman's harness shop, seen here, was one of several thriving businesses in Oakdale. Merchandise on display here includes saddles, gloves, and horse brasses. When cars replaced horses, harness shops faded and eventually disappeared. (ACHS.)

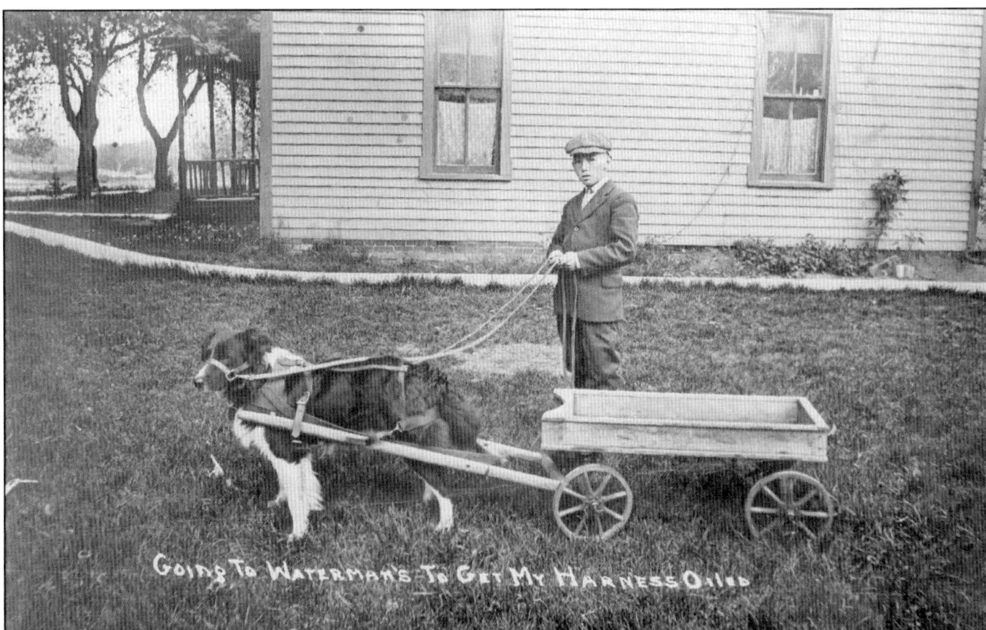

This dog is harnessed to a wagon on a postcard advertising free services at Waterman's harness shop. The postcard, signed by D.H. Waterman, states that he will give away $71.50 worth of goods and would oil harnesses without charge. (Courtesy of Lois Johnson.)

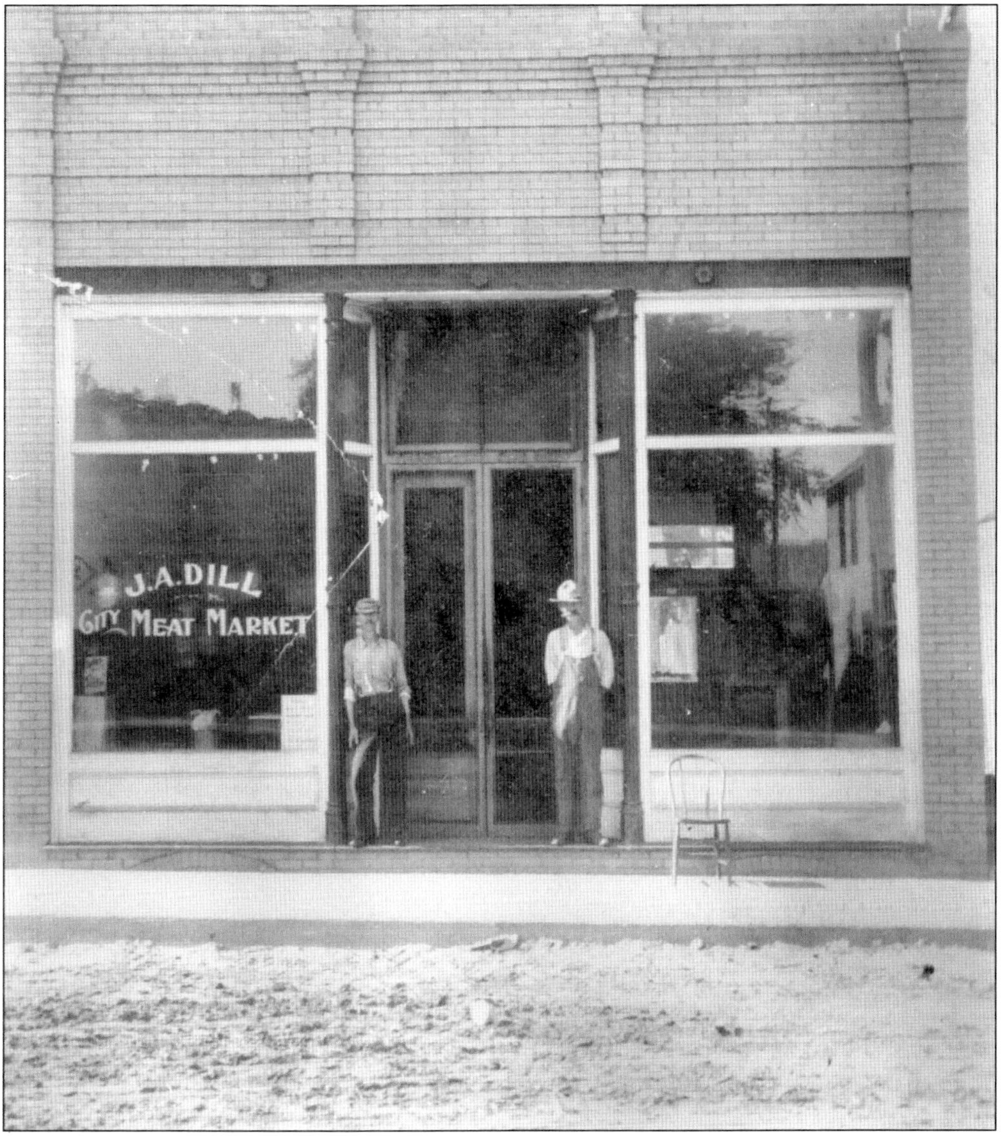

Around 1910, Jack Dill's meat market served Oakdale residents. Located on Main Street, the market had a chair sitting outside the store encouraging folks to sit down and rest or visit with people passing by. Standing in the doorway are Jack Dill (left) and Mr. Milliken, and the Commercial Hotel is reflected in the window. (Courtesy of Lois Johnson.)

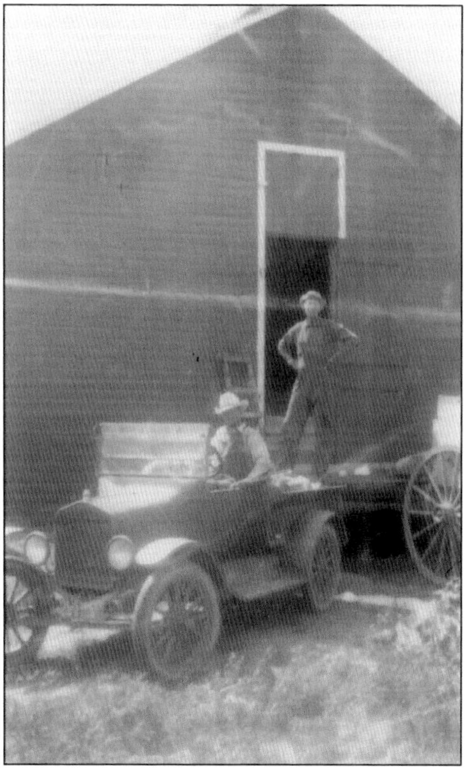

The Johnson Ice House (left) was about 60 feet by 80 feet and had approximately six feet of concrete wall below ground level. Workers cut the ice into 24-inch-by-36-inch cakes that were at least 12 inches thick. Bill Johnson constructed the ice saw (below) using a Ford Model T motor and rear end mounted on a homemade sled. He cut the rear axles off, mounted the saw blade on one side, and blocked the other side. The ice cakes slid to the house on a chute made of two-by-fours. They were placed on edge in the house, and three feet of straw protected them from the outside wall. The Chicago & Northwestern Railroad bought ice from Johnson. After the railroad cars were loaded with ice, they were shipped to Fremont. (Both, courtesy of Lois Johnson.)

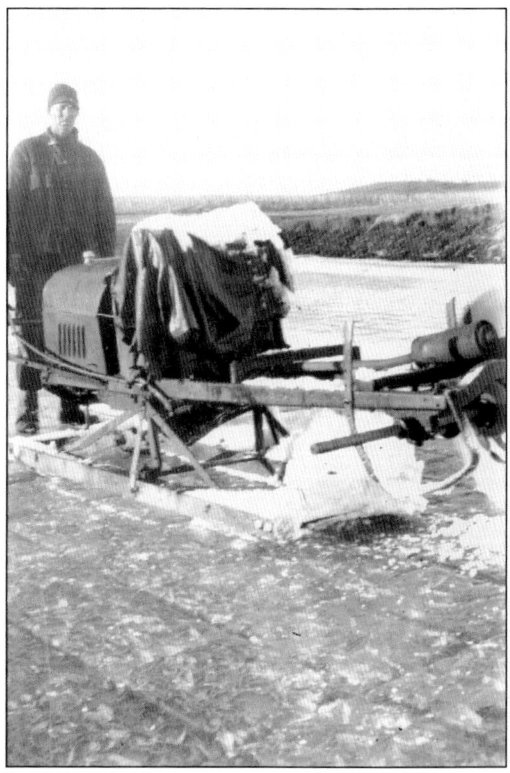

Three

Neligh
The County Center

John Neligh, an inventive and imaginative brick maker from West Point, Nebraska, traveled with two companions to Antelope County in 1872 and was impressed by the scenery. While he and his friends looked at the Elkhorn River, bordered by cottonwood trees, they also noticed an uninhabited valley filled with clumps of green and gold grasses swaying in the August breeze. Neligh decided that the area favored a townsite and traveled to Omaha to buy the land, where he found that the Omaha & Northwestern Railroad had already chosen the property for a future town and depot location.

Fortunately, a careless clerk failed to check the railroad's choice of town locations, allowing Neligh to purchase the 500-acre tract for $6 per acre. His friends encouraged him to name the town Neligh. He immediately arranged to build a brick flour mill and a dam across the Elkhorn River. He also installed machinery for a sawmill. After the county seat dispute with Oakdale was settled in 1883, the fledging town prospered.

Located in the middle of Antelope County, Neligh became the center of county government. Major improvements in milling occurred with each new owner of the Neligh mill, and unlike mills in some neighboring towns, it survived the Great Depression. Now the mill is an area tourist attraction. Neligh reached its population peak of 1,800 in 1980. The 2010 census reported 1,599 Neligh residents.

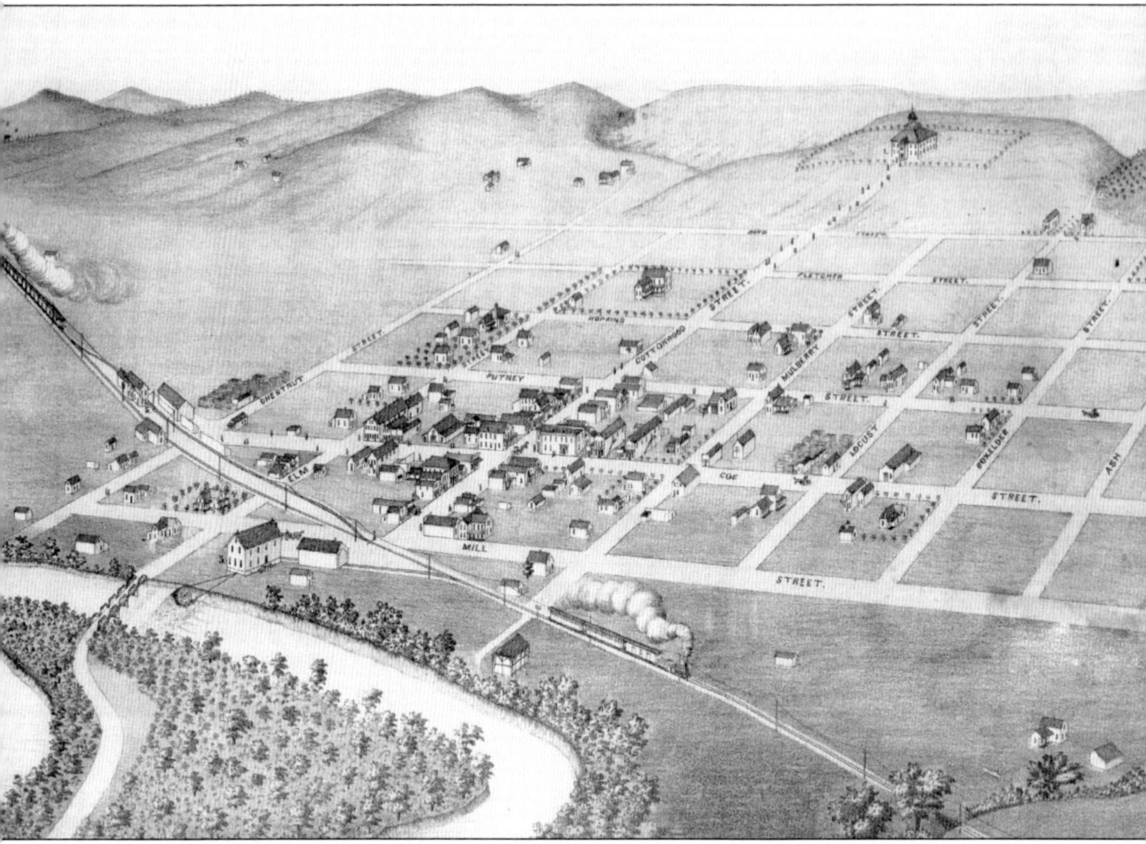

This advertising map of the town of Neligh was likely created prior to 1884, as the courthouse, which was dedicated in 1885, is not shown. Also, Gates College is in the wrong place, and it is likely that the college, founded in 1881, occupied a different building lot when it was first established. The map emphasizes the position of the mill, the railroad, and the bridge crossing the river. Main Street runs from east to west rather than in the present-day north-south direction. The rolling hills north of town are also drawn on the map. In 1893, the *Nebraska State Gazetteer* stated that Neligh was located on the Fremont, Elkhorn & Missouri Valley Railroad and was surrounded by good agricultural country that had been settled by "frugal and prosperous" people. (ACHS.)

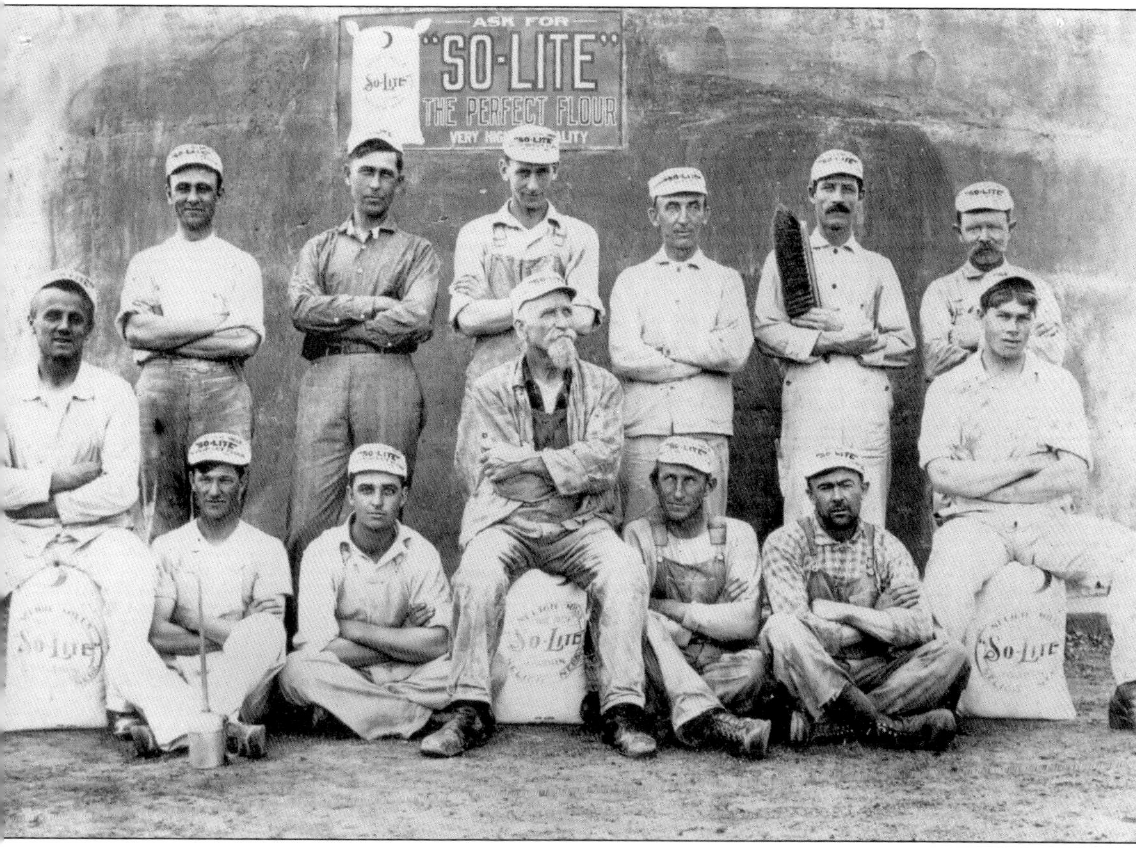

Workers pose for a photograph outside the Neligh mill beneath a So-Lite flour sign. Their caps also bear the So-Lite logo. In the 1880s, under the management of William C. Gallaway and William Lambert, the mill flourished. In addition to commercial orders, the mill shipped flour to Indian reservations in South Dakota and to military posts. It also shipped large amounts of flour to England. During this period, one of the mill's most dedicated workers, Philander D. Thompson, was working alone in the basement when his right hand was caught between a cogwheel and a belt. The force of the wheel pulled him through the belt and over the driveshaft. He managed to crawl upstairs for help and eventually recovered from his injury, but he lost his right hand. Seen here from left to right are (seated) Charles Kubacher, Art Tibets, unidentified, Philander D. Thompson, unidentified, Lou Haberstroh, and George Zemons; (standing) George Furgeson, unidentified, ? Henry, Jim Setzen, George Stein, and Matt Zeamons. (ACHS.)

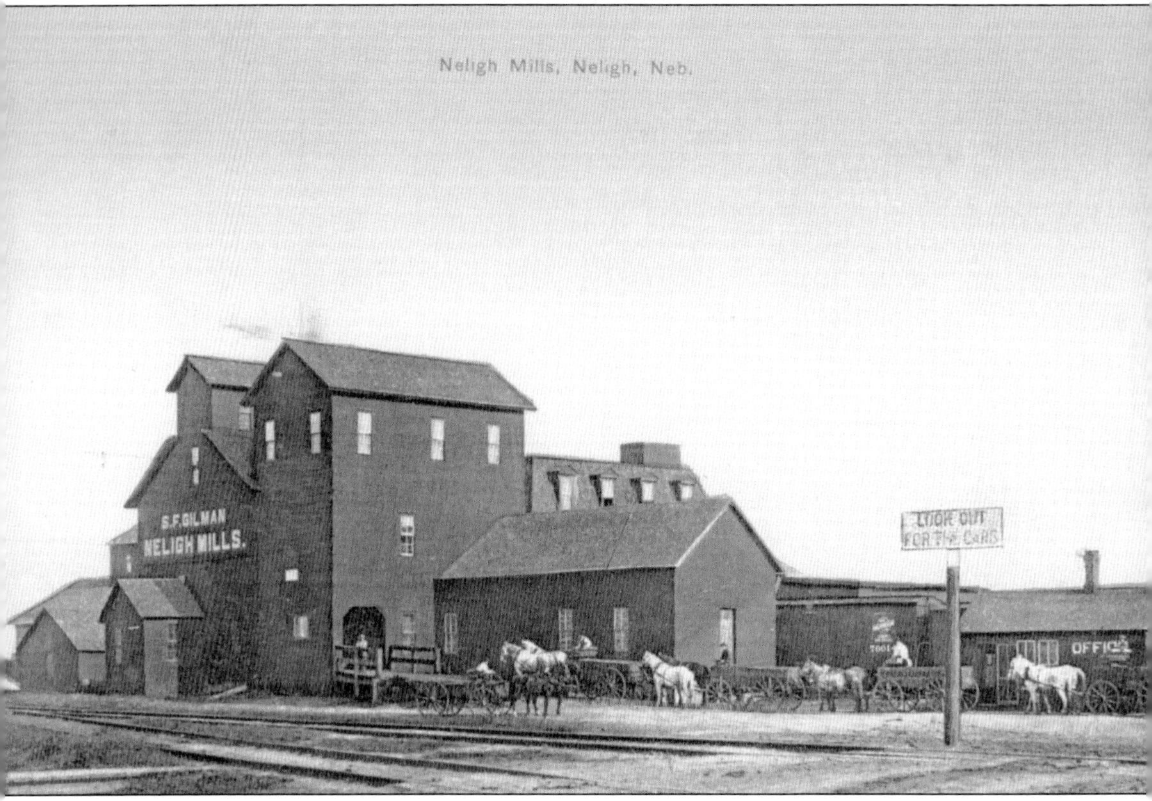

When the financial panic of 1873 interrupted John Neligh's plans for the town he had founded, he returned to West Point, Nebraska, selling his Neligh interests, including the mill, to William C. Galloway and William B. Lambert. By 1882, the mill had a capacity of 250 bushels a day. In 1886, steel rollers replaced the stone-grinding burrs, producing more finely ground white flour and also increasing the daily capacity. In 1898, Stephen F. Gilman purchased the mill and installed new machinery that increased the daily output to 500 barrels. He also purchased equipment that supplied electric power to Neligh citizens. As large corporations began taking over flour production, the operation ceased milling flour in 1952 but continued to produce livestock feed. In 1964, the mill closed its doors. The persistent efforts of Neligh citizen Margaret Pierson brought the mill and its machinery to the attention of the Nebraska State Historical Society, and the mill is now a Nebraska State Historical Site. (ACHS.)

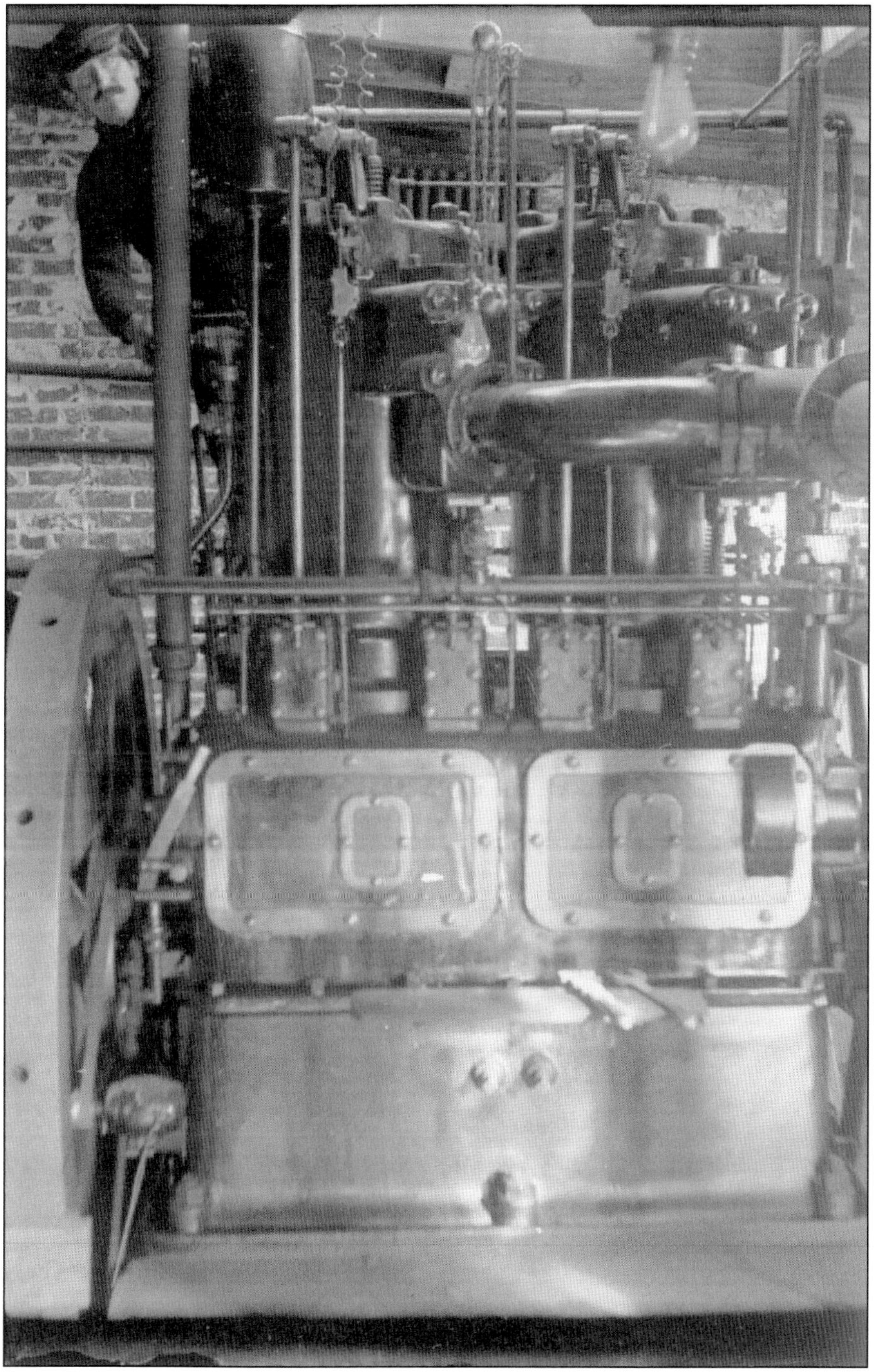

A mill worker peeks around the 100-horsepower gas engine that Stephen Gilman installed at the mill in 1904. It provided a backup to the hydropower system that provided power for the mill and for Neligh residents. Before the gas engine was installed, the water-powered turbines that provided electricity were dependent on the Elkhorn River. When the river changed channels or flooded, the mill and the town went without power. (Courtesy of George Strassler.)

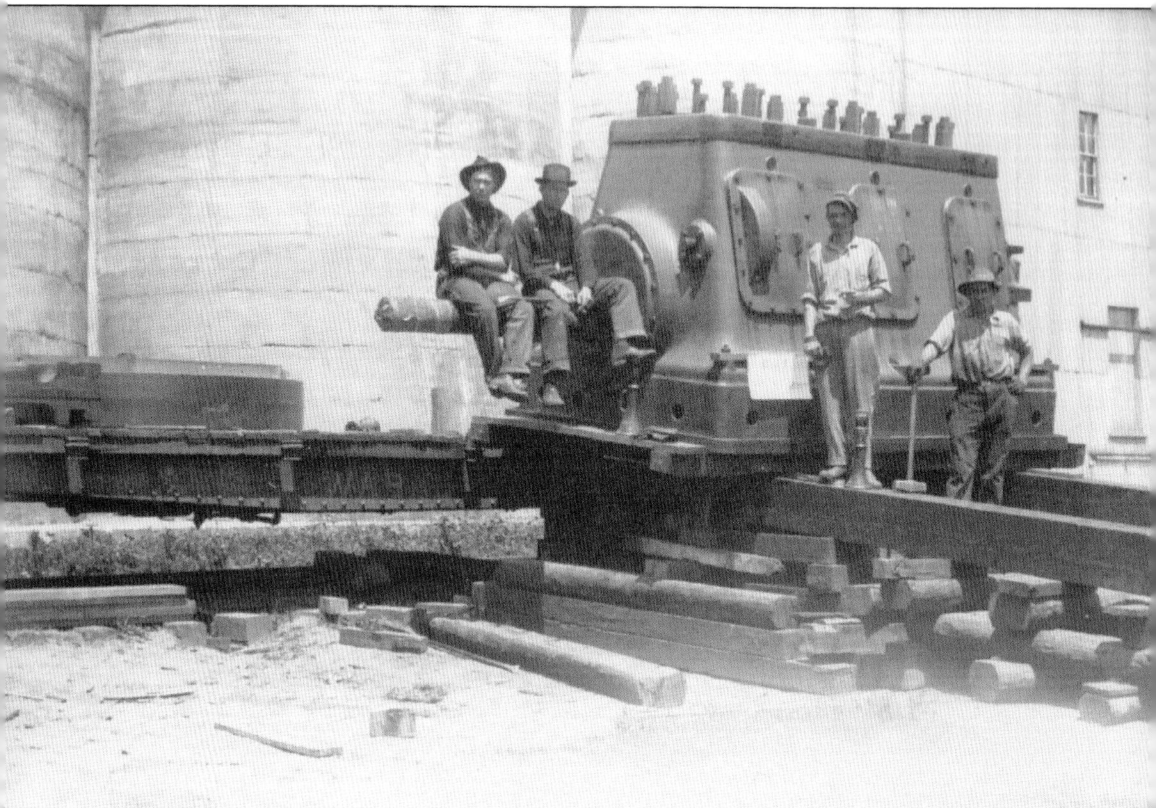

Four mill workers gather around the 225-horsepower diesel engine they are installing in 1915. It operated the electrical generator on a full-time basis, preventing the power outages that had inconvenienced the mill and Neligh residents. Unfortunately, Stephen Gilman did not live to see 24-hour electrical service offered to Neligh residents, which was finalized in March 1916. He had died the previous November on a hunting trip in Cody, Nebraska. Gilman's family retained ownership of the mill, with William Spirk continuing as manager. (Courtesy of George Strassler.)

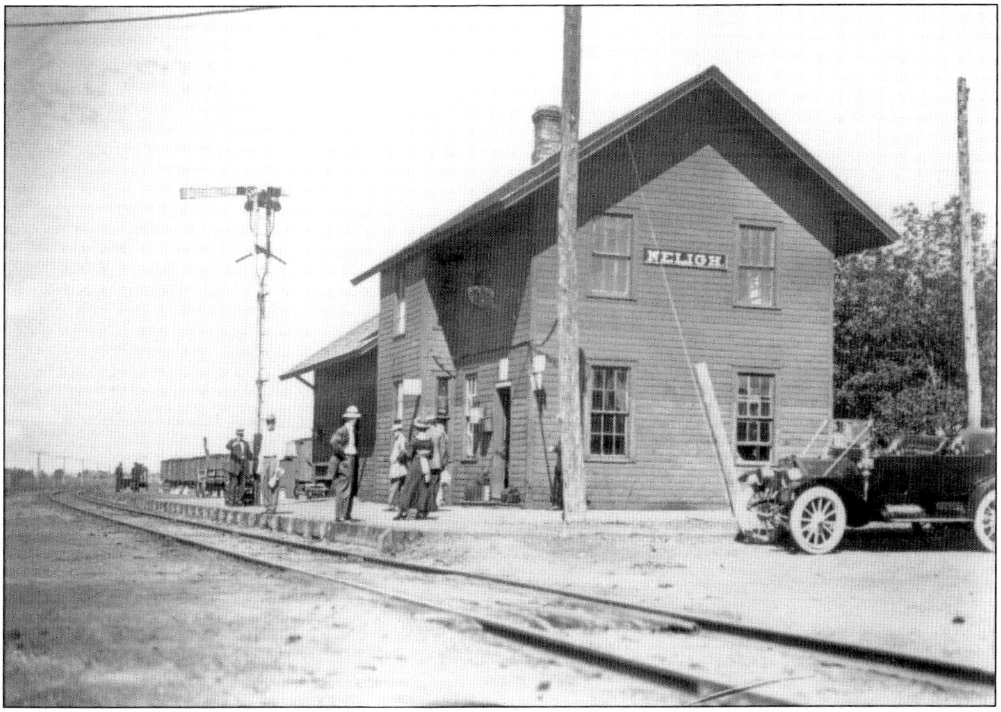

The first Neligh depot, built in 1880, became a busy center for passengers, freight, and mail by 1910. The Chicago & Northwestern had taken over the line by July 1884. In 1911, Neligh businessmen convinced the railroad superintendent that a new depot was needed. Passenger service ended in 1958, and the depot was demolished in 1969. (ACHS.)

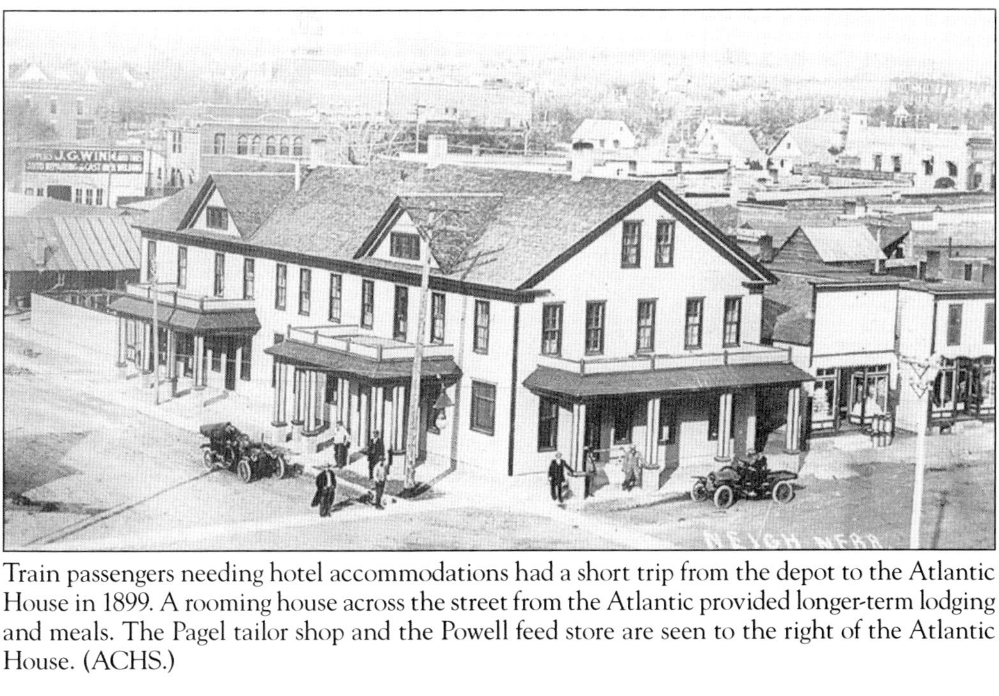

Train passengers needing hotel accommodations had a short trip from the depot to the Atlantic House in 1899. A rooming house across the street from the Atlantic provided longer-term lodging and meals. The Pagel tailor shop and the Powell feed store are seen to the right of the Atlantic House. (ACHS.)

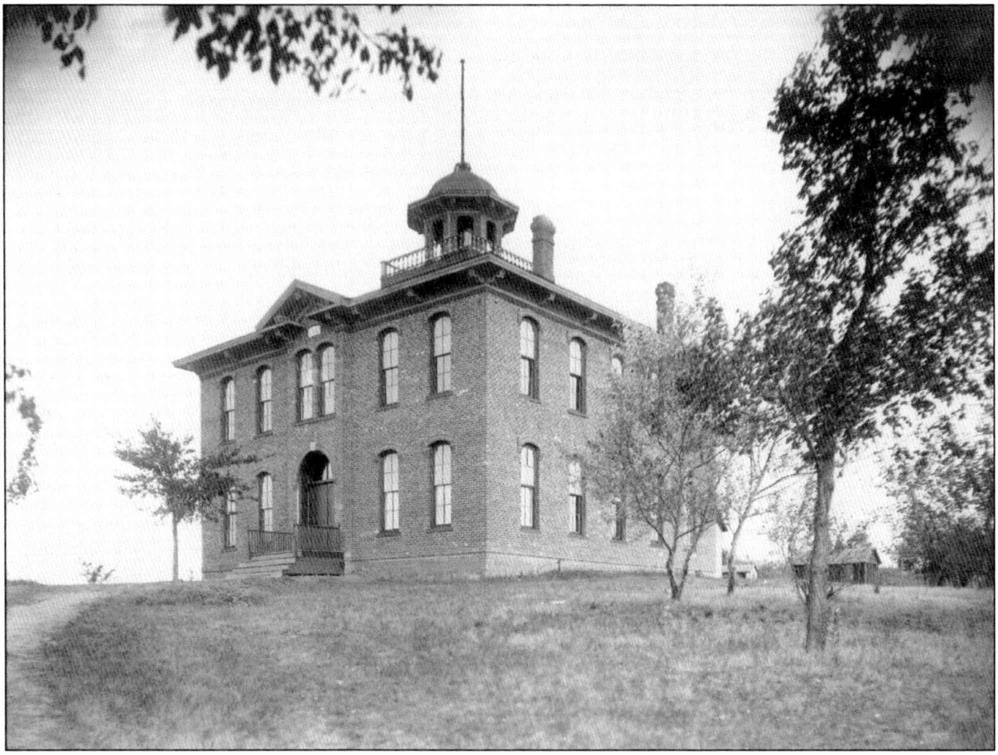

The Association of Congregational Churches established Gates Academy in 1881. The main building stood on a hill northeast of town. Gates became a college in 1892, attracting students from across the country. It was the only Nebraska college between the Platte River and the Dakota Territory for several years. Gates became an academy in 1899 and was discontinued in 1914. (ACHS.)

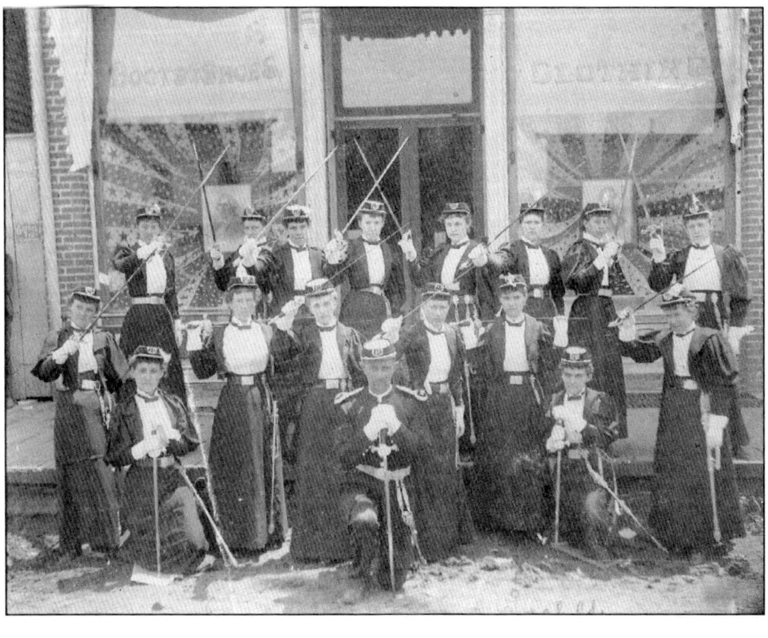

Female students at Gates College hold their swords high as they pose for this photograph in 1896, likely during a patriotic celebration of some sort. The store windows in the background have flag designs on display. (Courtesy of Kenneth Krohn.)

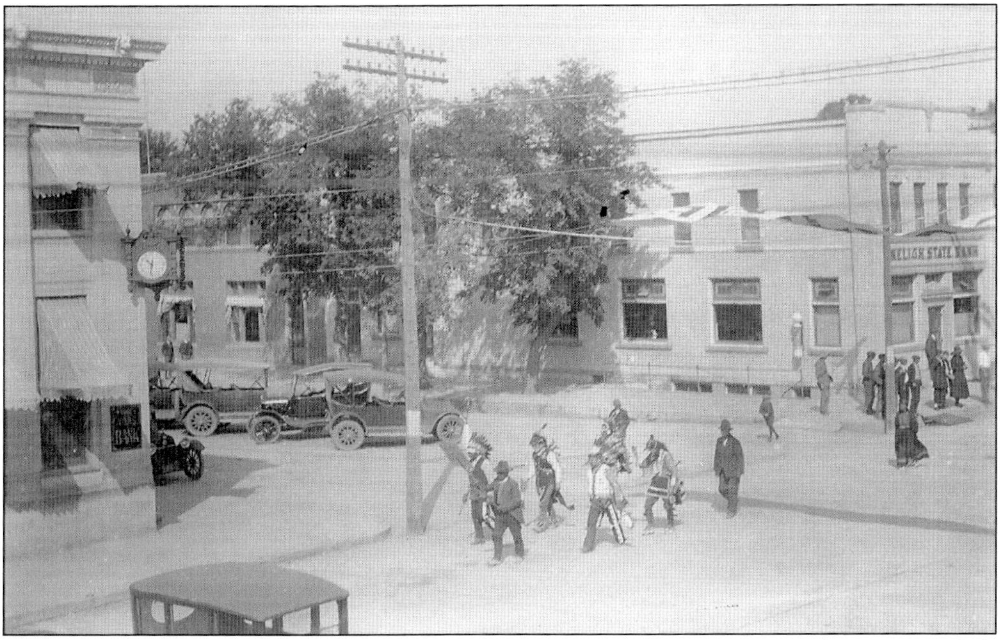

The Old Settlers' Association, founded in 1886, is seen holding a celebration in downtown Neligh in 1911. The association was active until the 1920s and was reestablished as the Antelope County Historical Society in 1955. A corner of the Atlas Bank is on the left, and the Neligh State Bank is across the street. (ACHS.)

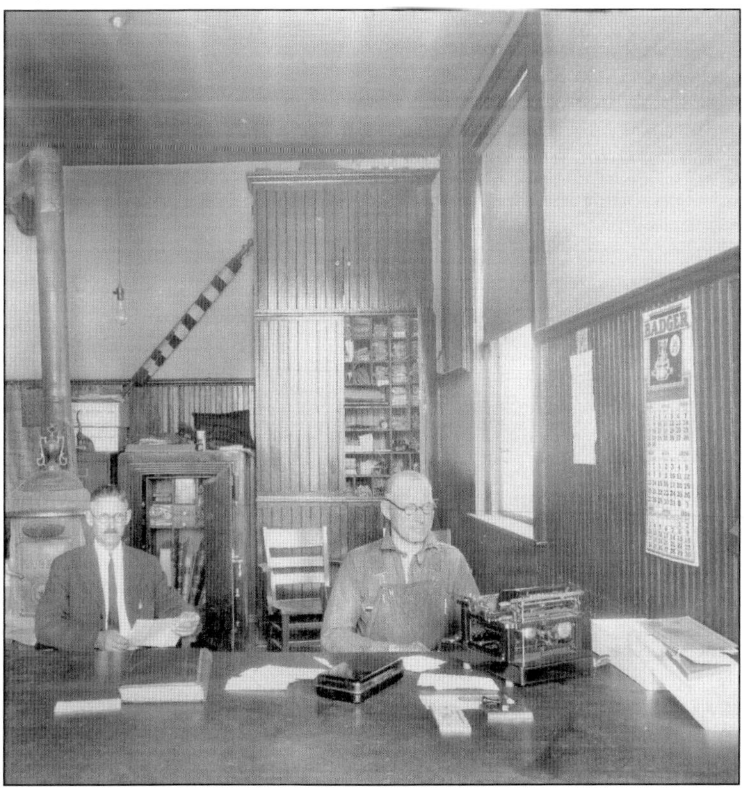

Neligh filed incorporation papers for designation as a second-class city in March 1888 and received confirmation on April 6. Neligh and Chadron were the only designated cities west of Norfolk. W.C. Estes was the first mayor. Seen here in the city office in 1928 are police judge Ed Godkin (left) and water commissioner Gus Reiss. (ACHS.)

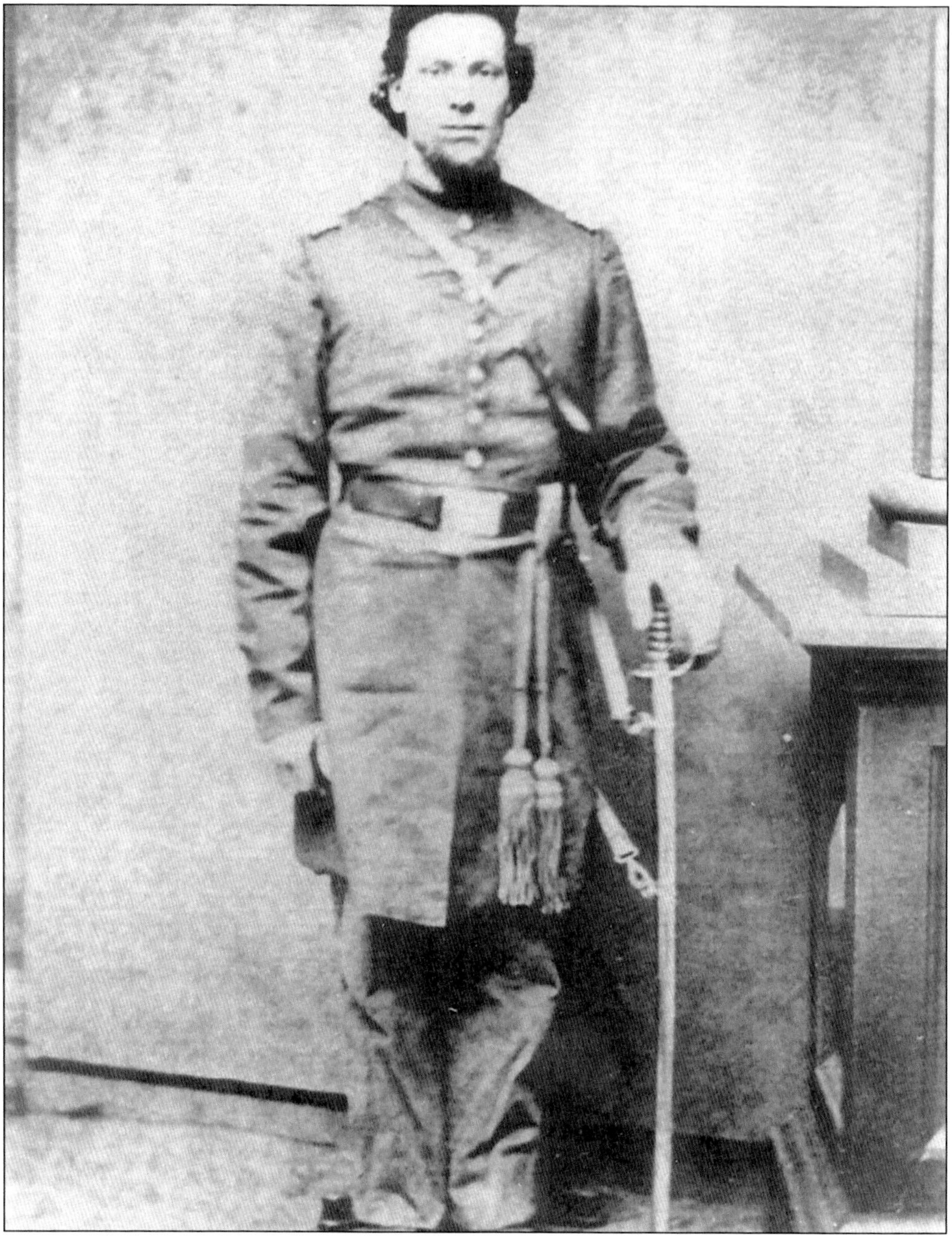

Capt. J.D. Hatfield arrived in Neligh in 1895 to look after land he had purchased. The former Union officer took part in Sherman's march through Georgia, survived a serious wound, and escaped from Libby Prison with fellow inmates by digging a tunnel. Captain Hatfield served as Antelope County treasurer and was elected to the state legislature in 1909. (ACHS.)

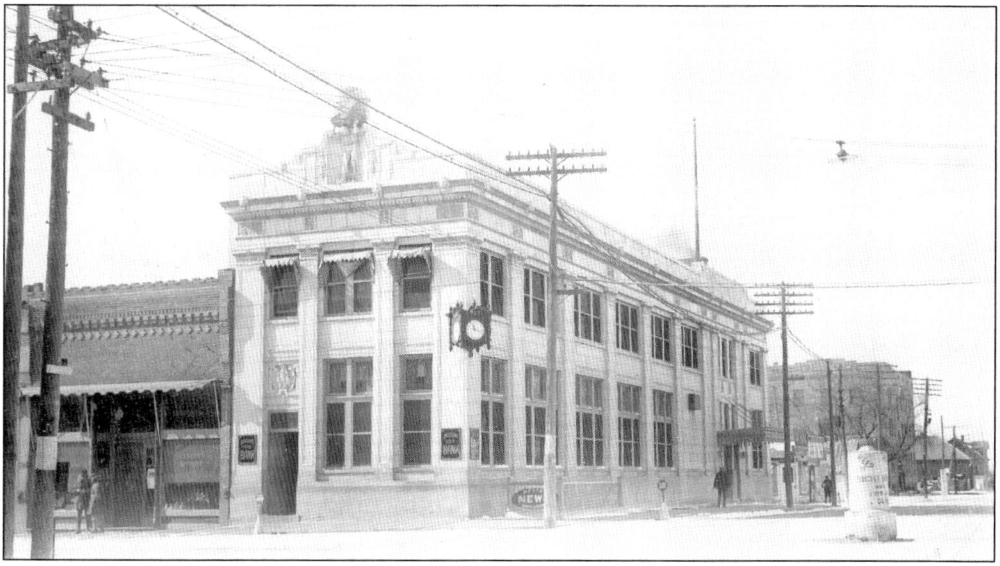

In 1918, the Atlas Bank opened its impressive doors. Faced with Indiana stone, it was considered the finest structure in the city. A cast or stone figure of Atlas supporting the world graced the top of the building. A three-sided clock extended from a corner of the bank and chimed the hours. During remodeling in the 1950s, the clock was removed, and Atlas's globe now resides on the bank's top floor. (ACHS.)

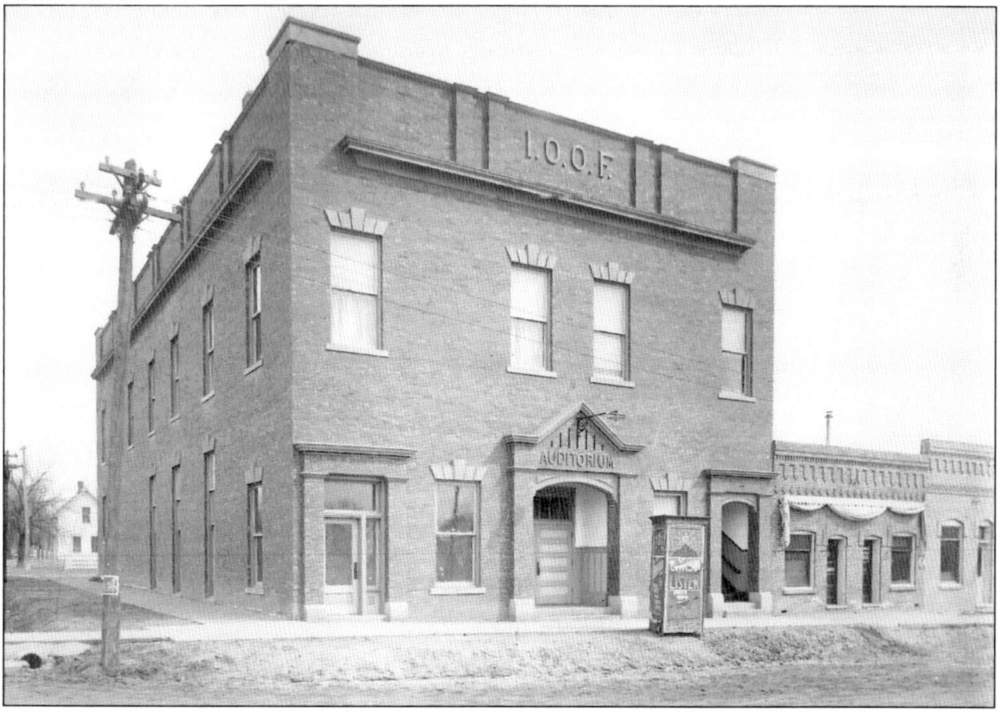

The Neligh Auditorium, erected in 1907, provided a meeting place for the Independent Order of Odd Fellows on the second floor. The Jenkins law office occupied rooms on the ground floor, and the main room provided space for lectures and other entertainment. C.J. Jenkins showed the first movies in town on the ground floor. An advertising kiosk stood outside the auditorium. (ACHS.)

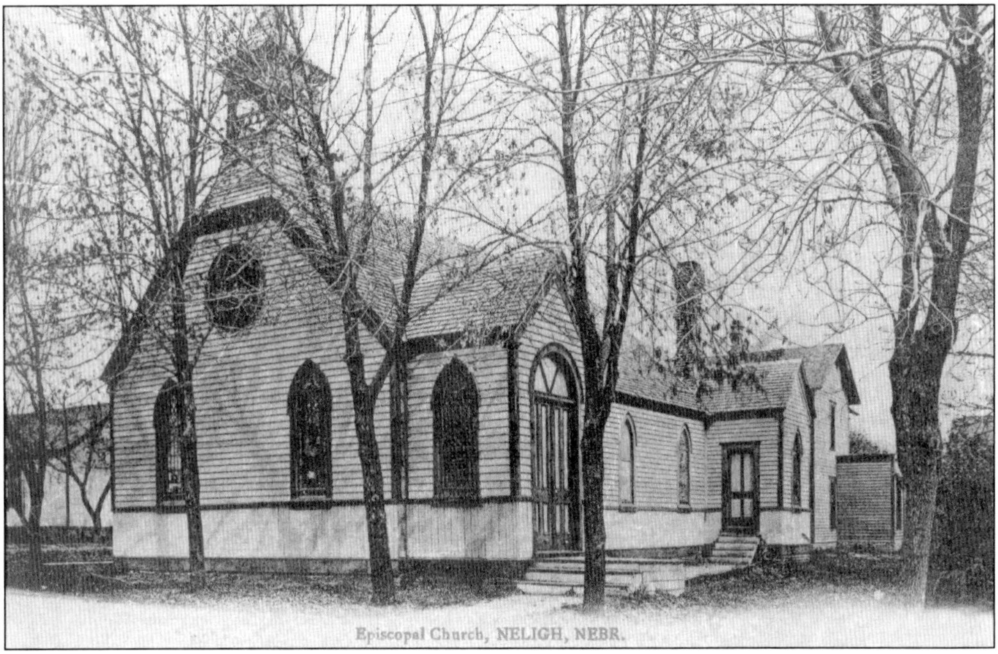

Before their church building was erected in 1887, Neligh Episcopalians met at Court House Hall (now Wanek Pharmacy). In 1886, the Women's Guild contributed the first $100 to buy three lots at Cottonwood and Main Streets (now Fifth and L Streets). This church was constructed on the newly purchased land. (ACHS.)

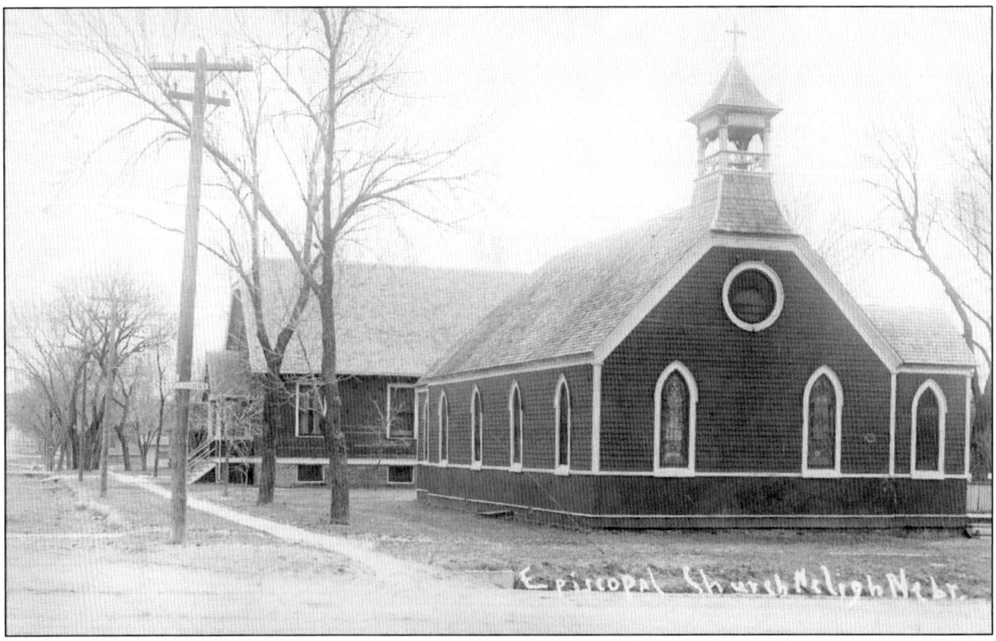

St. Peter's Episcopal Church, erected in 1887 in a simple Gothic Revival style, featured Eastlake stained-glass windows and an oil-on-canvas reproduction of Bernhard Plockhorst's *Good Shepherd*, painted in the early 1900s by Bishop Arthur L. Williams's wife, Adelaide McKinster Williams. The church is now part of the Antelope County Museum complex. (ACHS.)

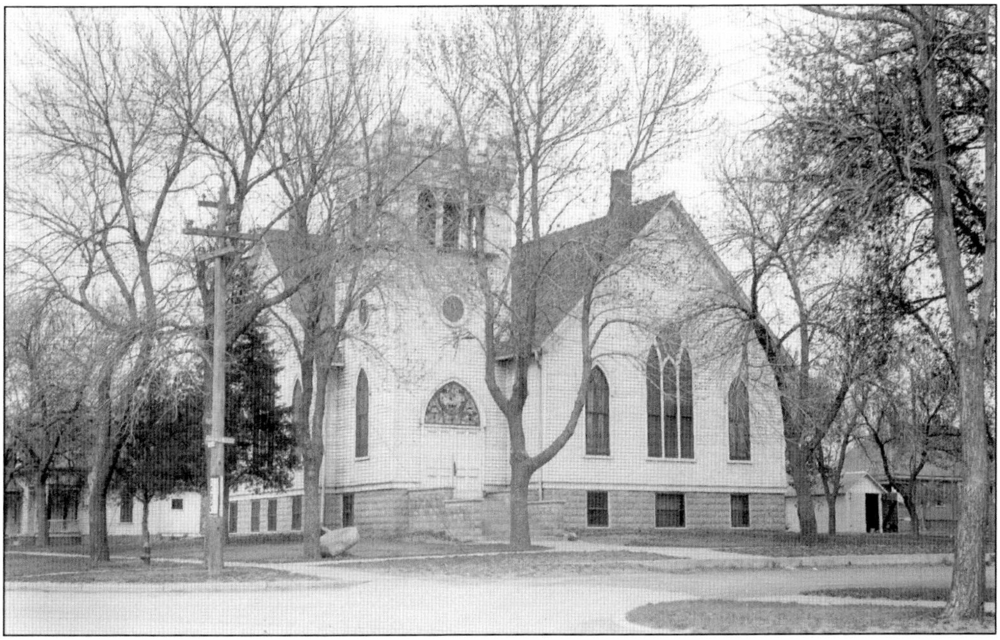

Rev. Henry Griffiths organized Neligh's First Congregational Church (United Church of Christ) on March 22, 1875, in the schoolhouse. Services continued to take place at the school until this church was erected in 1886 at Sixth and Main Streets. (ACHS.)

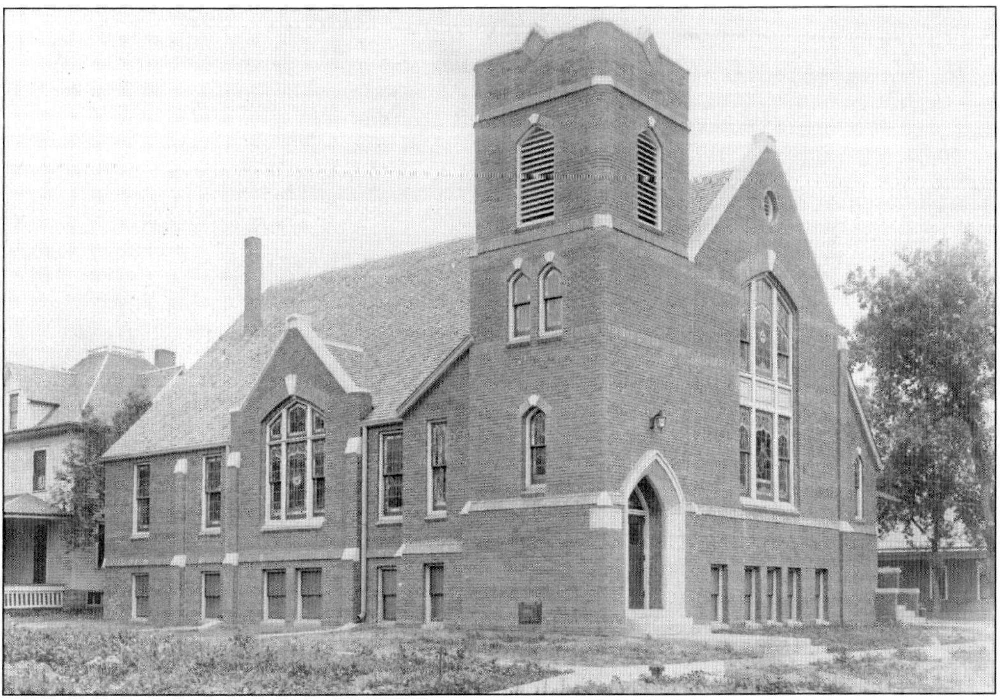

After a successful fund drive, the first shovelful of dirt for a new Methodist church building was dug on March 31, 1920. J.R. Smith of Lincoln was the architect, and Fred Thornton of Neligh was the superintendent of construction. On July 10, 1920, the cornerstone was laid, and the dedication took place on February 19, 1922. (Courtesy of Kenneth Krohn.)

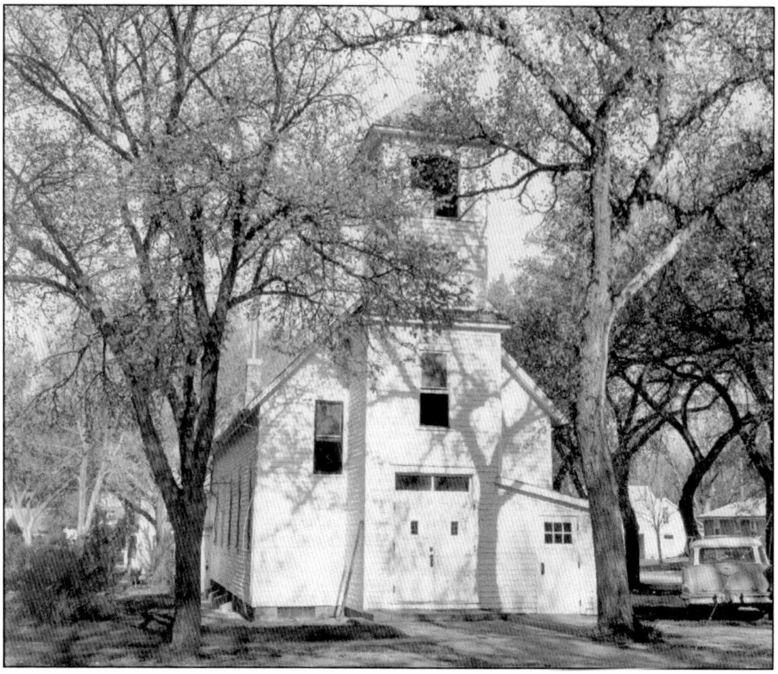

Two months after Barney Ryan purchased two lots on the corner of present-day Sixth and J Streets, he deeded the property to the Catholic bishop of Omaha. In 1900, a small frame church was completed, and it eventually came under the patronage of St. Francis of Assisi. A new church on Highway 275 was completed in 1962. (ACHS.)

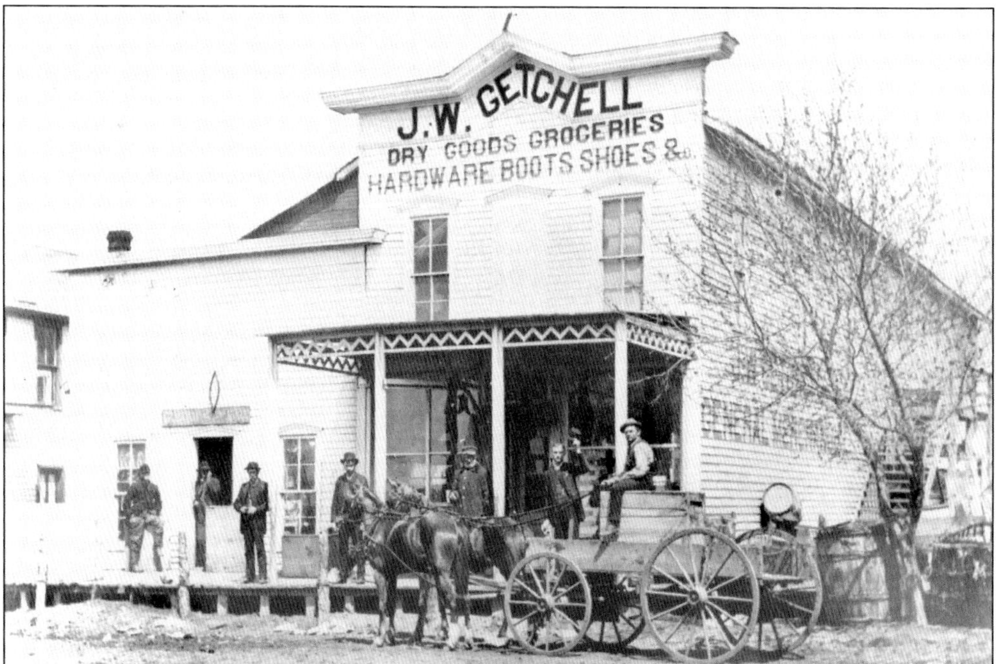

One of the earliest stores in Neligh, J.W. Getchell's general store is seen here in 1886. A newspaper advertisement stated that all kinds of country produce were taken in exchange for goods at the store. Seen in front of the store are, from left to right, an unidentified man, Bill Lawson, Gus Lancaster, John Getchell, unidentified, Will Lancaster, and Pete Lawson (on wagon). (ACHS.)

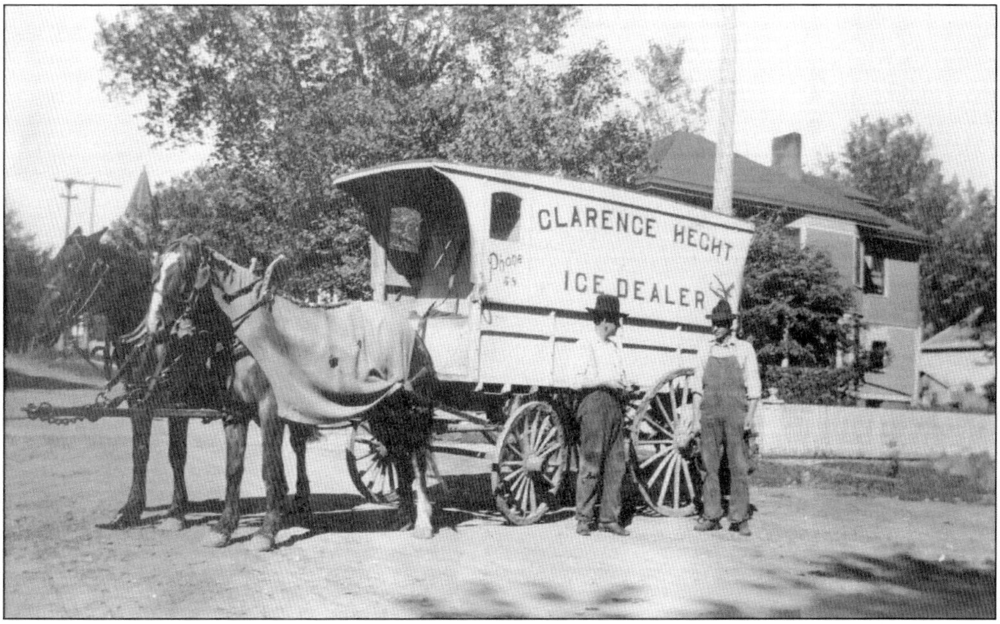

Clarence Hecht's ice wagon is seen here on a hot summer day around 1900. Before making a delivery, the driver (possibly Hecht) visits with an acquaintance. One of the horses pulling the ice wagon wears a burlap cover. The courthouse spire rises behind the trees in the right background. (ACHS.)

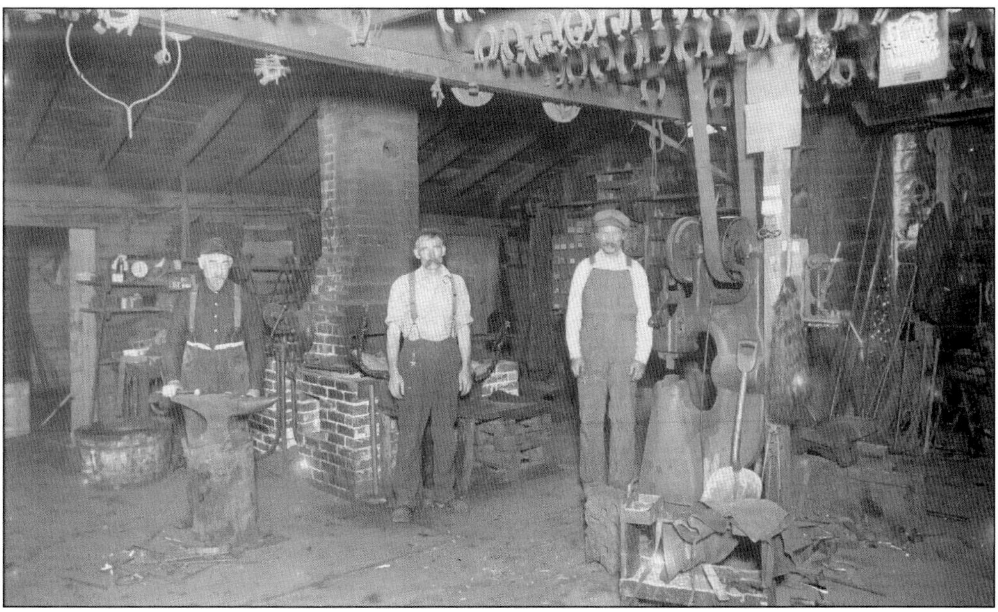

In 1907, a blacksmith and his two assistants stand beside their charcoal forge and behind the large anvil used to size horseshoes. In addition to shoeing horses, blacksmiths fabricated items for farm use and repaired wagon and carriage wheels. (ACHS.)

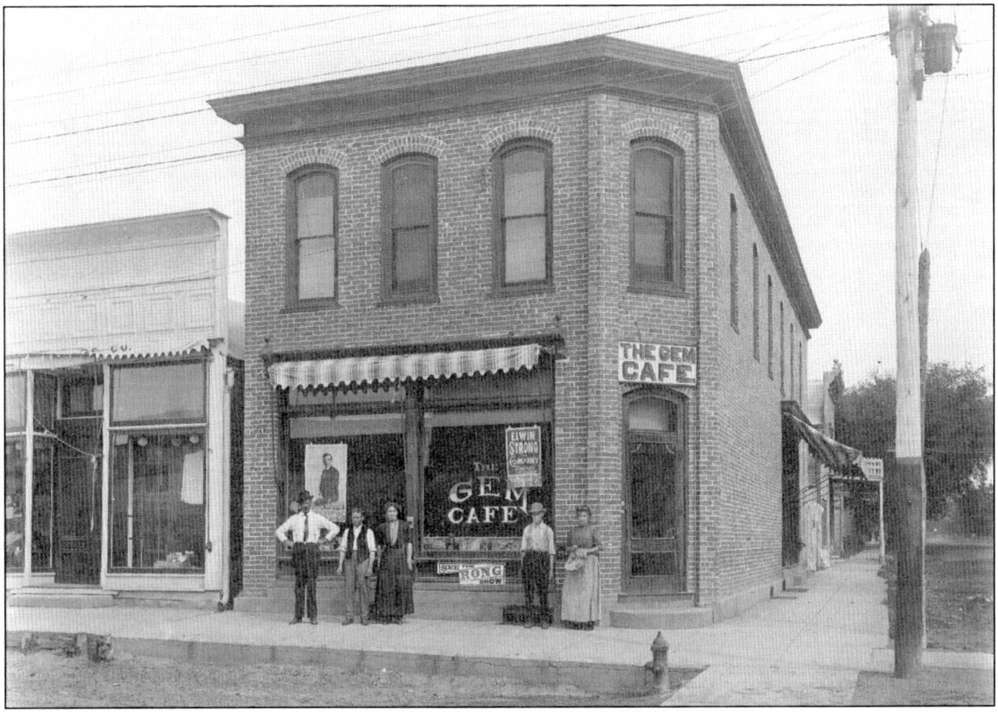

Pictured in 1915 across the street from the Union Store on the south end of Neligh's Main Street is the Gem Café. An edge of Anderson's Mercantile appears on the left, and a few customers stand in front of the café. (ACHS.)

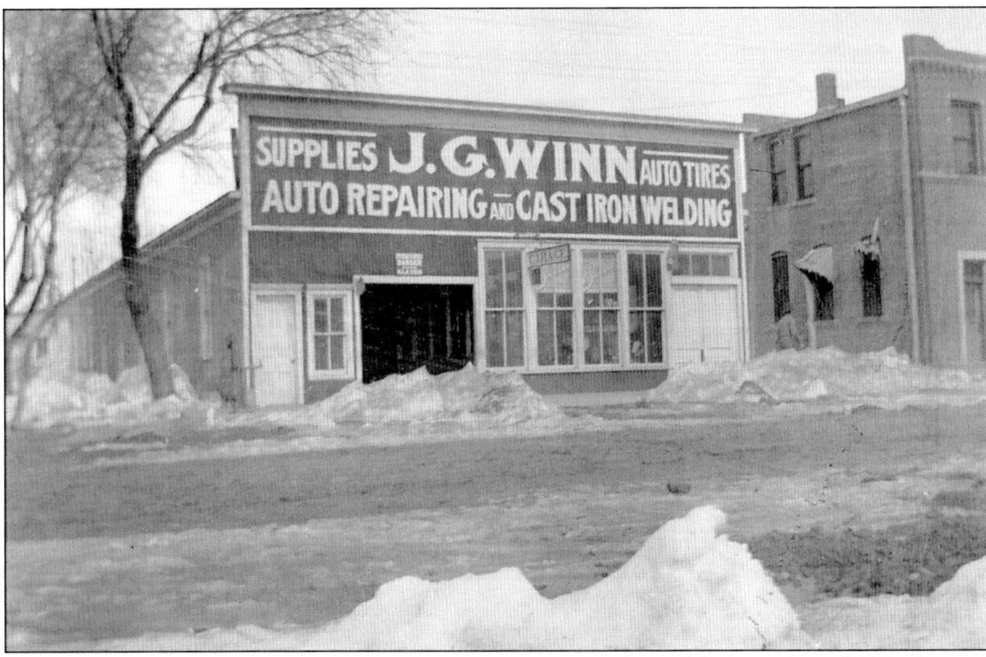

Jesse Grant Winn owned the Winn garage, where he served as a blacksmith, a skill he learned from his father, and a machinist/mechanic. He also sold Ford cars. While he was repairing a car in 1937, the engine caught fire and burned him to death. (ACHS.)

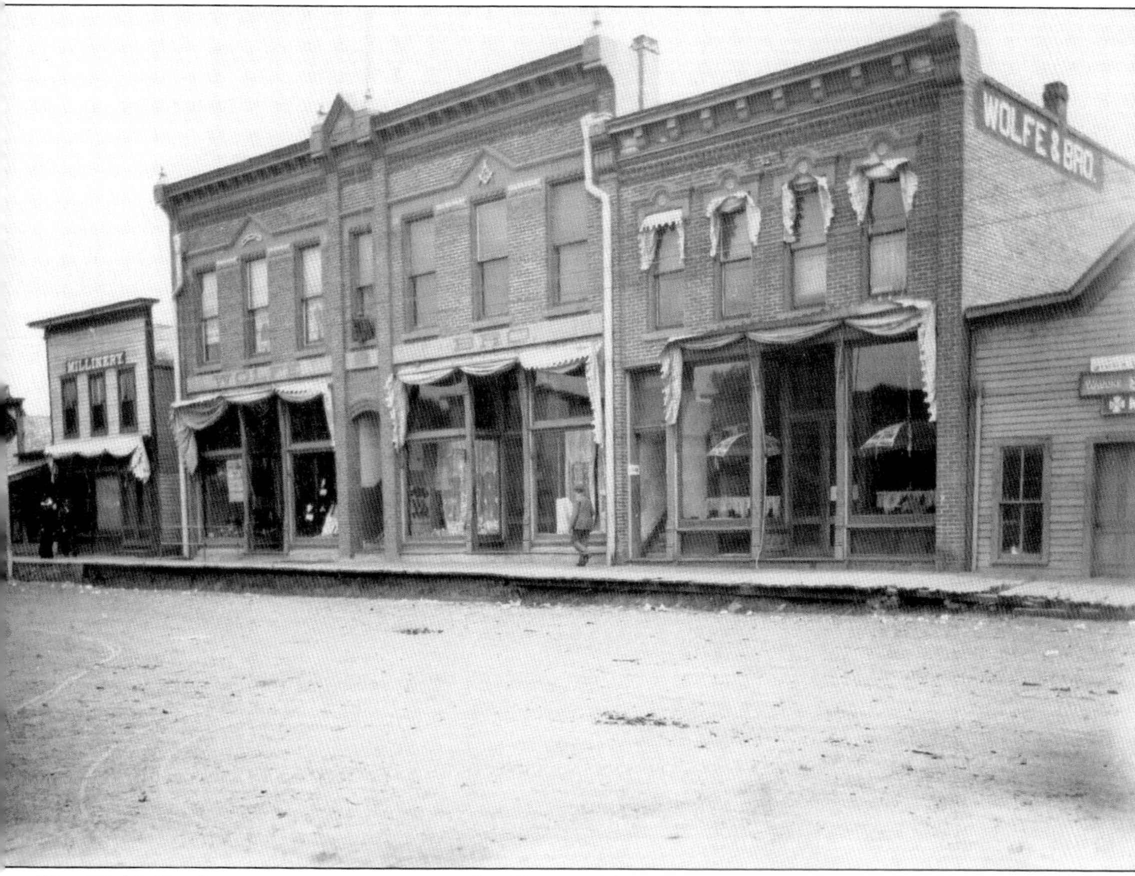

The Wolfe Brothers store was a prominent building on Main Street in 1894. Emanuel "Monte," Ira "Ike," and William Wolfe established the store in Neligh and then opened branches in Oakdale and Elgin. They owned the largest mercantile business in northeastern Nebraska west of Norfolk. Monte, an accomplished amateur photographer, recorded a pictorial history of Neligh. (Courtesy of Kenneth Krohn.)

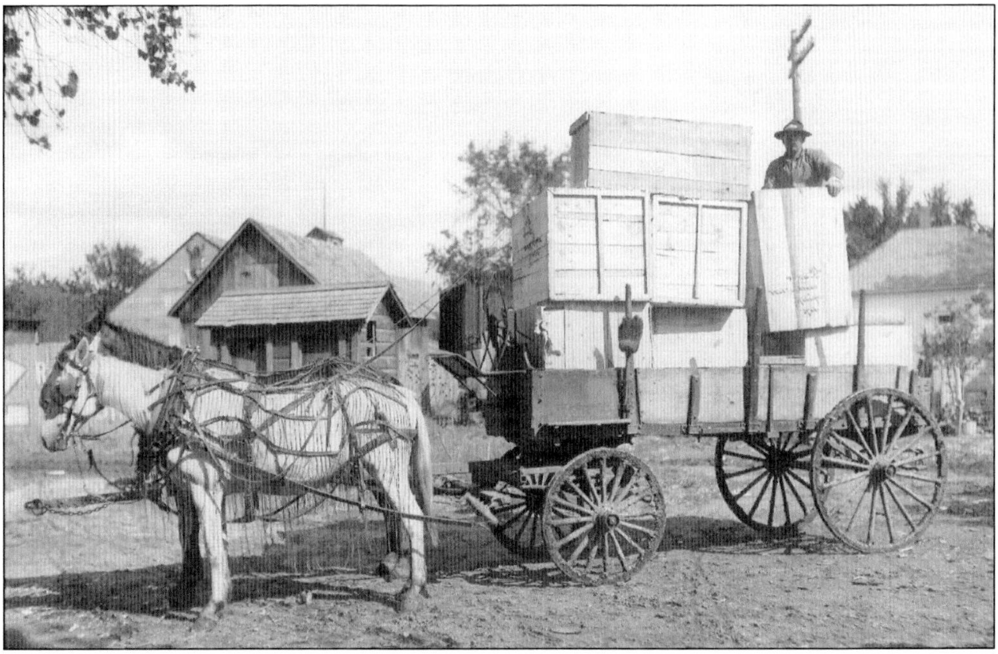

In 1903, the Wolfe Brothers delivery wagon is ready to depart after an unidentified man loaded it. The livery stable at Third and L Streets is in the background. (ACHS.)

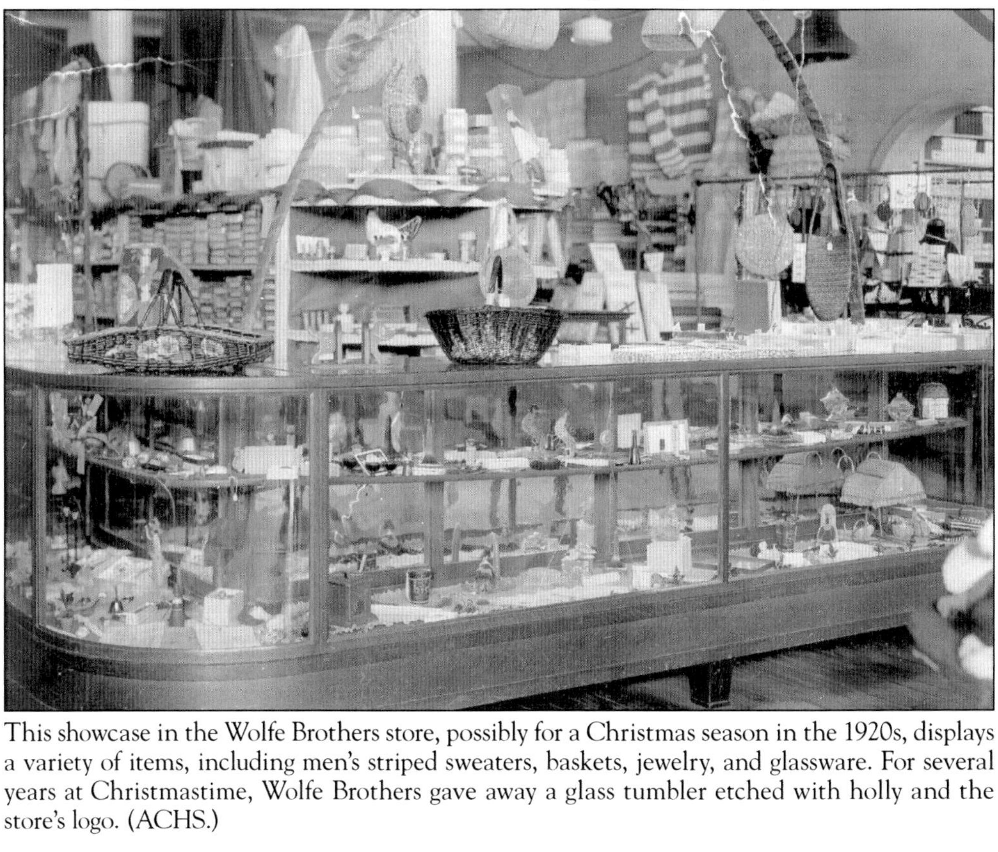

This showcase in the Wolfe Brothers store, possibly for a Christmas season in the 1920s, displays a variety of items, including men's striped sweaters, baskets, jewelry, and glassware. For several years at Christmastime, Wolfe Brothers gave away a glass tumbler etched with holly and the store's logo. (ACHS.)

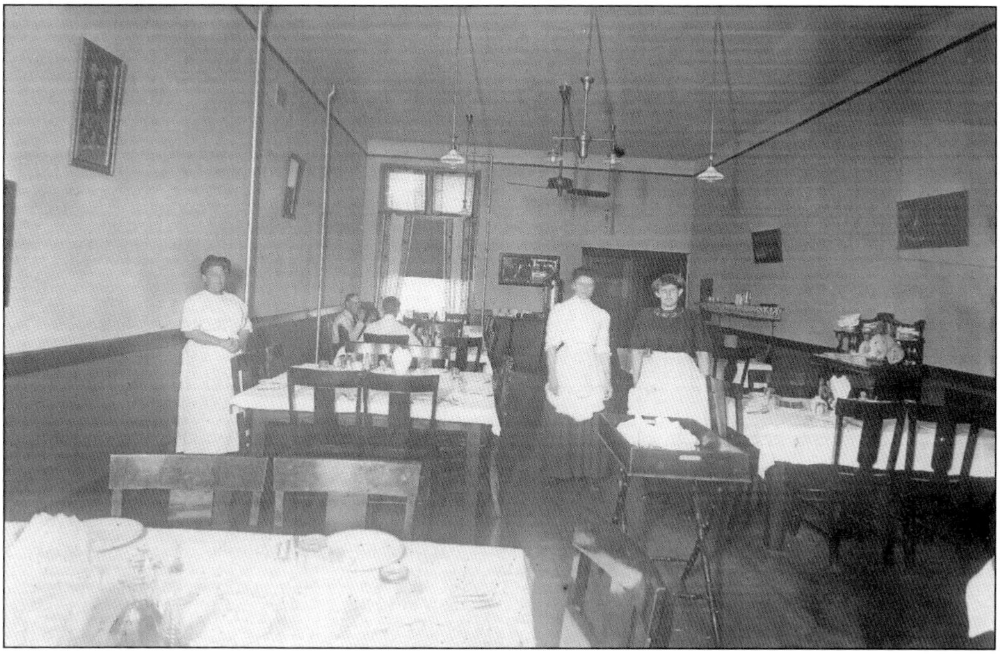

The Nehoco Hotel was built in 1913. The name was derived from the first two letters of each word in Neligh Hotel Company. Here, in 1915, waitresses stand ready to serve a meal in the dining room. (ACHS.)

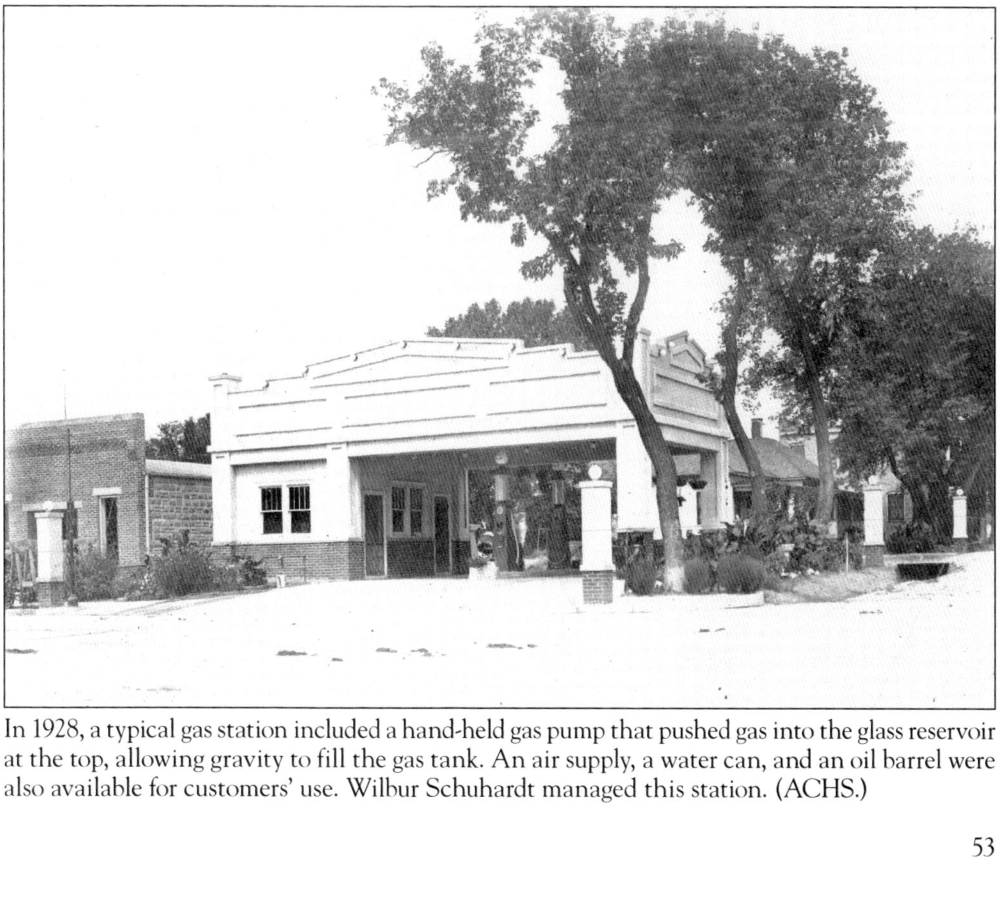

In 1928, a typical gas station included a hand-held gas pump that pushed gas into the glass reservoir at the top, allowing gravity to fill the gas tank. An air supply, a water can, and an oil barrel were also available for customers' use. Wilbur Schuhardt managed this station. (ACHS.)

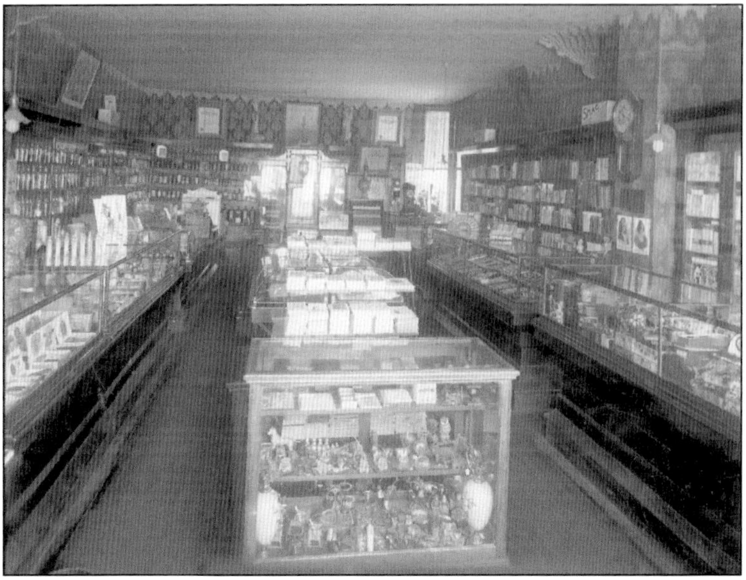

Seen in 1913, the Remington drugstore supplied Neligh residents with a variety of products in addition to filling prescriptions. Teachers bought classroom supplies, ladies purchased perfumes and makeup, and their husbands bought boxes of cigars. (ACHS.)

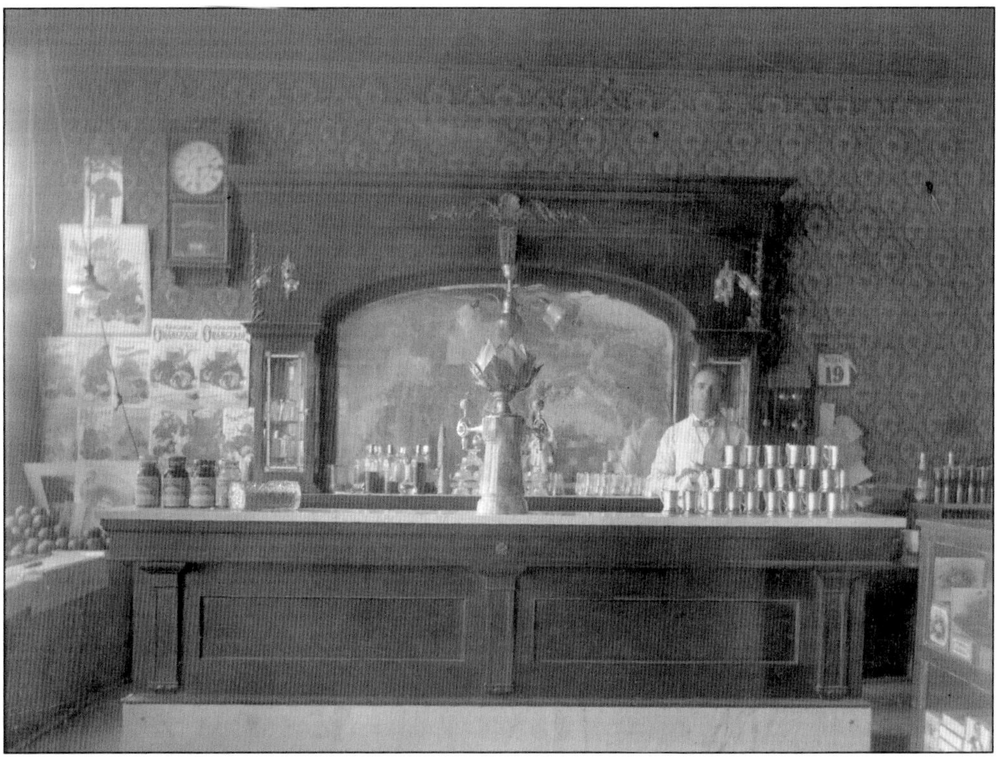

A clerk stands behind the Remington drugstore soda fountain in 1918 ready to serve customers. An ornate soda dispenser, syrups, glasses, and silver cup holders are a few of the accessories seen here, along with advertising posters pinned beside and below the Regulator clock. A large mirror is in the center of the fountain area. (ACHS.)

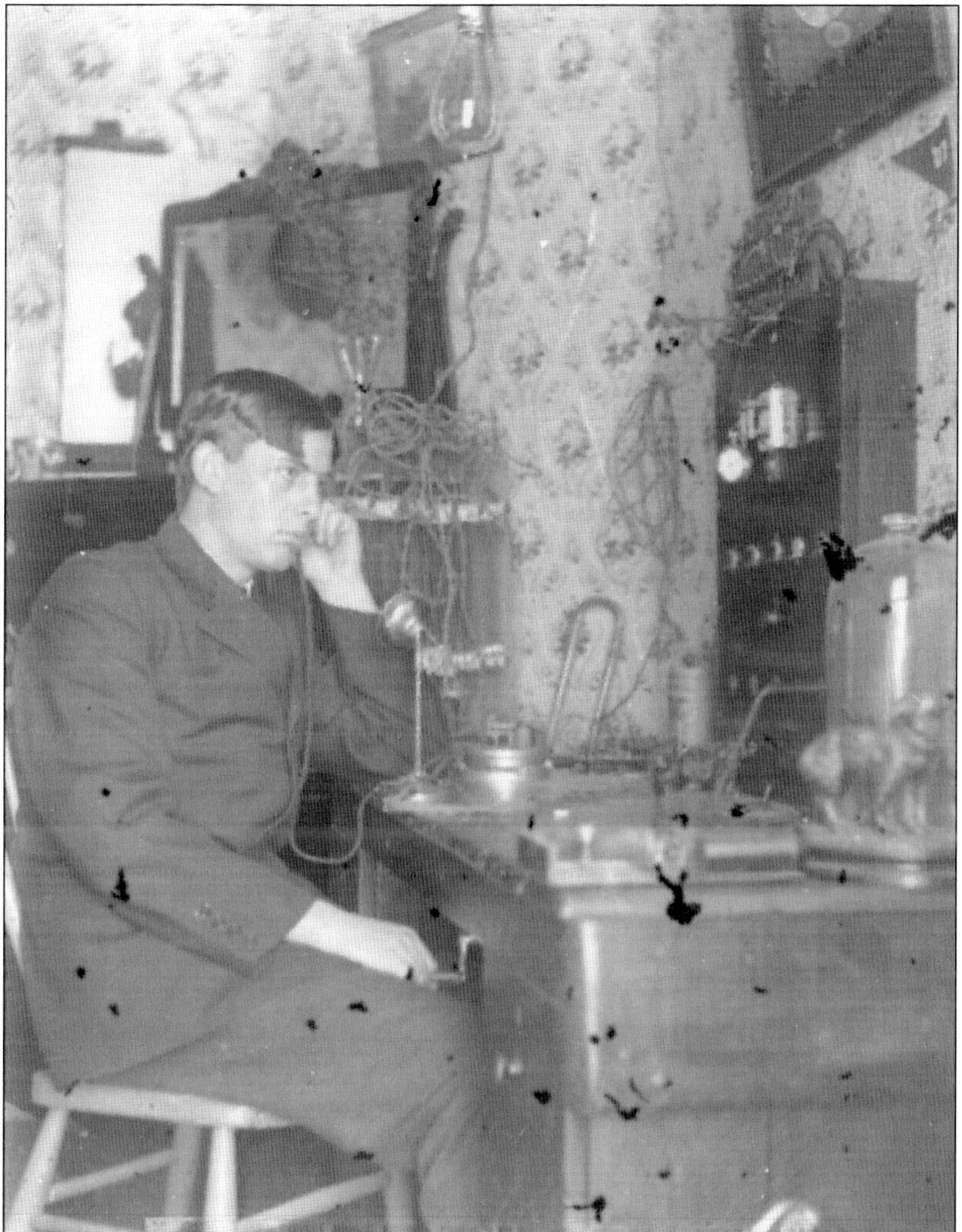

Telephone service was established in Neligh in March 1902. Milton Everson worked for the Hauser Telephone Company and helped set up the Neligh service. He is seen here in front of the new switchboard that served additional customers, including the county offices of treasurer, attorney, sheriff, school superintendent, and judge. A telephone was also placed in the public school. (ACHS.)

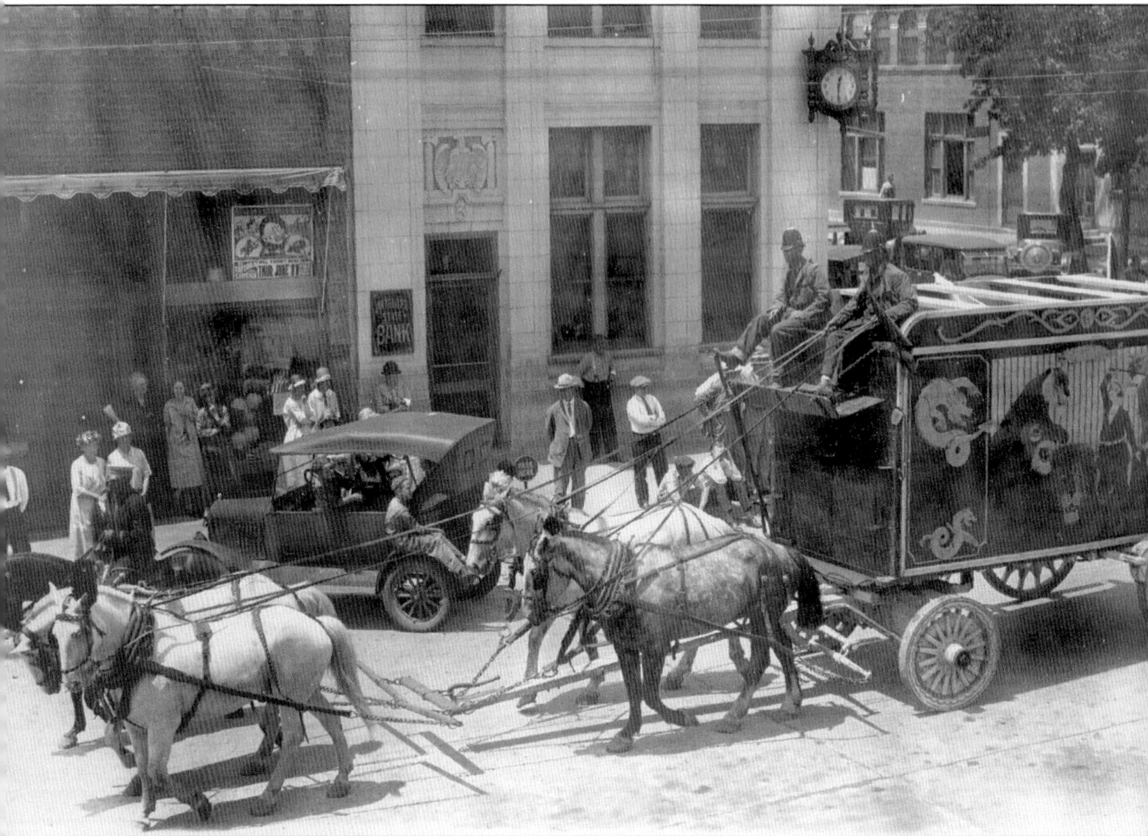

Around 1936, a circus parade proceeds down Neligh's Main Street, drawing the attention of those who were downtown. The gaily painted circus wagon pulled by a four-horse team is seen passing the Atlas Bank. (ACHS.)

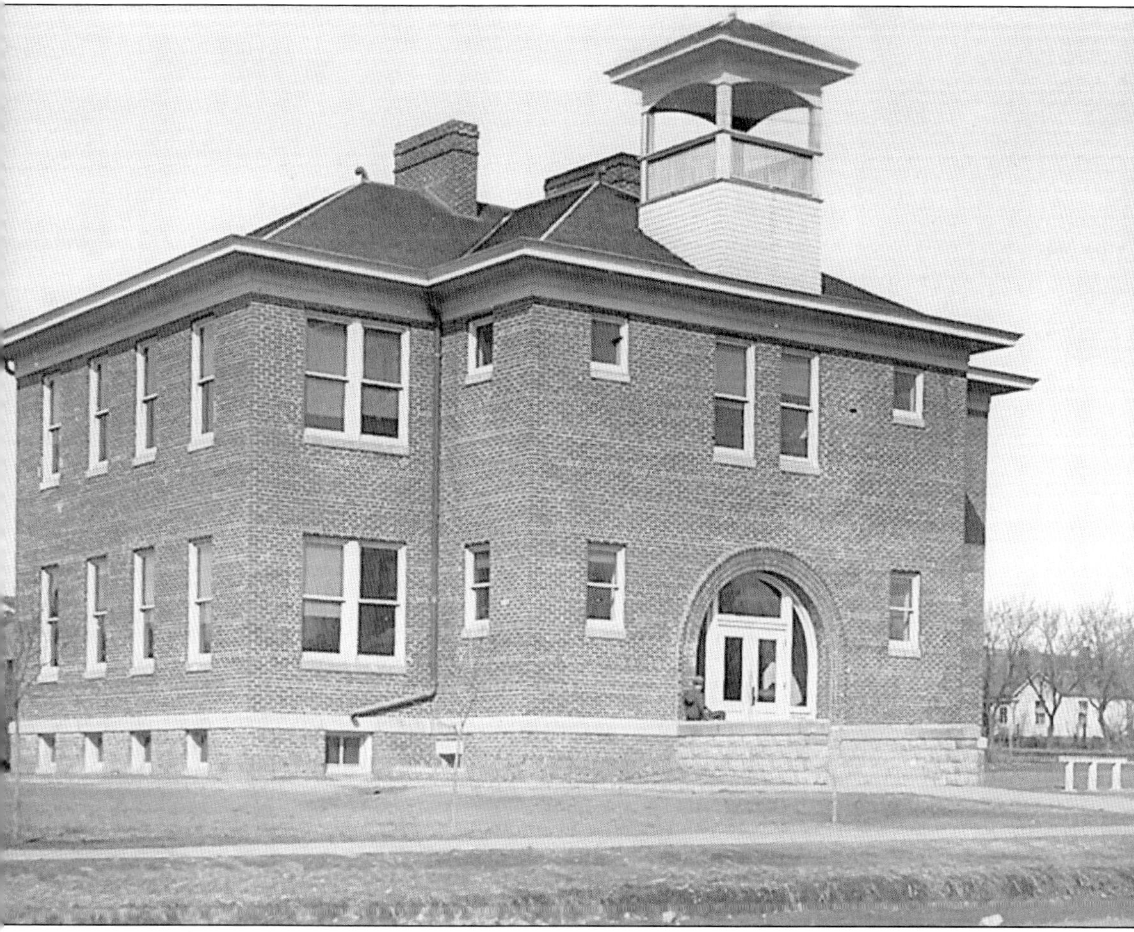

From 1916 until 1977, this two-story brick school, constructed by Neligh builder Howard Kester and his crew, served students in kindergarten through sixth grade who lived west of Highway 275. Those residing east of the highway attended the East Ward School. Kindergarten and first and second grades were on the first floor; grades three through six met on the second floor. (ACHS.)

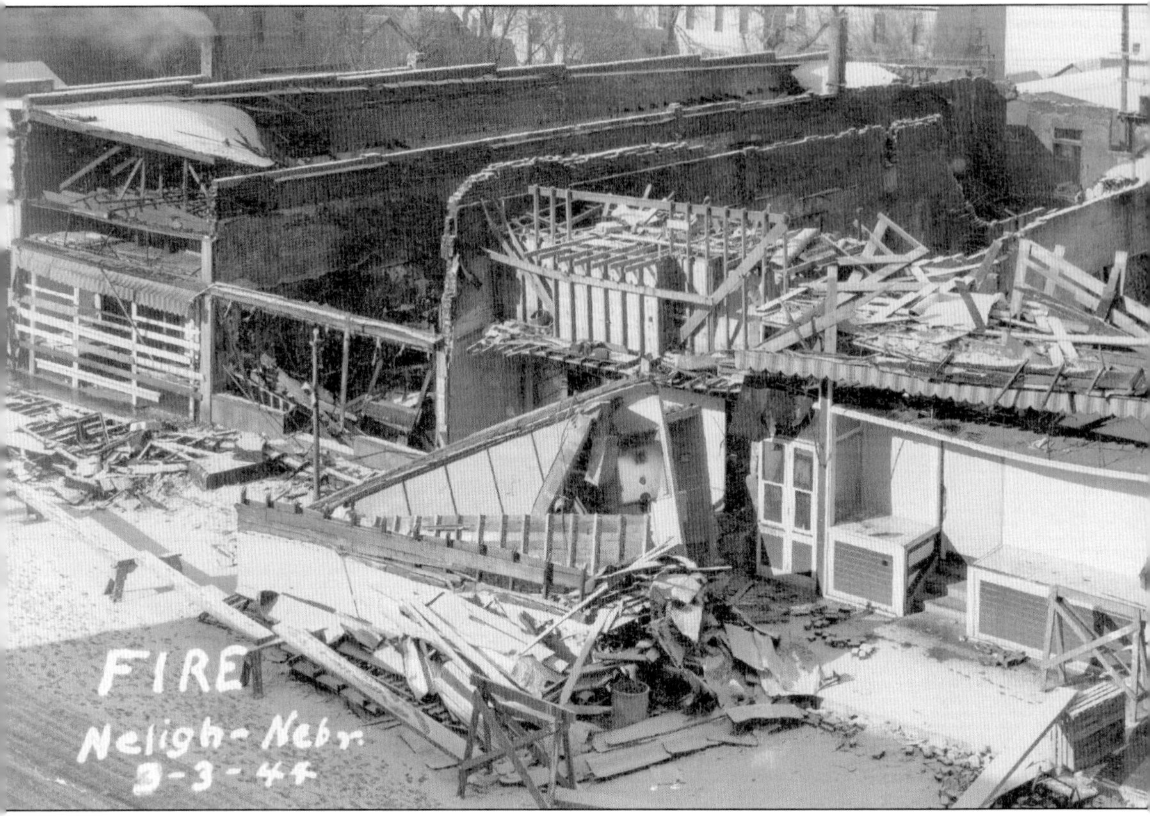

On March 3, 1944, fire departments from surrounding towns helped fight the early-morning blaze that destroyed Wanek Pharmacy, the Moon Theater, Hewitt Jewelry, and J.C. Penney. Eight other businesses suffered damage, and total losses exceeded $100,000. (ACHS.)

Four

Tilden

Straddling Two Counties

The Fremont, Elkhorn & Missouri Valley Railroad fulfilled the wishes of Tilden area settlers when it constructed a depot in 1879. The depot was on the line dividing Madison and Antelope Counties. In 1880, Charles Burnham, who helped build the depot, enlisted his son to help him erect a store on the Antelope County side; meanwhile, the railroad negotiated with landowners south of the depot to obtain property for establishing a town. By the spring of 1880, the town was platted and named Burnett. Two rectangular blocks were on the Madison County side, and two were on the Antelope County side.

In 1885, the Madison County side of the village was incorporated. Since the Antelope County part of town could not be incorporated due to the lack of a state law governing such a circumstance, Antelope County residents benefitted from improvements on the Madison County side. Also, the county line's position made it possible to disturb the public peace on the Madison County side and then run across Center Street to Antelope County and avoid arrest. Fortunately, future laws made a total incorporation of the two areas possible.

The confusion in mail delivery between Burnett and Bennett, Nebraska, resulted in the federal government urging Burnett to change its name. In 1889, Burnett was renamed Tilden after Samuel J. Tilden, a defeated presidential candidate whose loyal supporters lived in the area. In 1919, Tilden had about 1,000 inhabitants, and the 2010 census reported a population of 953.

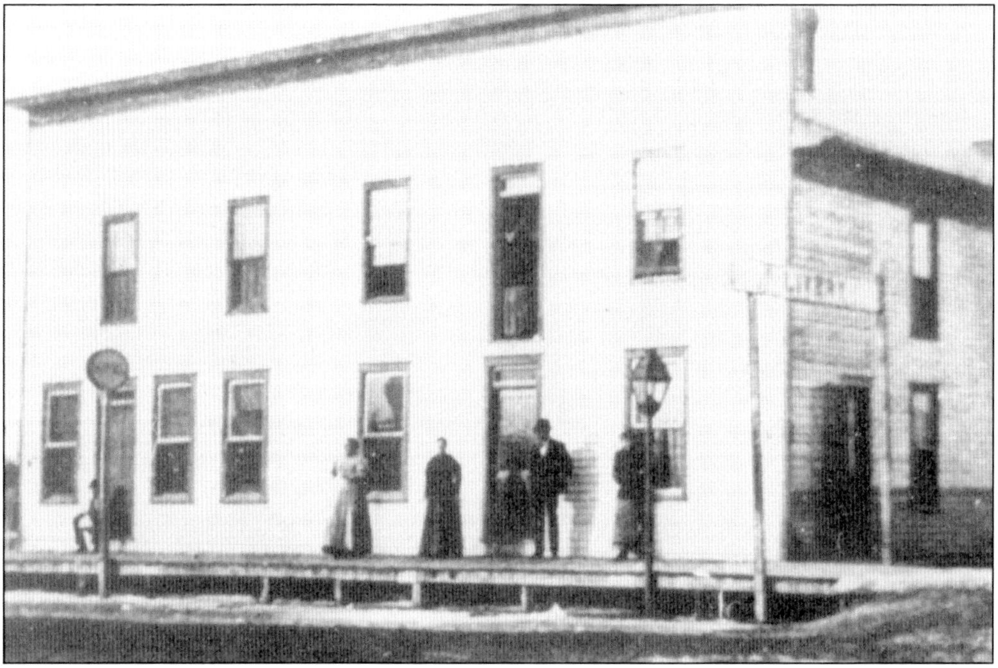

In the summer of 1885, Harry Davis, who had owned a rooming house near the depot, built a hotel just south of the depot on the west side of Center Street. The Davis House Hotel received a favorable review in the *Burnett Blade*. It was well built, well furnished, well kept, and offered good food. (Courtesy of Arlene Hofmann.)

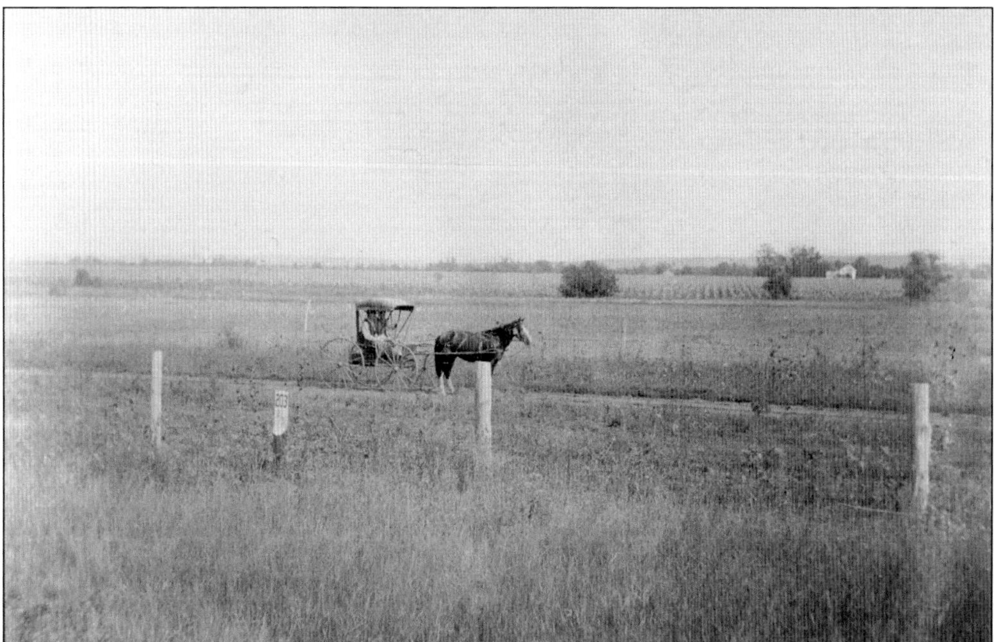

A couple riding along a country road in their horse and buggy have a view of a cornfield and a farmhouse in the distance. Pictured around 1890, they are likely on their way to church or to a social event in town. (Courtesy of Lois Johnson.)

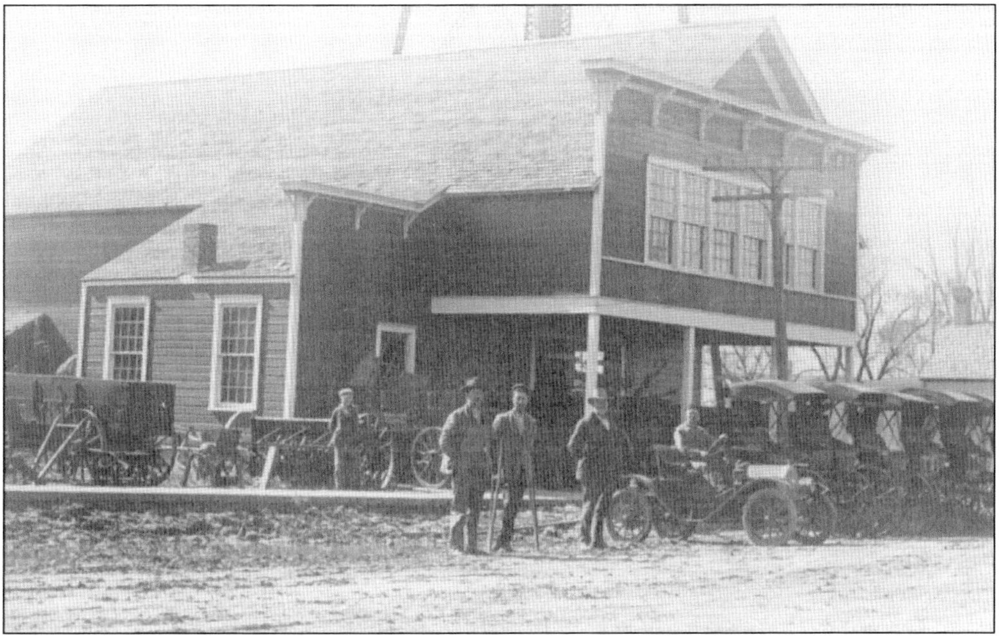

Tilden businesses added to their buildings in 1899, enhancing their appearances and adding storage capacities; this included Irving's implement store. Here, Irving's has several early automobiles on display. A group of wagons is also displayed. Wagons remained a practical and economical choice for agricultural work. (Courtesy of Arlene Hofmann.)

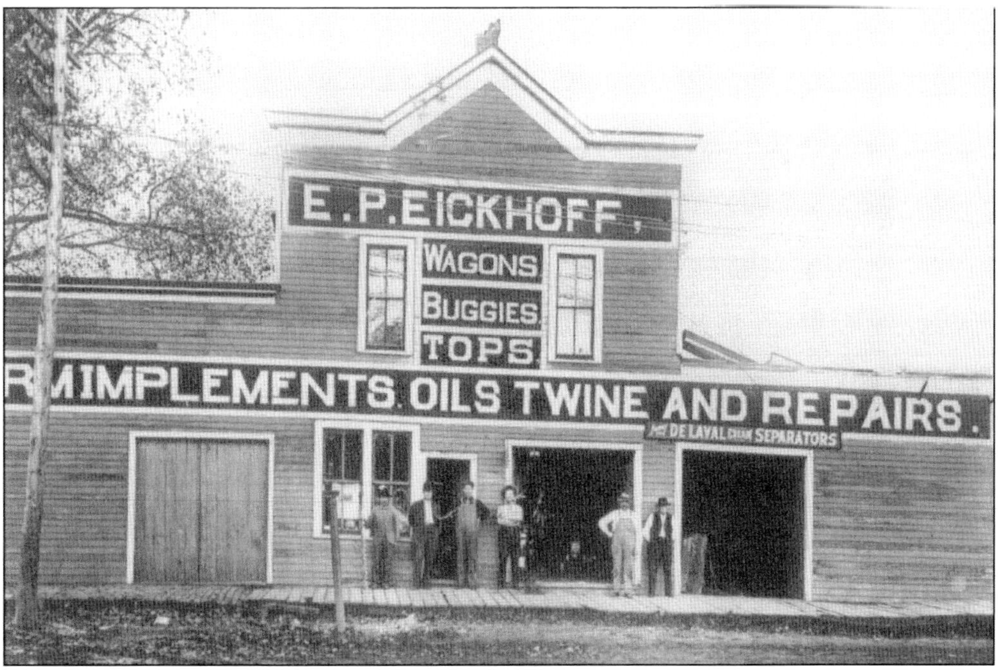

A group of men stands in front of E.P. Eickhoff's store around 1900. The board sidewalk in front was typical of the time; similar sidewalks had been installed in front of businesses since 1884. If they were not anchored firmly, the walks floated down the street when Giles Creek flooded, often carrying merrymakers on top. (Courtesy of Arlene Hofmann.)

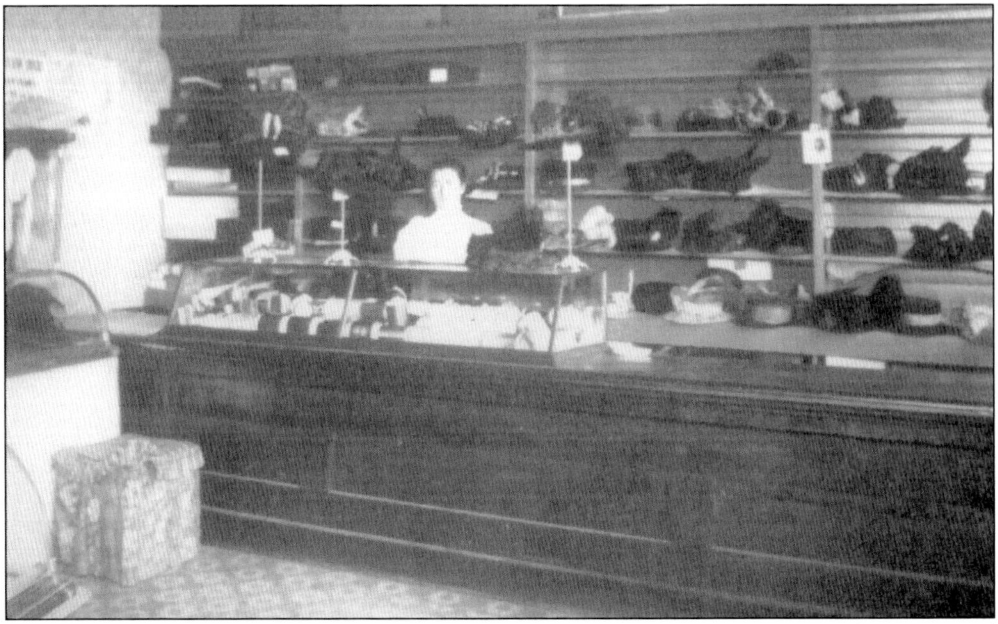

Hats were an essential part of an individual's attire around 1900, and enterprising milliners opened shops in frontier towns, where they designed and sold hats. From 1889 to 1895, the Botsford sisters owned a millinery shop in Tilden, and in 1904 J.H. Johnson opened a shop. Between 1910 and 1919, Mrs. E. Burnham, Mrs. Mayes, Mrs. S. Blackman, and Edith Cunningham all opened new millinery shops. An unidentified millinery shop is seen here. (Courtesy of Arlene Hofmann.)

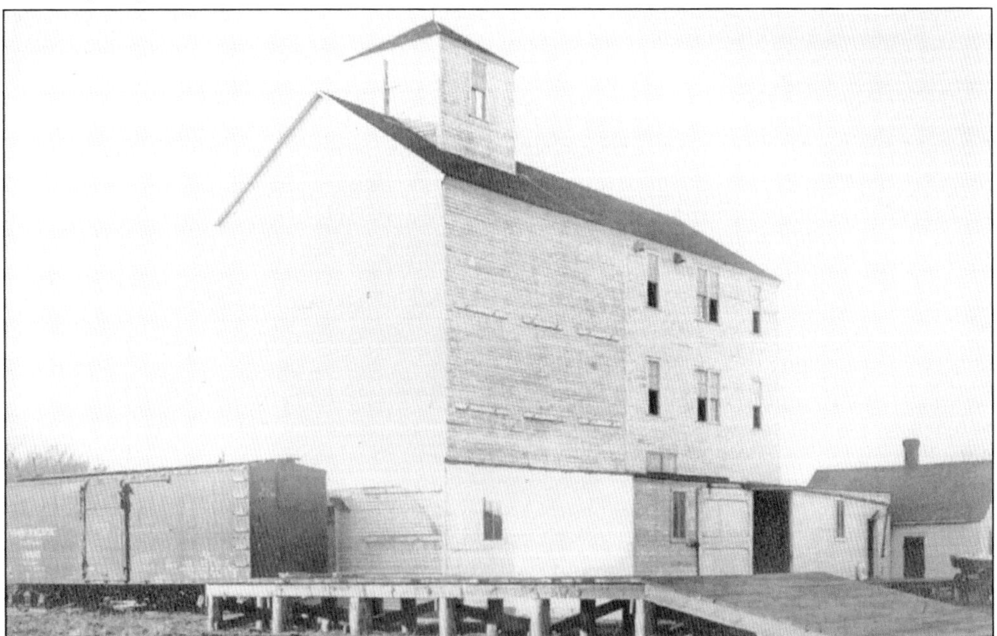

A long-awaited flour mill was built in Tilden in 1903 by partners Will Corkle and Dan Dauphin. It stood on the north side of the railroad tracks on the Antelope County side of Center Street. The first carload of flour was shipped to Stuart, Nebraska, in 1904. The mill produced the Our Best brand of flour. (Courtesy of Arlene Hofmann.)

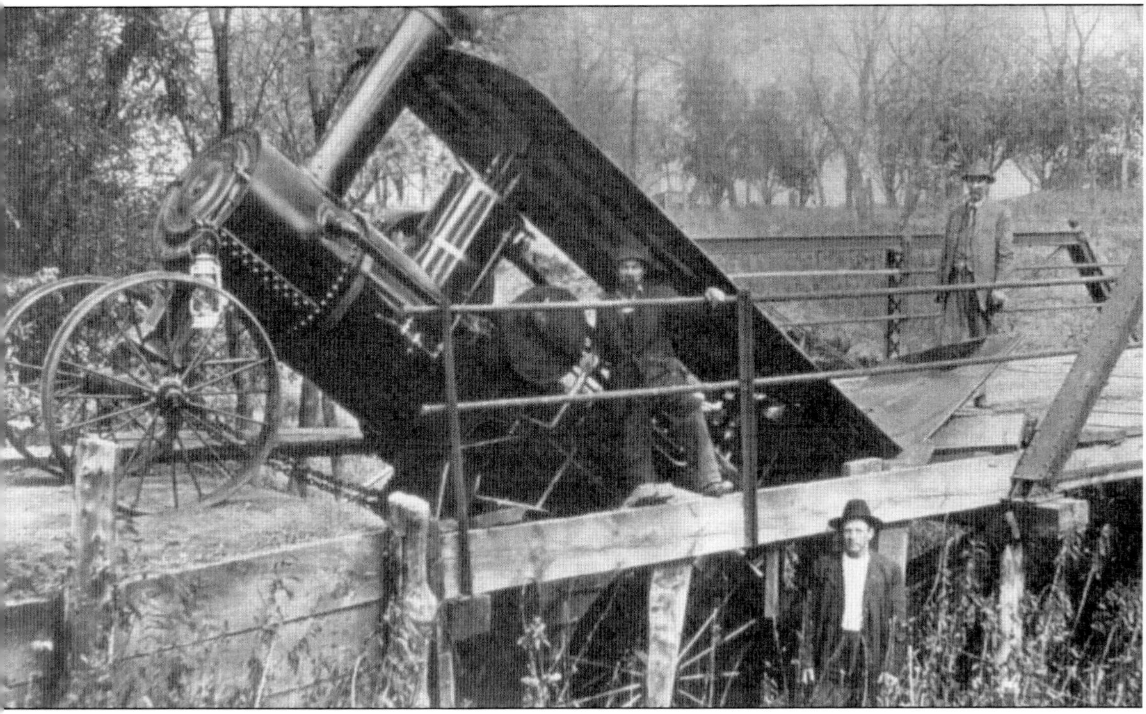

In 1915, this steam tractor broke through the bridge over a creek bed near Arnold Eggers's farm. Steam tractors weighed between 20,000 and 30,000 pounds and were bulky and hard to manage, even though they could plow six or more rows at once. Puzzling over how to lift the tractor are, from left to right, Bert Edwards, George Ullrich, and Ezra Moon. (Courtesy of Arlene Hofmann.)

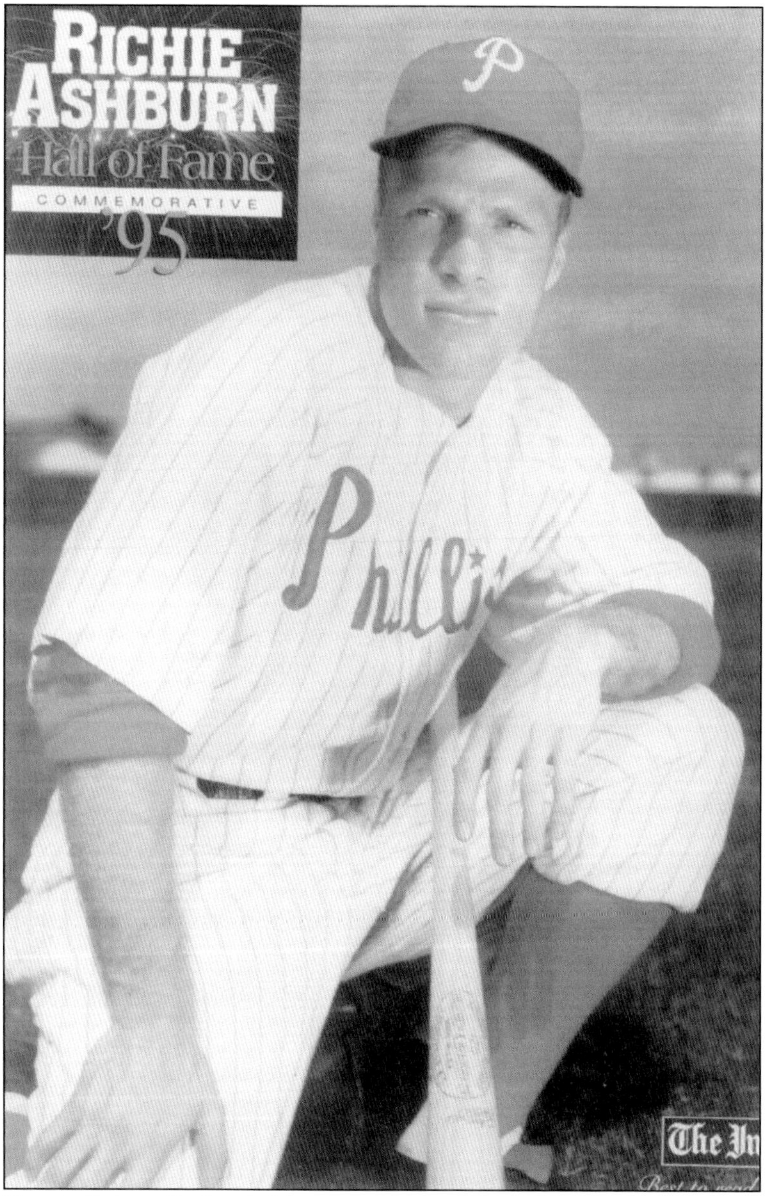

Professional baseball player Richie Ashburn was also known as "The Tilden Flash" and "Whitey." Born in Tilden in 1927, he played baseball in his high school years for the American Legion team in Neligh, and in 1944 he represented Nebraska in the Esquire All-Star Game. Ashburn signed to play minor-league ball for the Philadelphia Phillies organization in 1945, but he missed the 1946 season due to Army service. In 1947, he played with the Phillies' minor-league team in Ithaca, New York, and in 1948 he went into the Phillies' regular lineup. He remained with the team as a center fielder until 1959. After playing with the Chicago Cubs and the newly organized New York Mets, he became a radio and television commentator for the Phillies in 1963, a post he retained for the rest of his life. He died in September 1997 after completing his broadcast of a Phillies-Mets game. Ashburn was elected to the National Baseball Hall of Fame in 1995 after fans campaigned for his election. Approximately 25,000 fans attended the ceremony in Cooperstown, New York. (Courtesy of Arlene Hofman.)

Five

Clearwater

Good Water, Good Farming

Named for the sparkling, clear water in the creek that flows south and east of town, Clearwater was founded in 1881 as a railroad stop for the Fremont, Elkhorn & Missouri Valley Railroad. It was originally known as Clearwater Station. The railroad purchased land for the town from Francis M. Snider.

Beginning in 1880, a windmill and water tower serviced steam engines there as they hauled passengers and freight farther west. On October 18, 1881, H.L. Phelps, Practical Builder and Surveyor, recorded the town plat at the Antelope County Courthouse. There was a post office in Clearwater by 1880, serving residents as well as the railroad workers who laid track and built quarters for themselves. They also erected a depot, which provided housing for the agent and the telegraph operator on the second floor. In 1886, a flour mill began operating on Clearwater Creek about a mile south of town. It had a capacity of 25 barrels of flour a day. Because it was too far from the railroad, the mill was abandoned, and the machinery was sold after only a few years of operation, probably in 1889.

The year 1888 was a remarkable one for Clearwater, when it was a boomtown for a short time. Rumors of plans to build a railroad from Sioux City to Denver that would cross the Elkhorn River northeast of Clearwater and run through the town's western side encouraged the establishment of new businesses. Even though the railroad did not materialize, the additional commerce boosted the town's growth. The population has remained around 400 throughout the years. The 2010 census reported 419 residents.

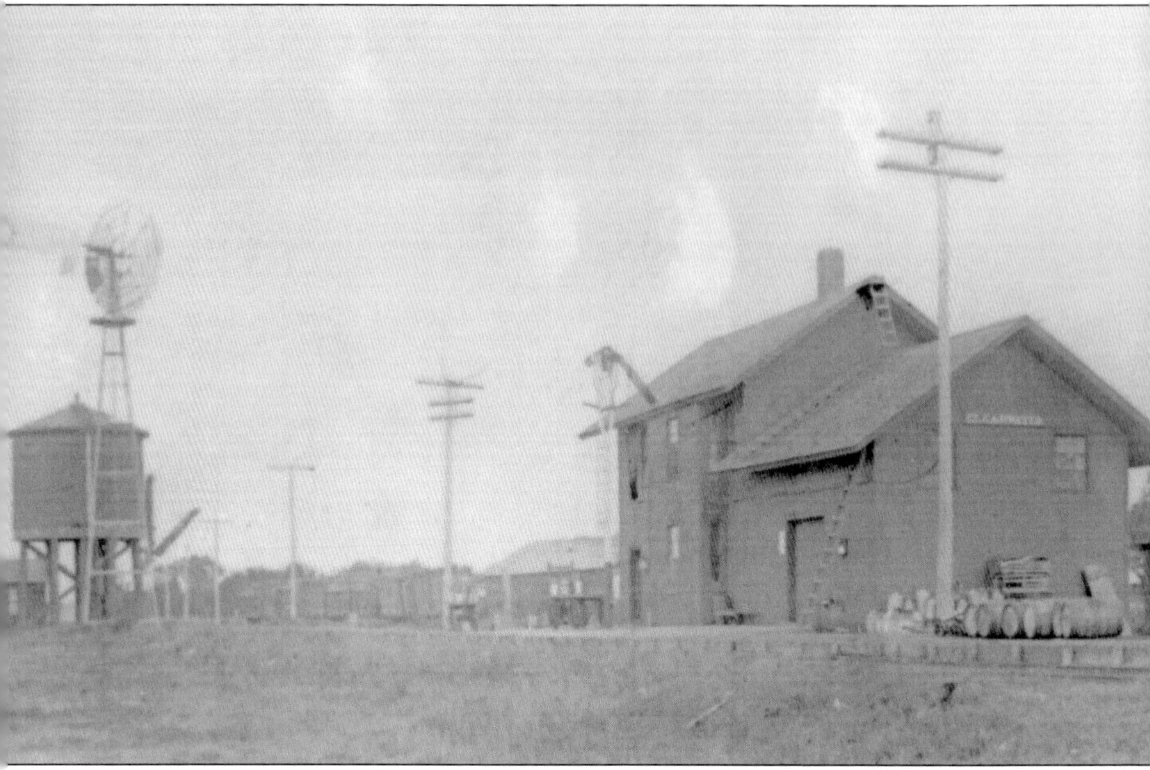

The first Clearwater railroad depot was erected in 1880 and 1881 along with a windmill, a water tower, and a pump house. The pump house contained a gasoline engine, and the windmill was 75 feet high. The original water tower was replaced in 1904. In October 1955, the water tower, pump house, and windmill were torn down because the railroad began using all-diesel engines that did not require water equipment. On November 12, 1933, a fire started in the west room of the depot's warehouse. A 50-mile-per-hour wind fanned the blaze, and firefighters were unable to save the depot. Firefighters from Neligh, Ewing, Orchard, and Elgin arrived to stop the several hundred fires that had started all over town by sparks carried by the wind. Only books and typewriters were salvaged from the depot. Joe Hague and his family, who lived on the depot's second floor, lost their clothing, bedding, and furniture. They had $100 in pennies, dimes, and nickels, but only salvaged $20 from their horde by washing it through a sieve. (Courtesy of Walter Patras.)

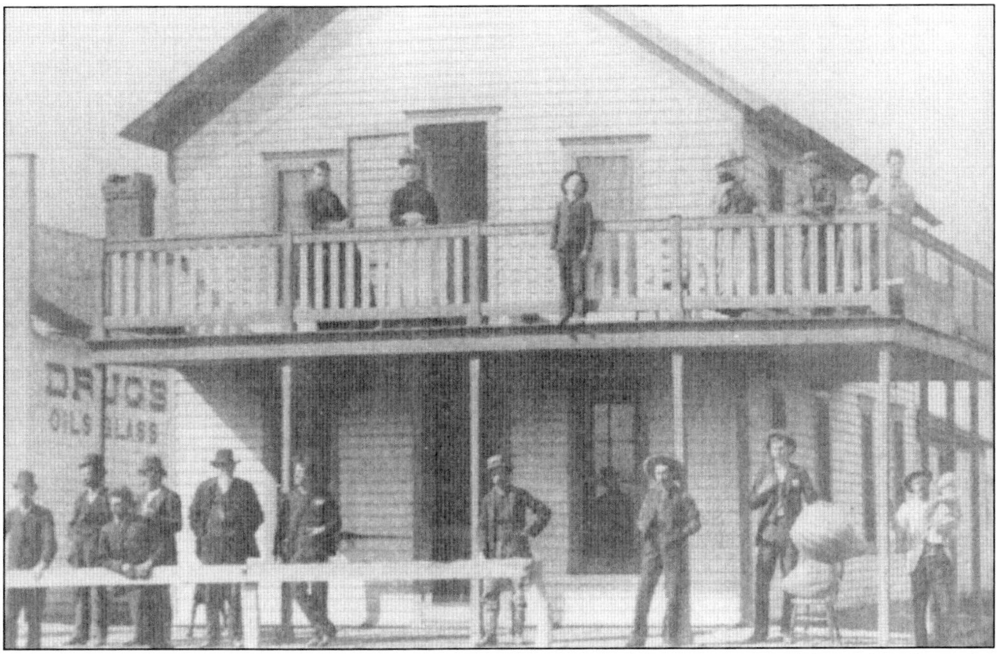

Benjamin Calder, an early Clearwater settler, opened the Calder House Hotel (seen here) on the southwest corner of First and Main Streets in 1881. Located near the depot, the hotel provided lodging for salesmen and display space for their goods. Local merchants examined the displays and placed orders. Doctors and dentists from larger towns also set up temporary offices at the hotel once a month and offered their services to Clearwater citizens. (Courtesy of Walter Patras.)

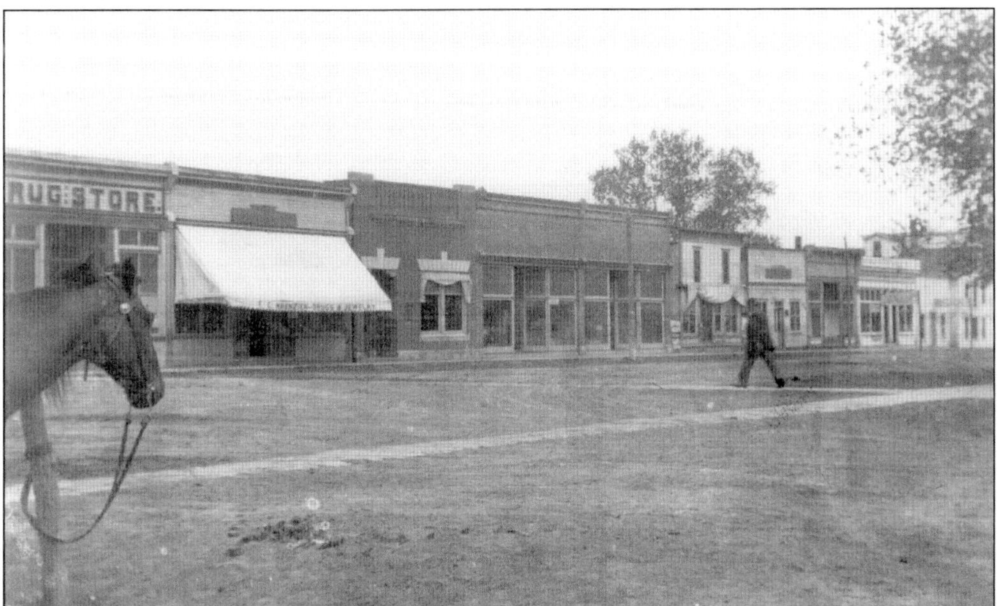

After a disastrous fire on October 20, 1896, destroyed the east side of Main Street from First to Second Streets, businesses had to rebuild. By 1902, the newspaper announced that block two of the northwestern side of Main Street had three new street crossings. Here, an unidentified man strolls along one of the new crossings. (Courtesy of Walter Patras.)

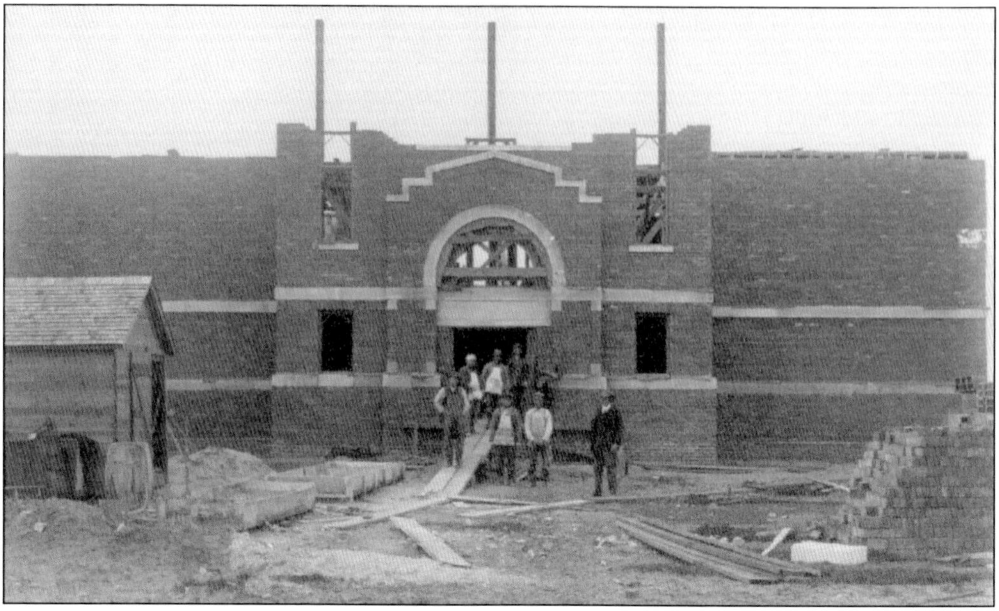

Prior to 1890, several schools existed in the Clearwater vicinity. The first school met in the back room of the drugstore in 1882. By 1890, this two-room schoolhouse was built, but it soon became overcrowded. The school district continued expanding with new buildings and additions to existing structures until 1999, when it merged with the school districts of Orchard and Verdigre. (Courtesy of Walter Patras.)

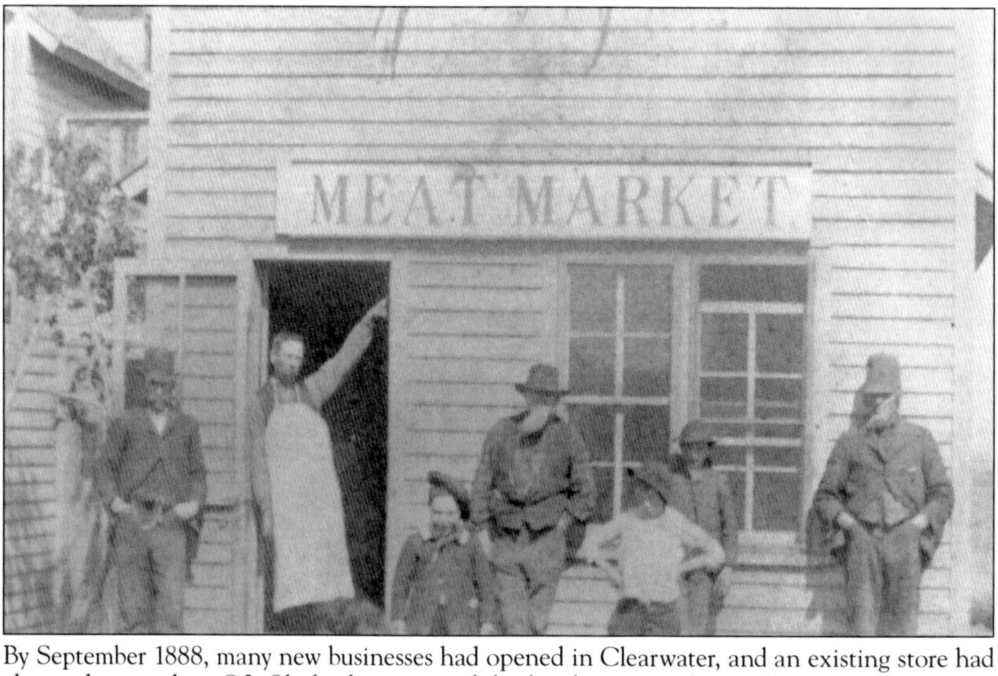

By September 1888, many new businesses had opened in Clearwater, and an existing store had changed ownership. C.J. Clark, the owner of the local meat market, sold it to J.S. Burnett of Ewing. Burnett then moved his family into town. Standing here are B.M. Macauley (far left), Mr. Burnett (in doorway), and Francis Snider (on left edge of window). The boys and the man on the far right are unidentified. (Courtesy of Walter Patras.)

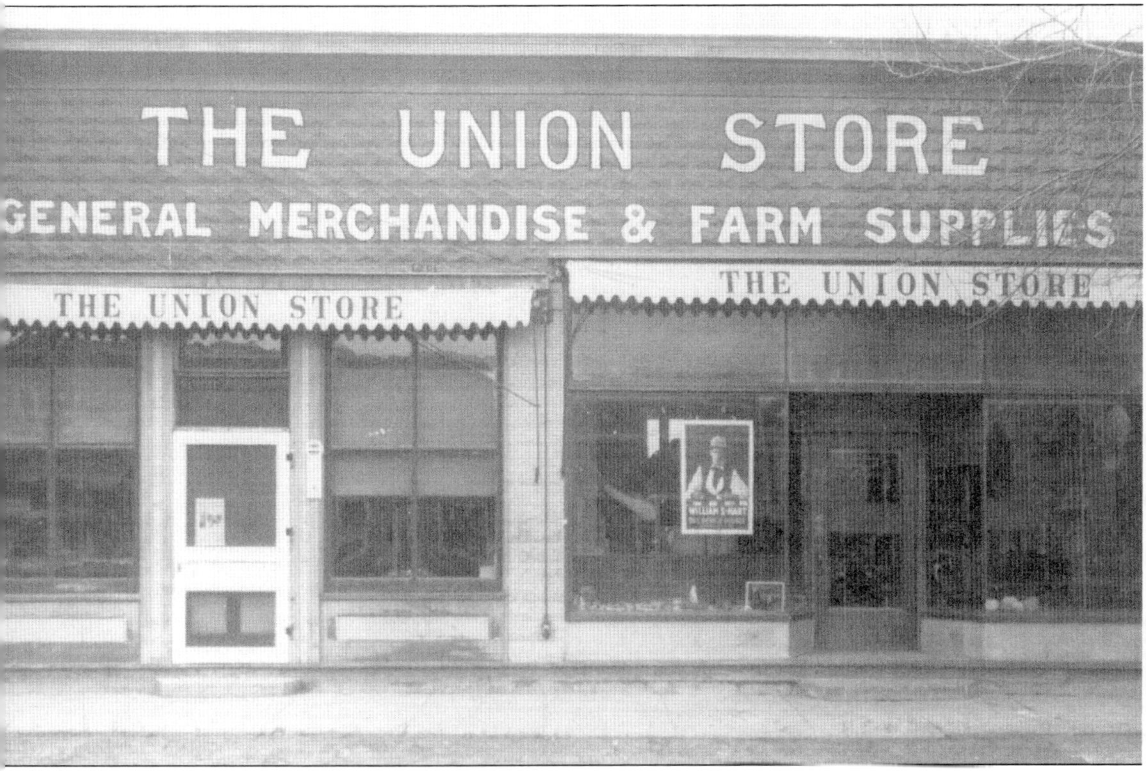

Union Stores were part of the National Farmers Union, founded in the United States in 1902 to protect and enhance the economic well-being and quality of life for family farmers, ranchers, and their nearby rural communities. Organizing efforts began in Nebraska in 1911 with the formation of local cream and agricultural supply cooperatives. In February 1910, farmers in the Clearwater area circulated a petition enlisting people to sign up for stock in a farmers' cooperative grain, lumber, coal, and hog business. By 1919, the Clearwater Union Store opened, and it served the community until 1925. In November 1926, Rundquist and Sons opened a store in the former Union Store building. The National Farmers Union still represents a quarter-million family farms, and union officials meet every spring and fall to talk with legislators about the problems farmers face. (Courtesy of Walter Patras.)

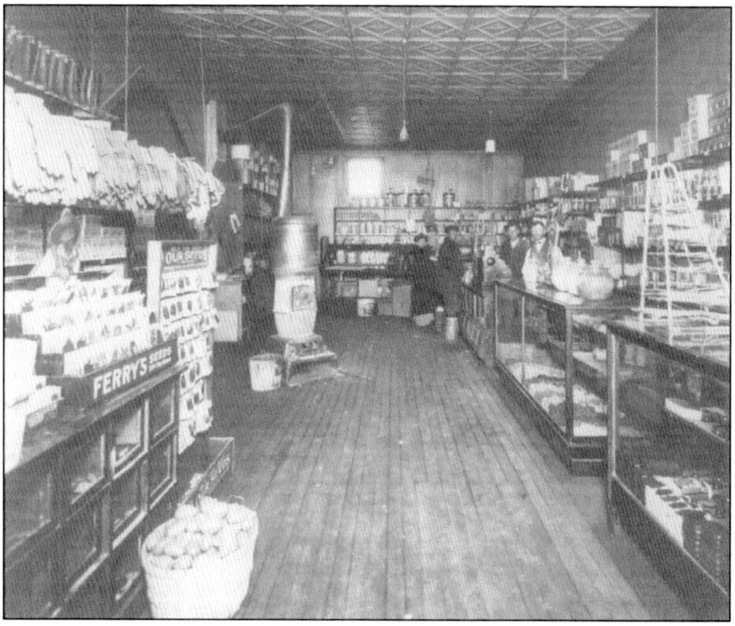

The display of Ferry's Seeds on the left and the basket of seed potatoes indicate that this photograph was taken during planting time in the Clearwater area. Glass cases on the right contain year-round merchandise, and grocery items are stacked along the back wall. The wood-burning stove, tin ceiling, and wood floor are typical features of stores established around 1900. (Courtesy of Walter Patras.)

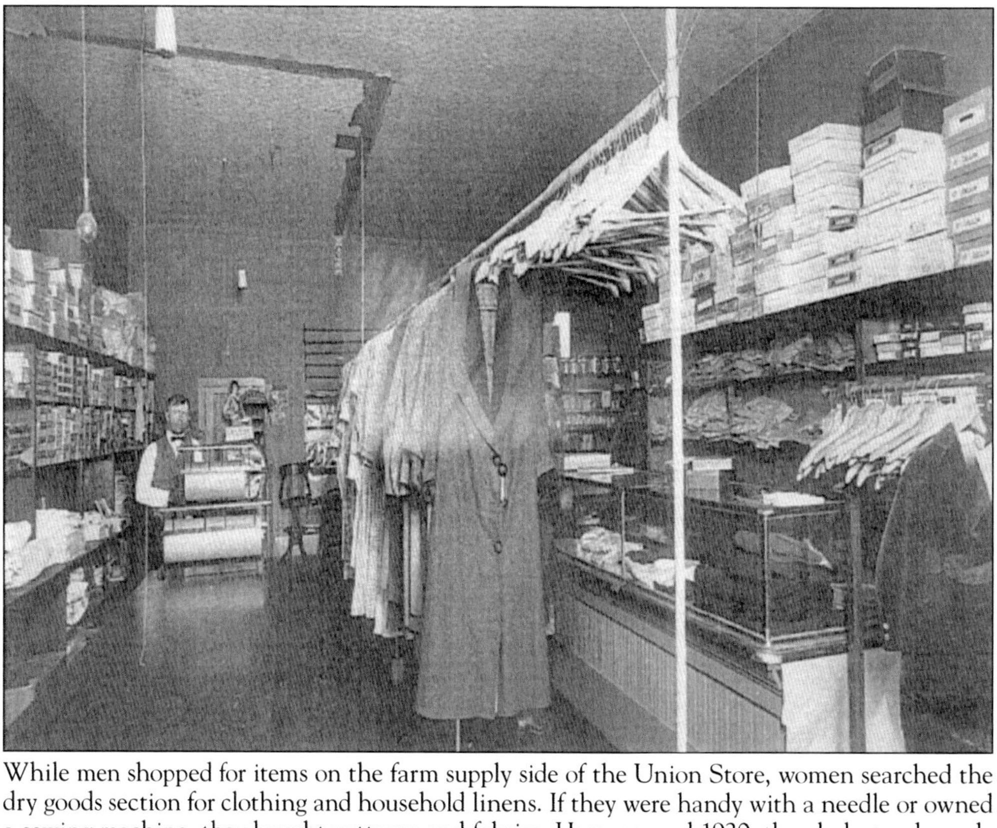

While men shopped for items on the farm supply side of the Union Store, women searched the dry goods section for clothing and household linens. If they were handy with a needle or owned a sewing machine, they bought patterns and fabrics. Here, around 1920, the clerk stands ready to wrap purchases by tearing paper from the rolls and tying the packages with string. (Courtesy of Walter Patras.)

George Mead installed the first Clearwater telephone exchange in 1902. In the first year of operation, calls could only connect to Clearwater residents and those living close to town. By 1918, lines had been extended, and connections were made with nearly every town and city in the United States. Iris Mead is seen here at the switchboard in 1918. (Courtesy of Walter Patras.)

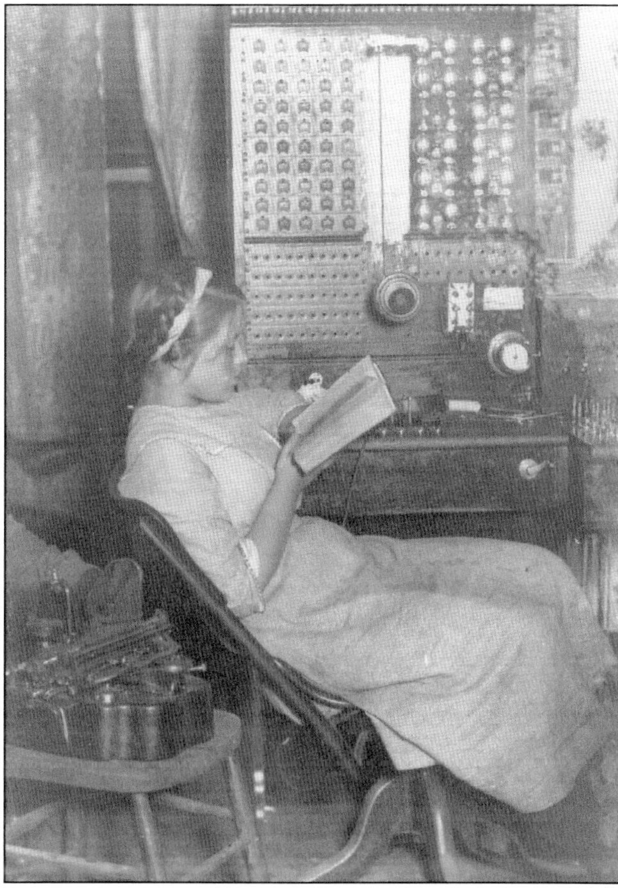

Barbershops were popular male socializing places from 1880 to 1940. Men stopped in weekly, or even daily, for a haircut and shave and to mingle with friends. Regular customers kept their personal shaving mugs and brushes at the shop. The decor was often elaborate; note the wallpaper and leather chairs in the Clearwater shop seen here in 1905, with barbers George Meyers (left) and Clyde Paine plying their trade. (Courtesy of Walter Patras.)

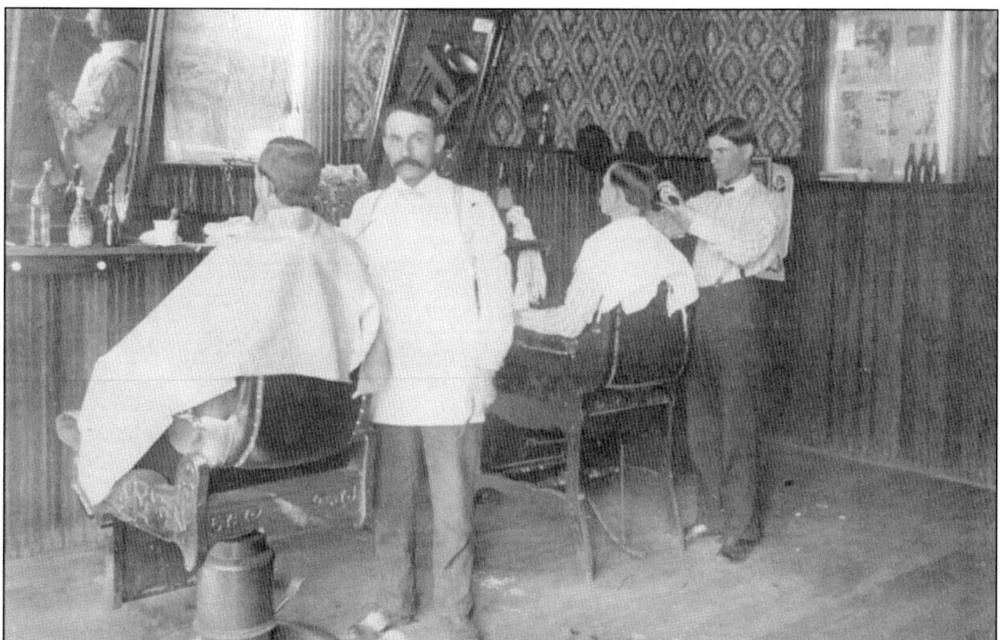

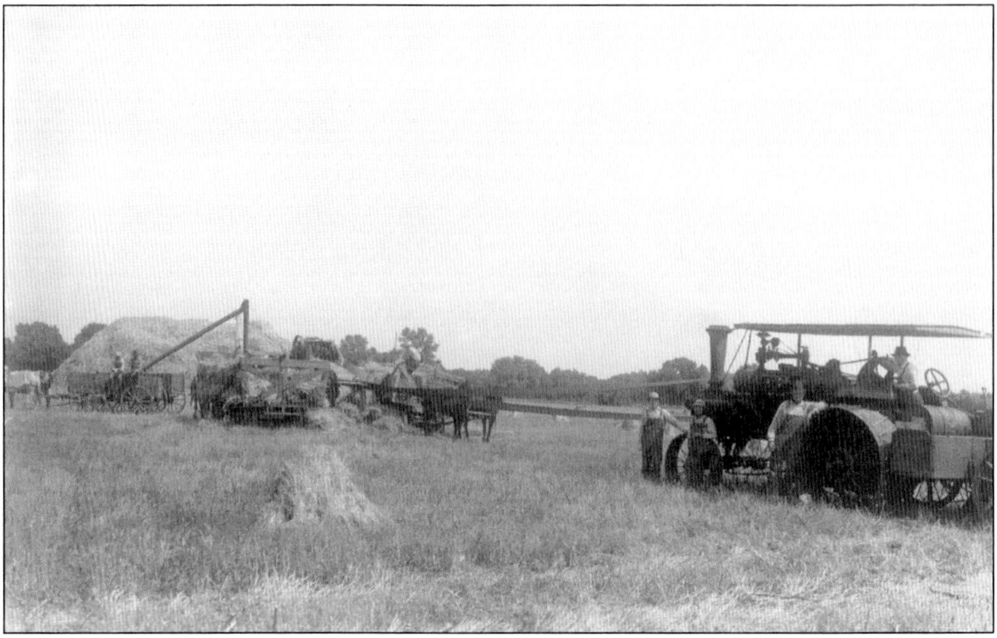

This Bill McDonald threshing crew harvests wheat on a Clearwater area farm in 1919 using a steam-powered threshing machine. Farmers often depended on custom threshing crews to do the work. Harvesting wheat took place in midsummer and was hot, dusty, and labor intensive, with each member of the crew having a specific job. (Courtesy of Walter Patras.)

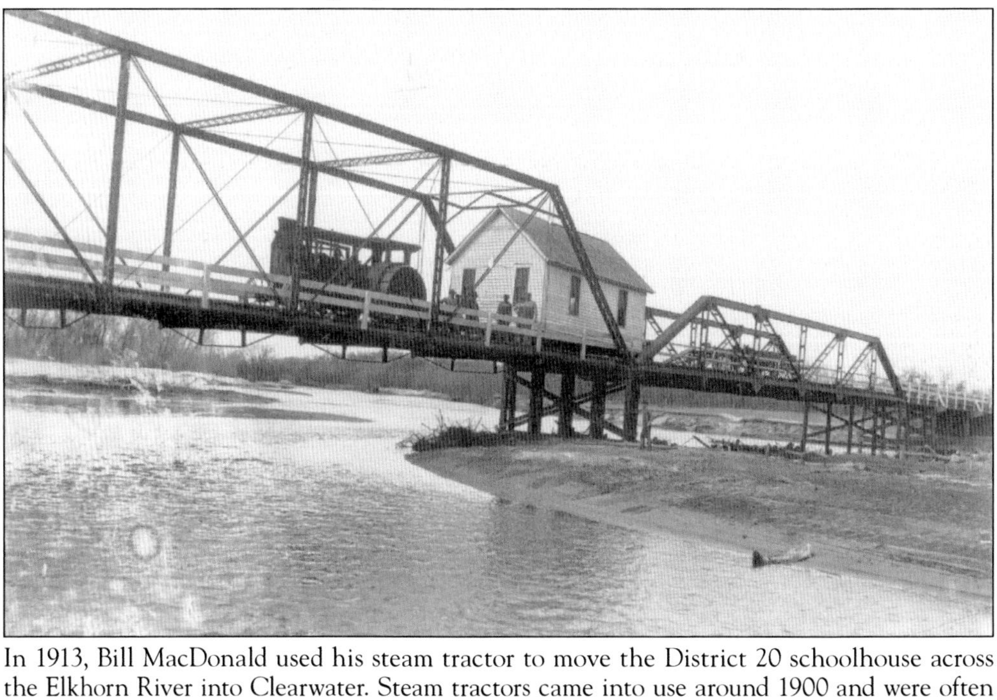

In 1913, Bill MacDonald used his steam tractor to move the District 20 schoolhouse across the Elkhorn River into Clearwater. Steam tractors came into use around 1900 and were often referred to as traction engines because of their ability to haul heavy equipment. After serving as a clubhouse for a time, the schoolhouse was eventually used for public restrooms in Clearwater. (Courtesy of Walter Patras.)

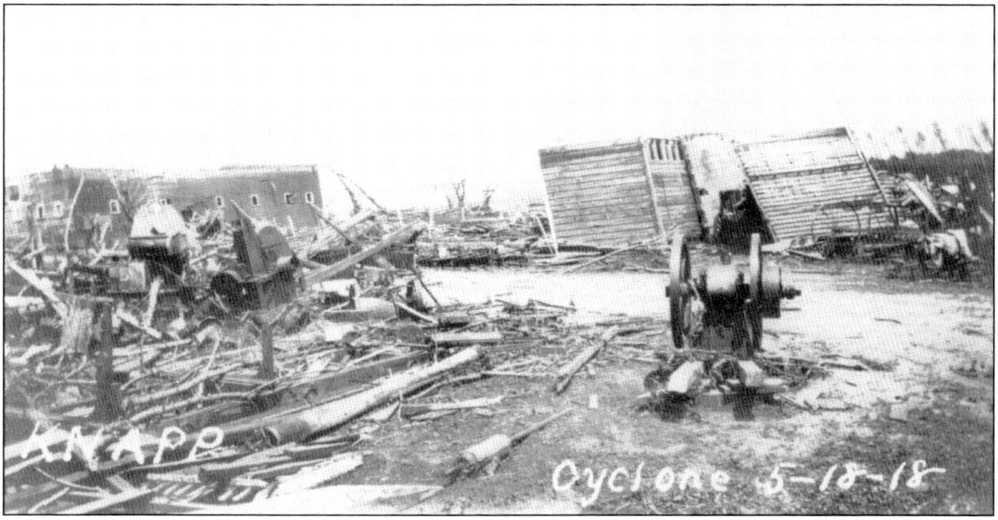

On Saturday, May 18, 1918, at about 6:00 p.m., a tornado passed through the edge of Clearwater and crossed the Elkhorn River, damaging trees and buildings in the rural areas. On Charles Knapp's farm, the tornado destroyed outbuildings but left the house. The family took shelter in their cave, and no one was hurt. (ACHS.)

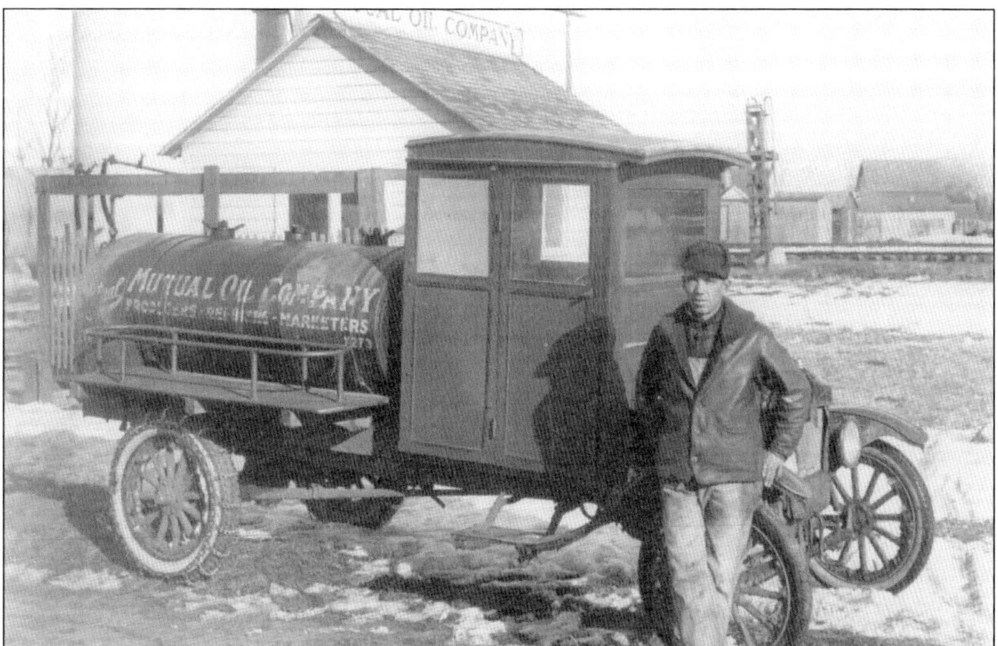

In September 1920, Standard Oil Company erected buildings and tanks and established an oil station in Clearwater. This enterprising citizen likely designed and built his own cab to transport oil to homeowners for the Mutual Oil Company. Heating oil fueled stoves and furnaces during the cold, snowy winters. (Courtesy of Walter Patras.)

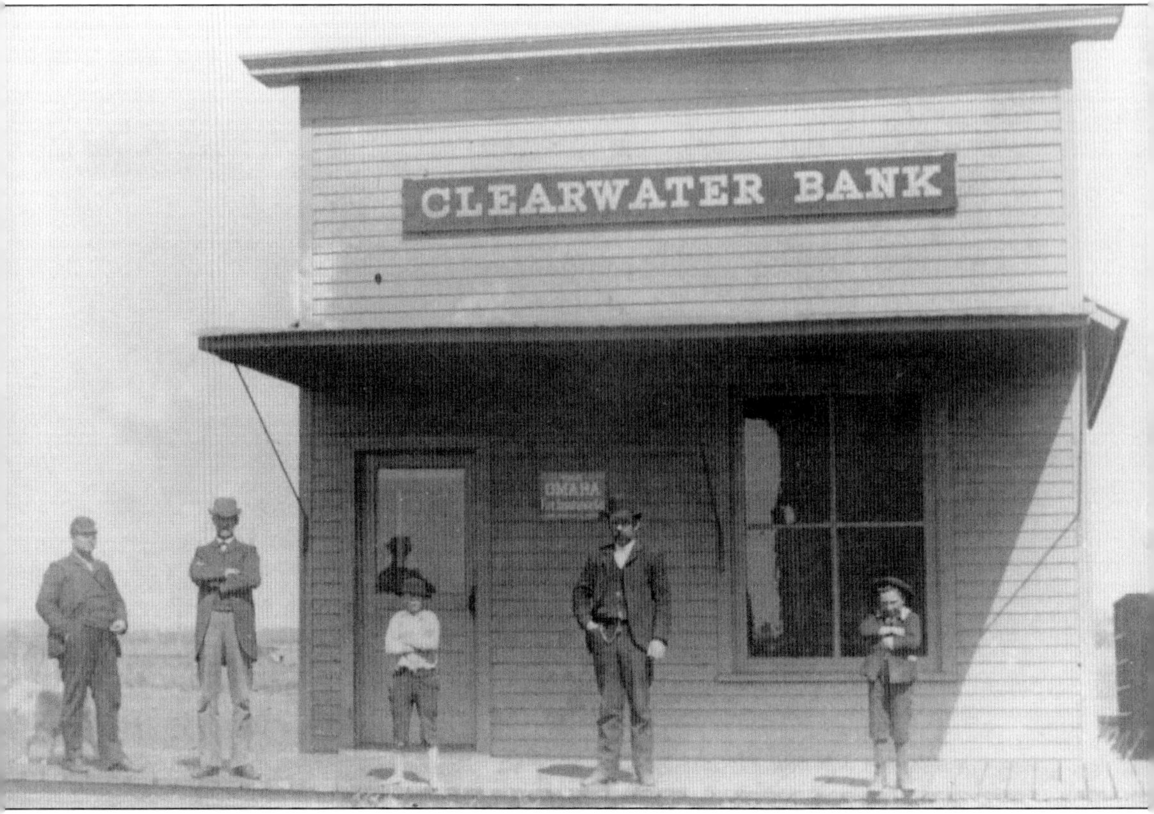

The first Clearwater Bank was established in 1888. It also housed J.C. Smith's law library and office. After the bank closed in 1890, the building served as the post office until December 1901, when it reopened as a state bank. Here, standing in front of the bank are, from left to right, Francis Snider, B.M. Macauley, an unidentified boy, Mr. Faunt, and an unidentified boy. (Courtesy of Walter Patras.)

Six

Elgin

Surviving Fires

In 1883, William Eggleston settled in the West Cedar Valley, two miles north of present-day Elgin. He immediately circulated a petition to establish a post office at his farm home, and it was granted. Eggleston wanted the post office named Eggleston for its founder, as was customary in those days, but postal authorities thought the name too long. In choosing another name, Eggleston consulted Gene Gailey, the Oakdale postmaster. Gailey opened a postal guide at random, stabbed blindly with his index finger, opened his eyes, and noted the name on which his finger rested: Elgin, Illinois.

Eggleston had emigrated from Illinois, and he decided to name the postal station for the town in his native state. On June 20, 1887, the Western Town Lot Company platted the town, but the lots were not put up for purchase until July 4. In 1895, a fire started in Blazer's hardware store, and it was impossible to save the surrounding buildings. The Elgin outlet of the Wolfe Brothers store had a narrow escape; the building caught fire several times, but hard work on the part of citizens saved it. The fire's origin was never determined, but strong winds strengthened the blaze.

After a period of rebuilding, rapid progress continued from 1895 to 1904. On April 28, 1909, another fire broke out, destroying an entire block of businesses. After that disaster, a volunteer fire department was organized. Since then, all Elgin fires have been controlled. The 2010 census reported 661 Elgin residents.

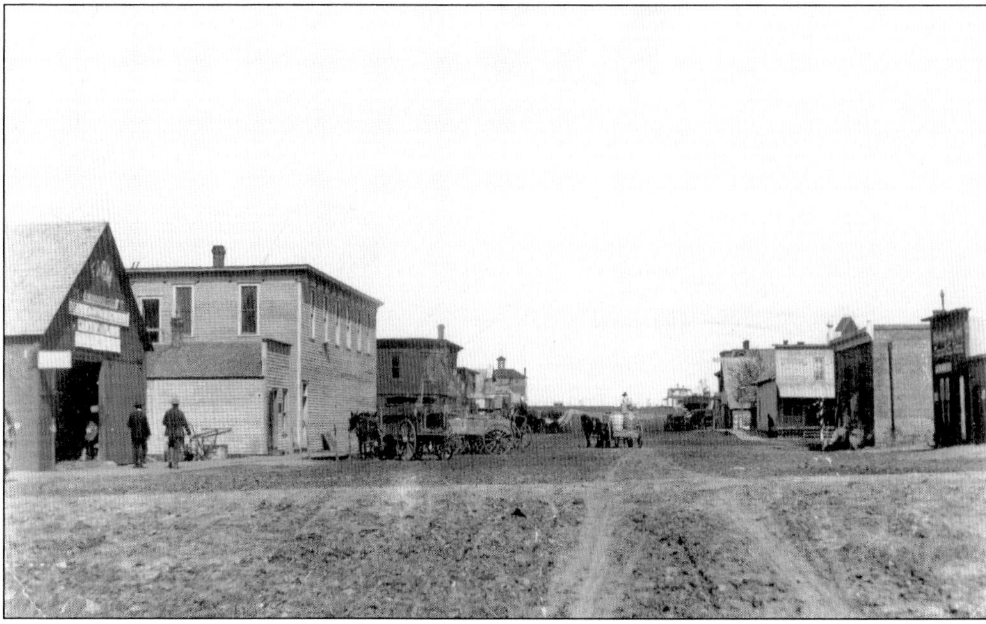

Seen around 1885, Elgin's Main Street runs east to west on what is now Pine Street. When the railroad was laid from Albion to Oakdale, Main Street was changed to a north-south direction to correspond with the direction of the railroad. (ACHS.)

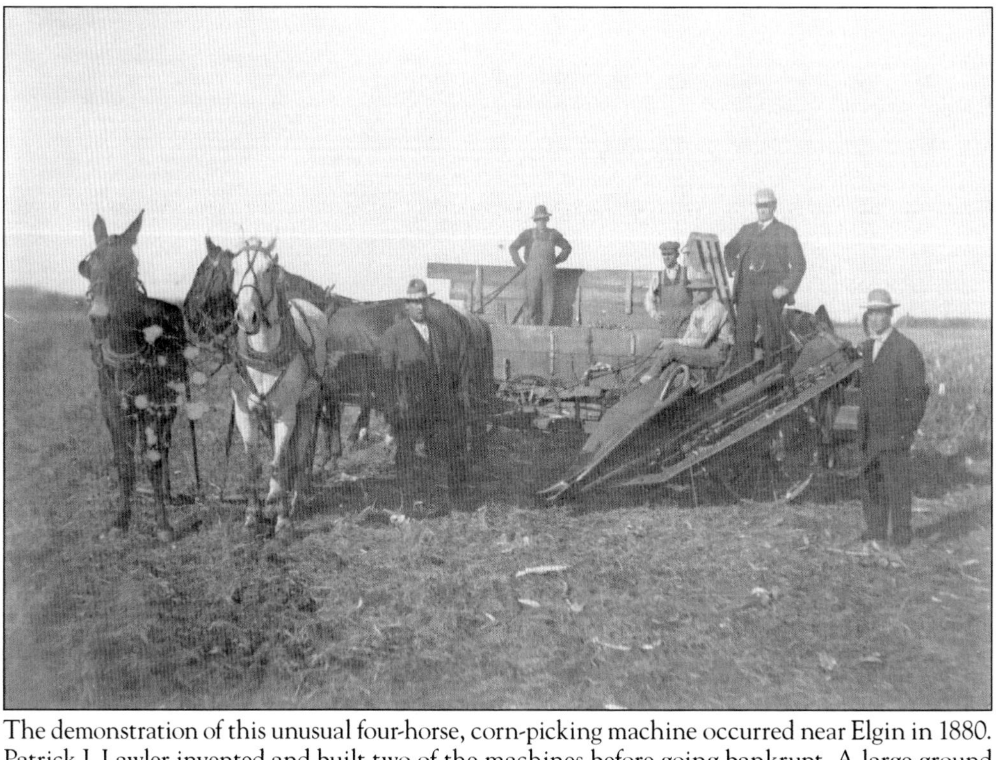

The demonstration of this unusual four-horse, corn-picking machine occurred near Elgin in 1880. Patrick J. Lawler invented and built two of the machines before going bankrupt. A large ground wheel provided motion and picking power for the device. From left to right are unidentified, Mr. Fink, W. Fraser, Paul McKay, August Buhler, and an unidentified salesman. (ACHS.)

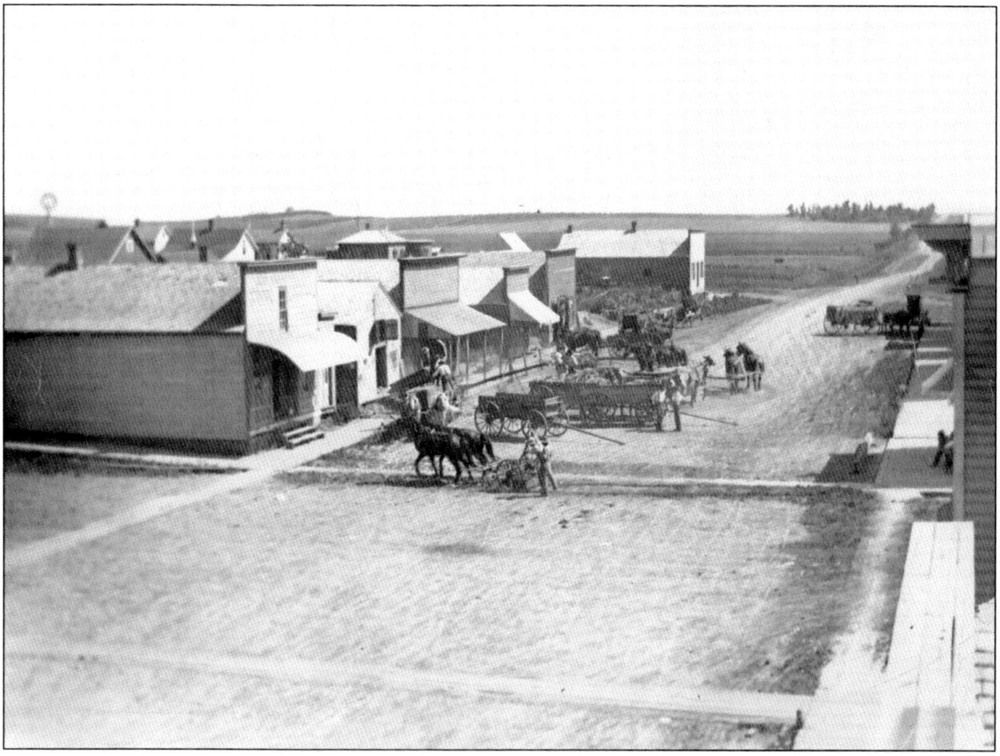

Corn has always been a stable and often profitable crop for Antelope County farmers. Around 1890, this corn-shelling cooperative event took place on Elgin's Main Street. Farmers brought their corn harvest to town and shared the use of one machine to strip corn from the cobs. (ACHS.)

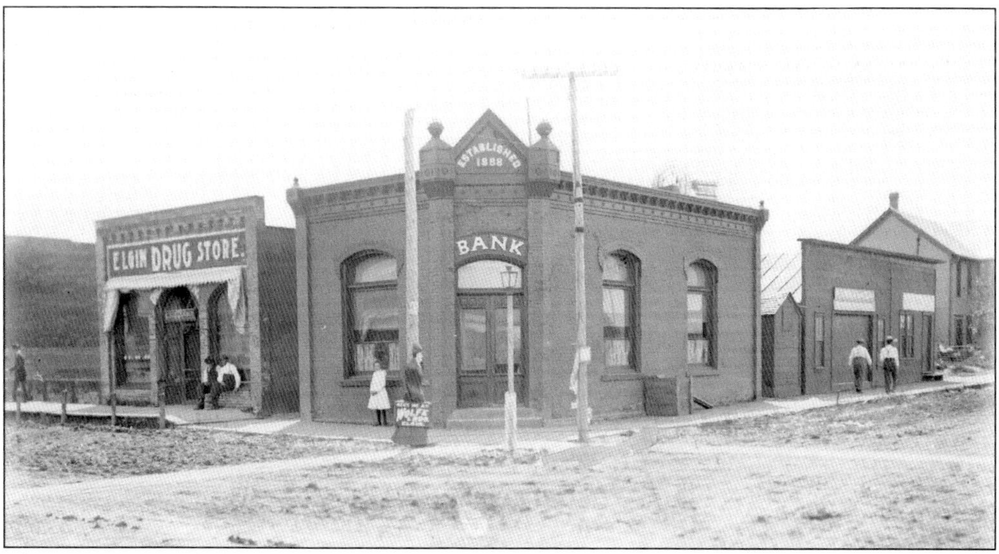

This 1908 view of Elgin's Main Street shows the Elgin State Bank, established in 1888. An advertisement on the sidewalk features a wooden cutout of a woman with a sign reading, "Meet Me at Wolfe & Bro. Elgin." A carbide light and telephone pole are in front of the bank, and there is a windmill behind the building. A sign above Elgin Drug Store advertises Wrigley's Juicy Fruit gum. (ACHS.)

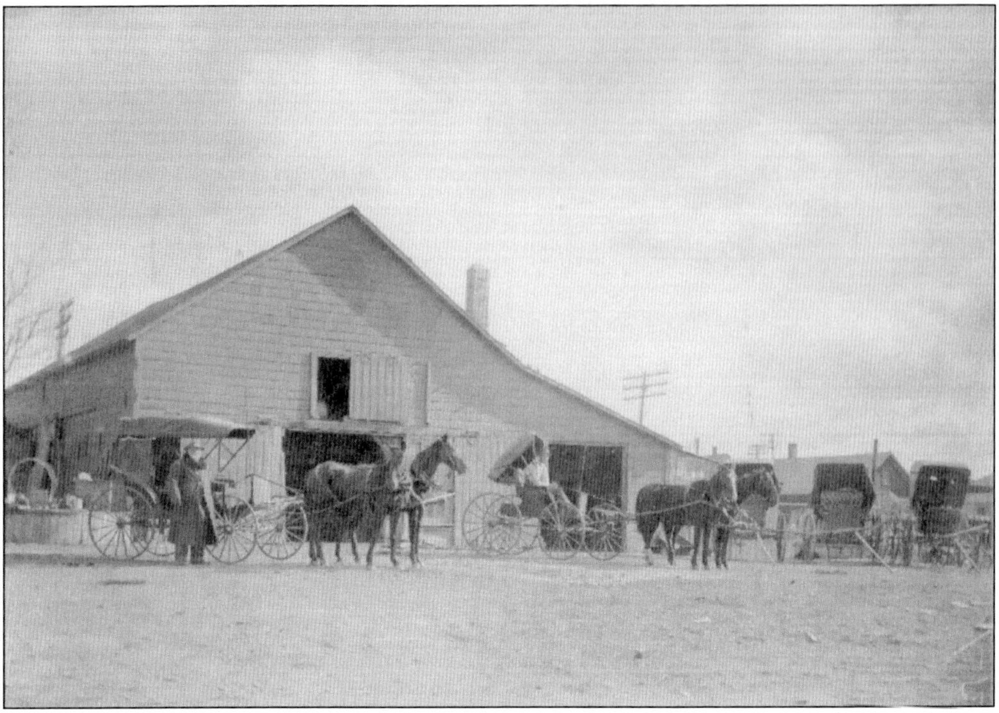

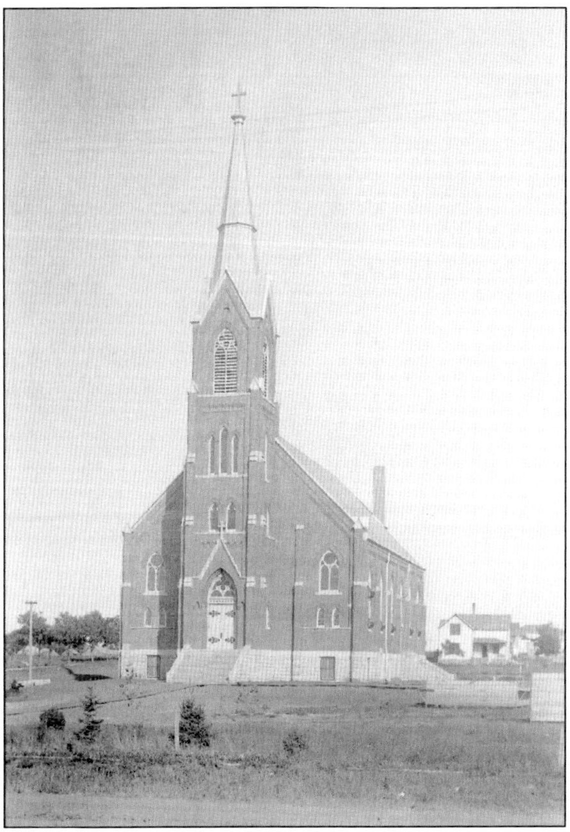

C.C. Roberts erected this large barn behind the Depot Hotel in 1899. He and his wife owned the hotel. Roberts bought new rigs for his livery stable and drove hotel guests and community residents to all parts of the surrounding county. (ACHS.)

In 1899, Fr. John Mueller, the pastor in Raeville, organized 25 families in the Elgin area into the St. Boniface Parish. On March 3, 1900, Father Mueller, John Joseph, and Meinolph Meis bought the block now containing the nucleus of the St. Boniface Parish for $450. A frame church was erected, and the first Mass was held on Christmas Day in 1900. The dedication occurred on January 1, 1902. Fr. Adam Brass was the first resident pastor. (ACHS.)

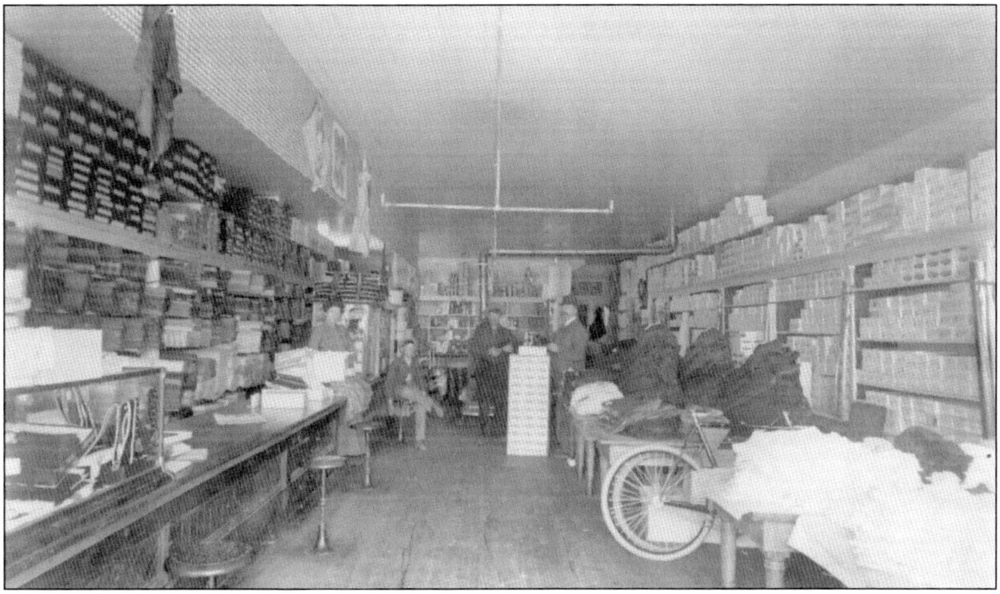

Eugene Gailey and his wife, Mary, opened this general store in Elgin in July 1901. In the 1800s, general stores served rural communities with almost anything their customers might need. Here, a bicycle is positioned ready for purchase, and shelves are filled with boxes of various merchandise. The Gaileys sold their store in 1904. (ACHS.)

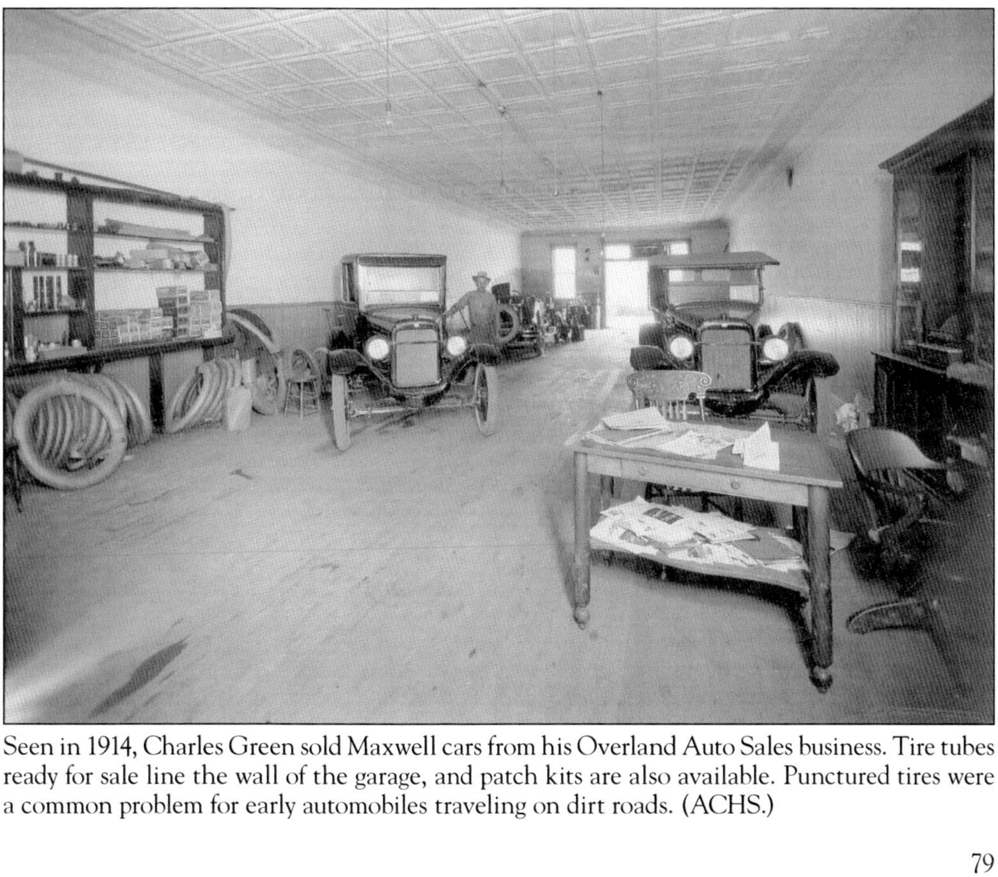

Seen in 1914, Charles Green sold Maxwell cars from his Overland Auto Sales business. Tire tubes ready for sale line the wall of the garage, and patch kits are also available. Punctured tires were a common problem for early automobiles traveling on dirt roads. (ACHS.)

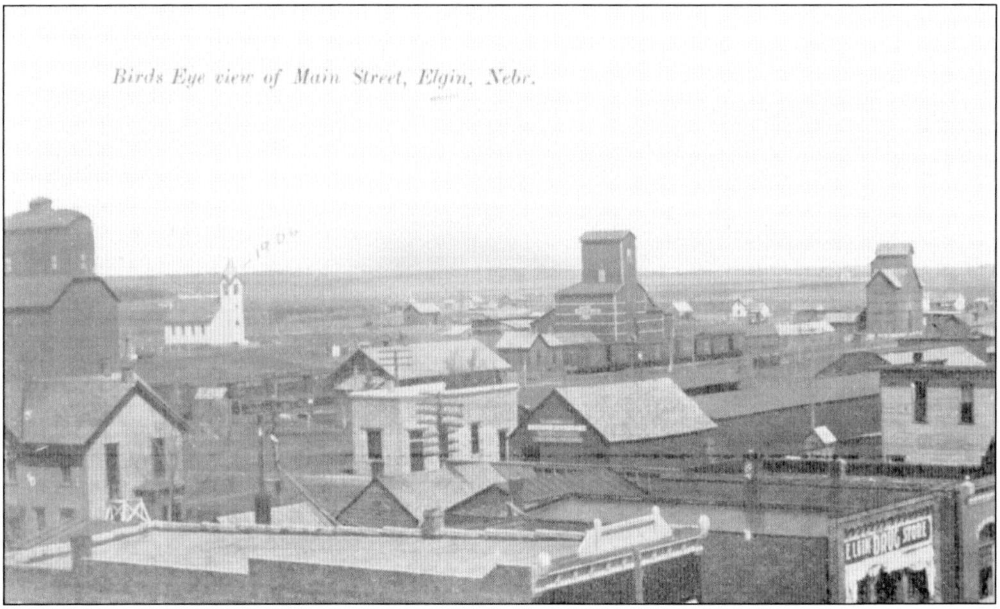

This 1906 bird's-eye view of Elgin shows several Main Street rooftops, including that of the Elgin Drug Store. A corner of Elgin State Bank is on the right. The railroad line ran in front of three grain elevators seen from left to right in the background. The Lutheran church is in the far background. (ACHS.)

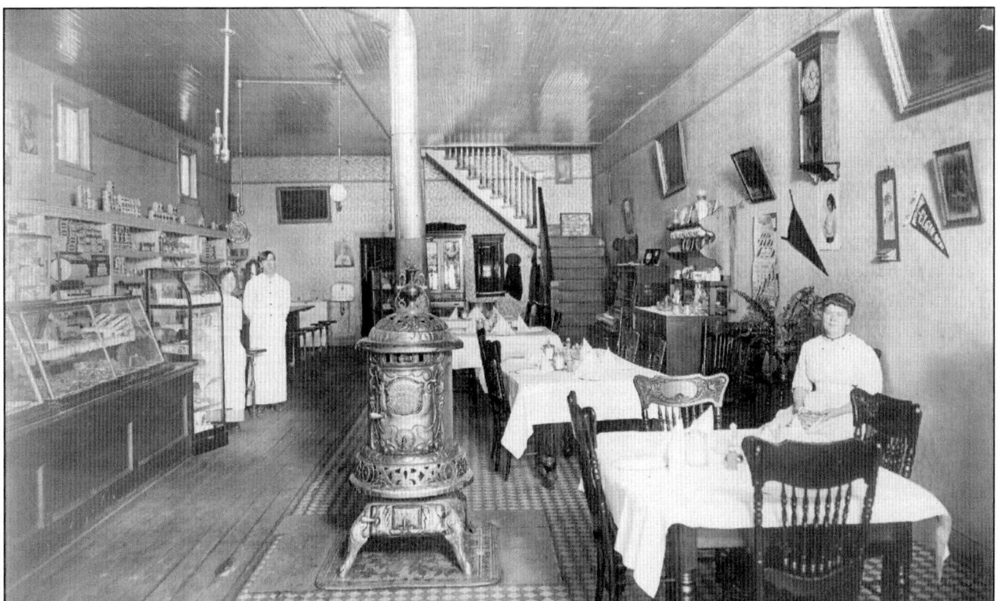

Maude Roberts Earl's restaurant, seen here in the early 1900s, was a forerunner of the modern-day delicatessen. Shelves of canned goods and baked goods fill one side of the store, a wood-burning stove in the center of the room kept customers warm, and gas or kerosene lights provided illumination. (ACHS.)

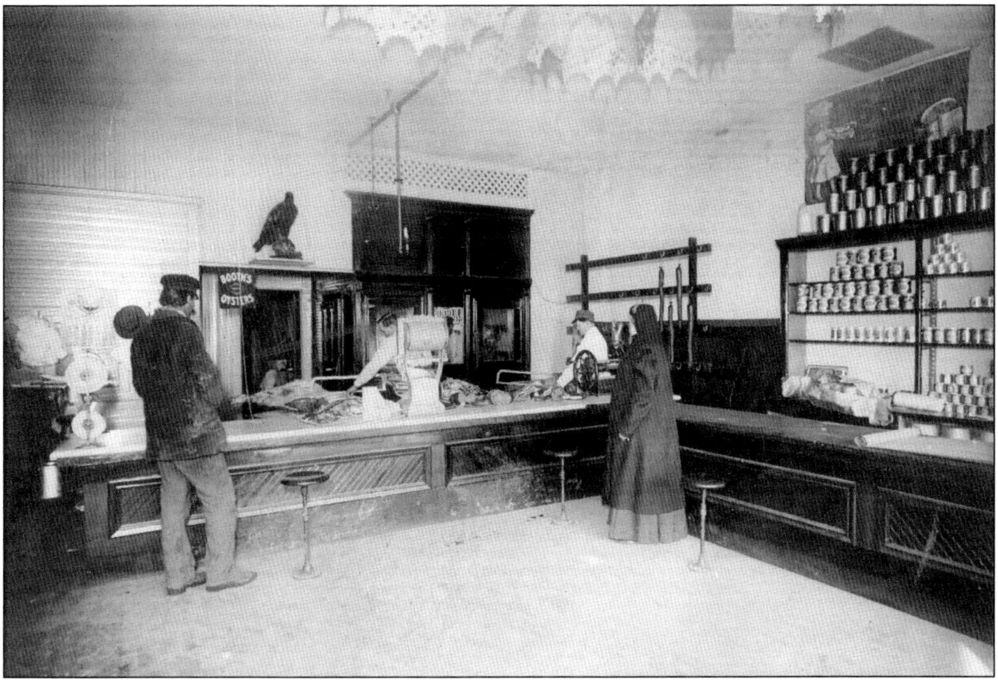

In this c. 1910 image, a stuffed eagle guards from his perch in a spacious Elgin meat market as customers wait for butchers to fill their orders. A gas light fixture hangs from the ceiling, and stools are available so customers could sit down. (ACHS.)

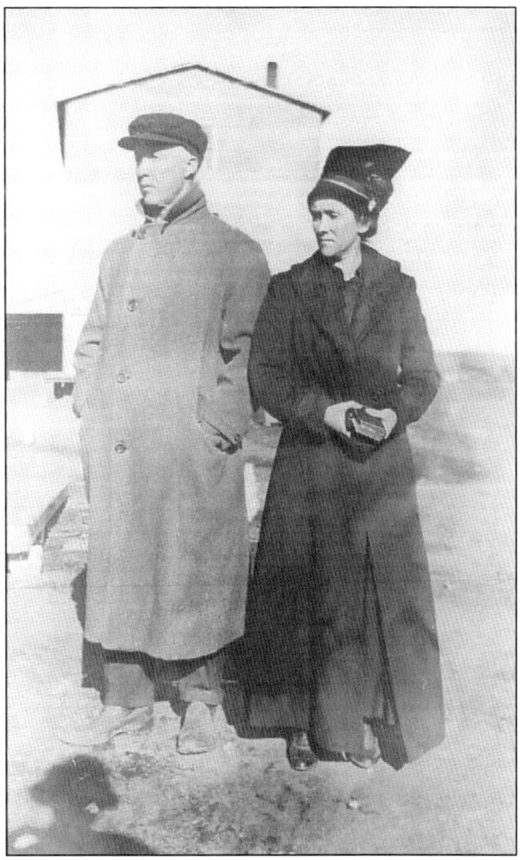

After their marriage in David City, Nebraska, in 1898, Henry and Emma Vanderheiden (seen here) moved to Elgin in 1908. They had 11 children, two of whom died in infancy. Henry had trained in the milling trade, and over time he and four of his sons were part owners of Elgin Mills. (Courtesy of Marie Vanderheiden.)

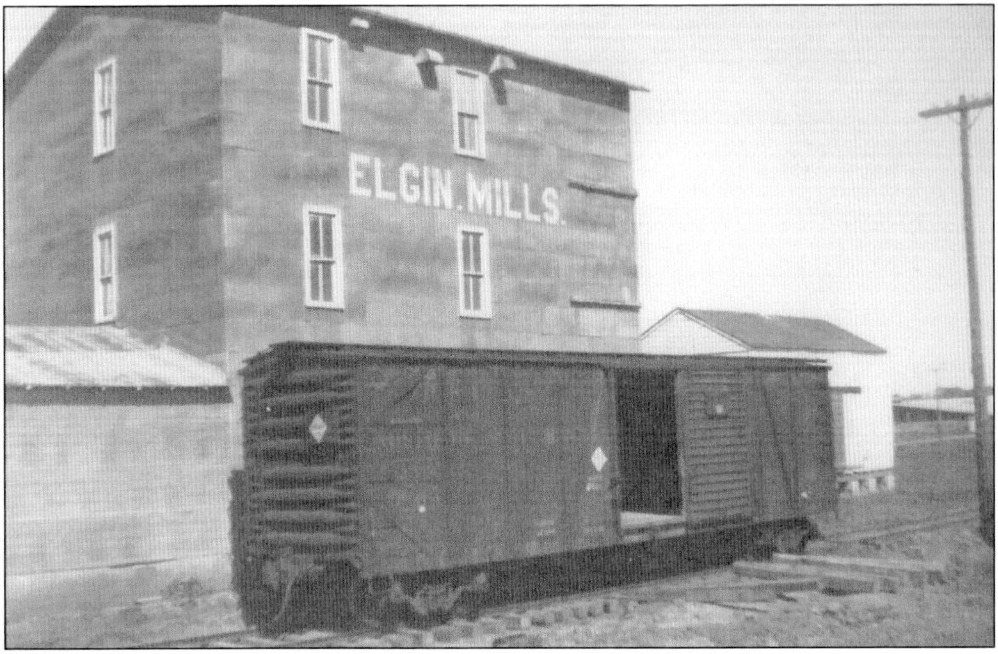

Elgin Mills, built in 1908, was owned by Henry, Ted, and Louis Vanderheiden, Paul Borgmeyer, and Frank Kalvelage. Flour brands milled there included O'Boy, Our Pride, Cream Loaf, and Big Chief. In 1944, another Vanderheiden, Lambert "Bert," bought the mill from his father. In 1951, milling equipment was replaced with vetch- and rye-cleaning machines. When fire destroyed the original building in 1968, it was reconstructed for storage as a stacking shed. (Courtesy of Marie Vanderheiden.)

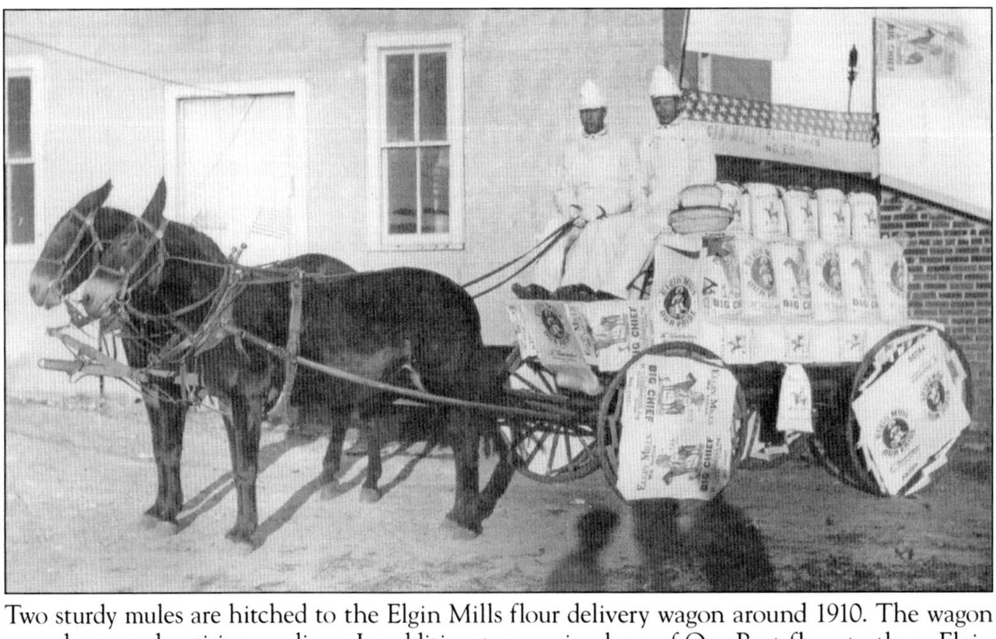

Two sturdy mules are hitched to the Elgin Mills flour delivery wagon around 1910. The wagon served as an advertising medium. In addition to carrying bags of Our Best flour to three Elgin Bakeries, the wheels also showcase Big Chief flour. The unidentified deliverymen are wearing white uniforms. (Courtesy of Marie Vanderheiden.)

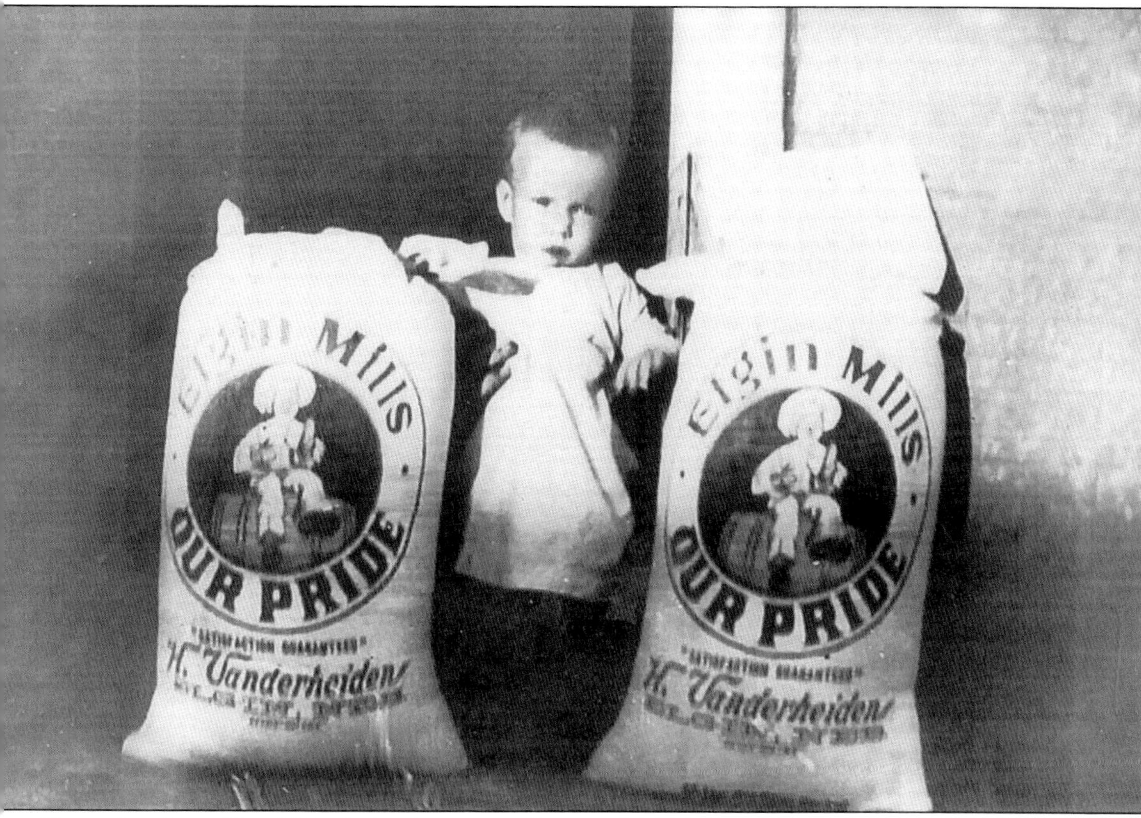

Young Lambert "Bert" Vanderheiden, one of nine surviving children of Henry and Emma Vanderheiden and the future owner of Elgin Mills, poses in 1922 between two sacks of Our Pride flour produced at the mill. Bert and his wife, Florentine Pelster, raised four children: Ann, Joe, Florentine, and Marie. In addition to his ownership of the mill, Bert was active in the Elgin community. On October 17, 1968, a fire of undetermined origin caused an estimated loss of $75,000 and destroyed the mill. (Courtesy of Marie Vanderheiden.)

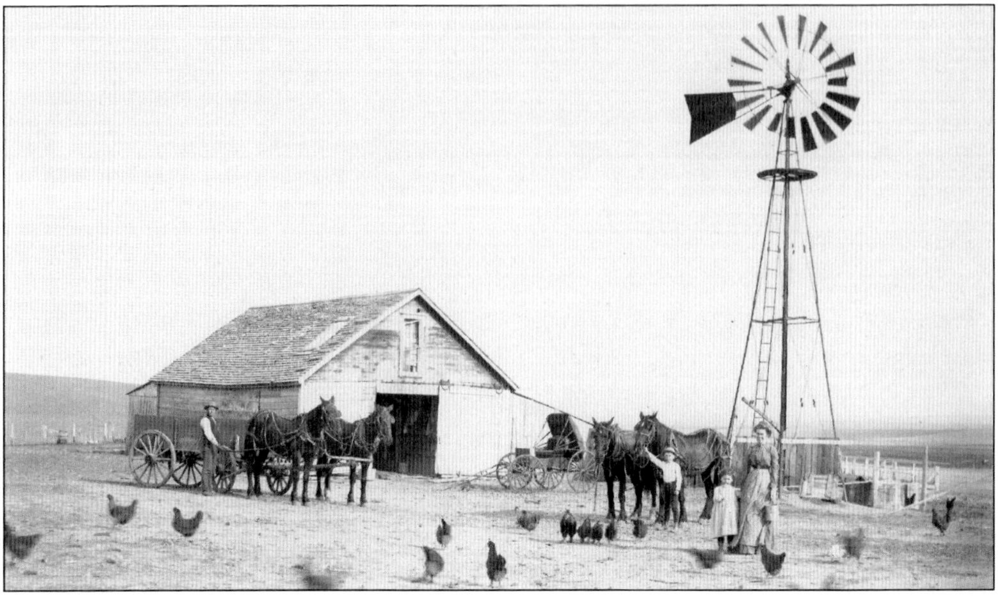

The Arthur Robbins farm, one mile south of Elgin, had a typical farmyard at the turn of the century. A large barn, a windmill, several horses, wagons, and a buggy share the treeless space with free-range chickens. Here, Arthur Robbins (far left) poses around 1900 with his wife and two children in the farmyard. (ACHS.)

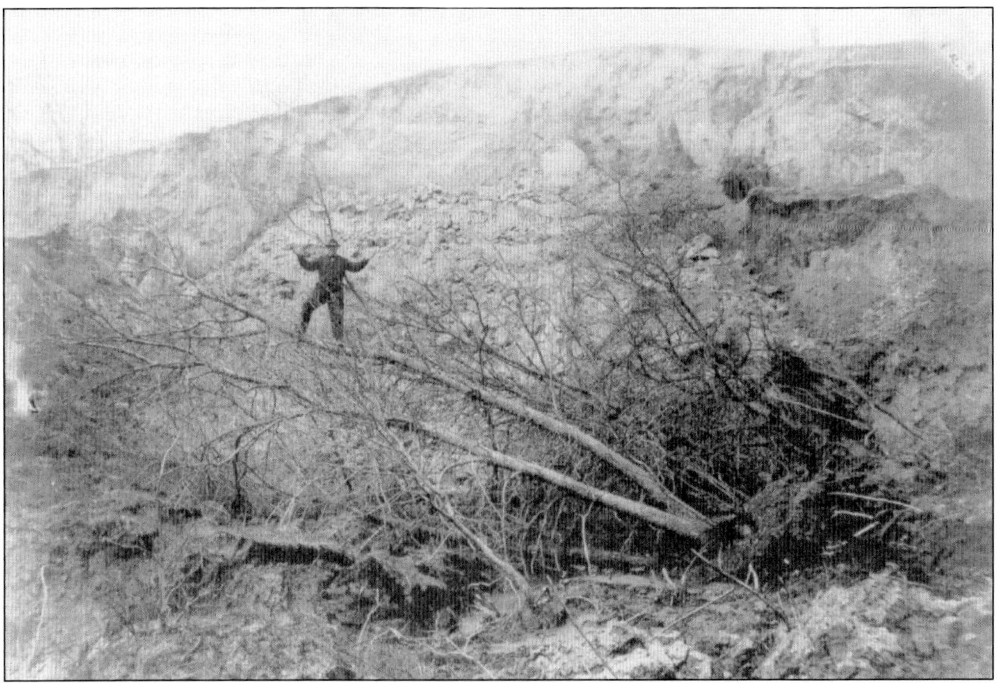

When springs beneath a hillside on W.A. Elwood's farm washed out the hill's soil on April 27, 1927, it formed a 75-foot crater. In 1961, Bert Vanderheiden purchased the property and constructed an earthen dam to form a lake. Vanderheiden named the lake Floberg Springs, combining his and his wife's names: Florentine and Bert. Here, Cliff Carlson stands on the north bank of the sinkhole in 1927. (Courtesy of Marie Vanderheiden.)

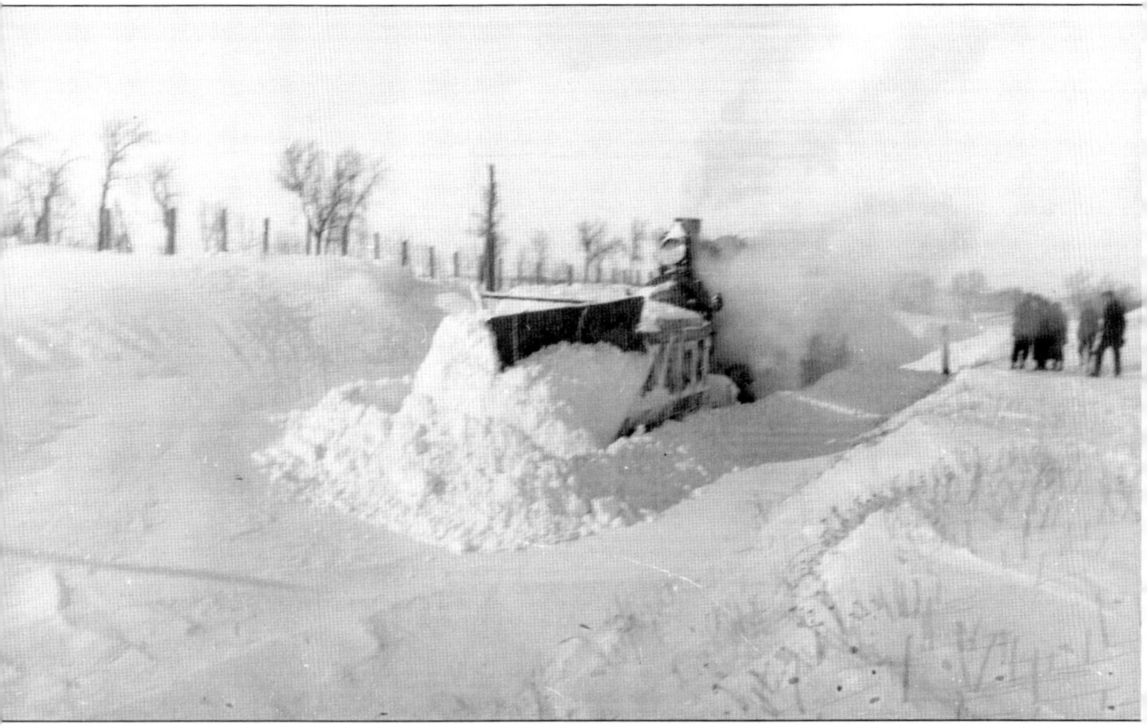

In the winter of 1897, the worst snowstorm since 1888 struck the Elgin area. It lasted 36 hours and deposited 15-foot drifts. This wooden snowplow coupled to a steam locomotive clears the track near Elgin. (ACHS.)

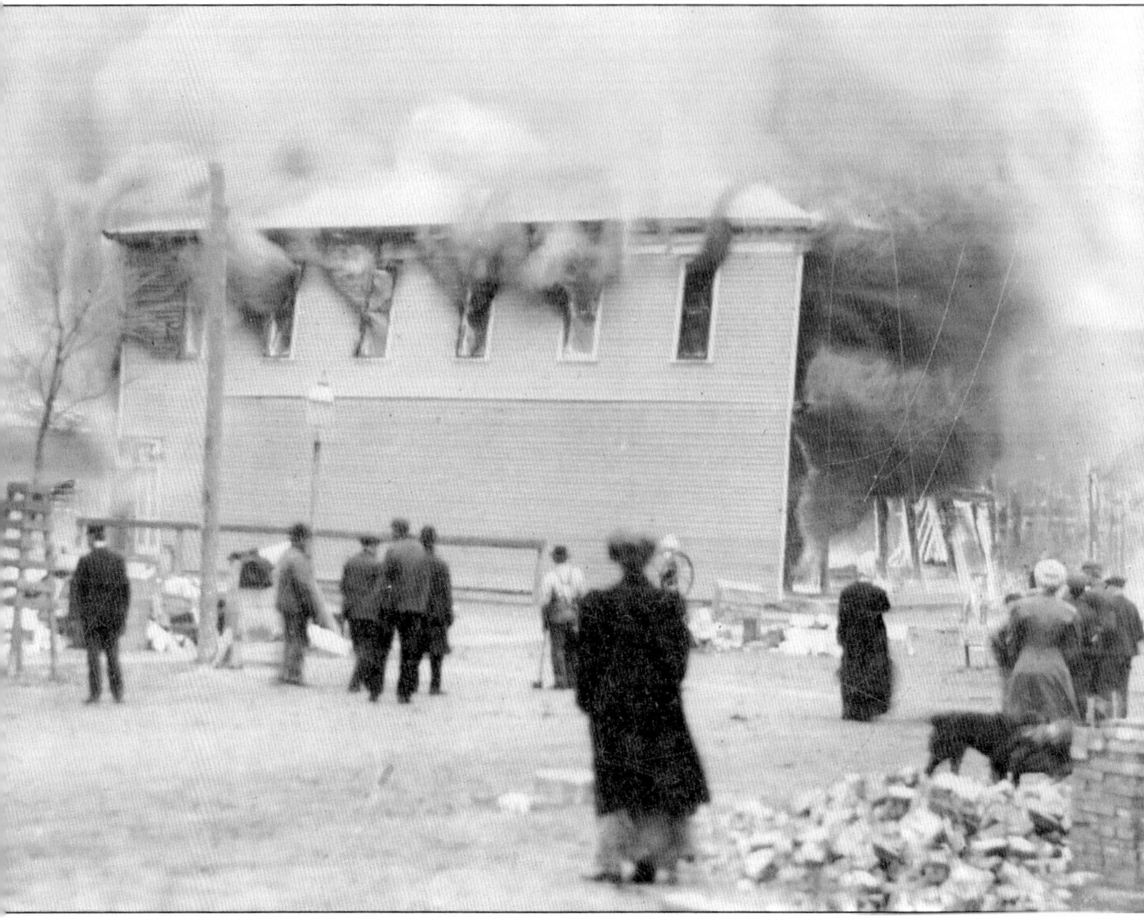

On April 29, 1909, a defective chimney in Brown & Green's restaurant ignited the worst fire in Elgin's history. After the alarm sounded, citizens organized a bucket brigade, but the fire persisted, destroying every wooden building on the block and damaging structures on the east and south sides of the street. This disaster prompted villagers to organize a volunteer fire department. (ACHS.)

Seven

Orchard
The Windmill Town

Henry Harvey, the first permanent settler in the Orchard area, arrived with his family in October 1878 and homesteaded near Verdigris Creek. Initially named Pacific Townsite, Orchard was one of several towns that the Chicago, Burlington & Quincy Railroad built along a line from Sioux City, Iowa, to O'Neill, Nebraska. The first train arrived on June 20, 1890, and the town remains on a railroad line. The Nebraska Northeastern Railway now serves Orchard's large grain terminal.

Pacific Townsite became Orchard because S.P. Cramer, the postmaster, had planted a large apple orchard on his farm. Cramer's application for a post office had been granted in 1881. Due to the many early residents who had their own wells with pumps, windmill power, and cisterns, Orchard earned the title Windmill Town. The first gristmill had a large windmill with wooden fans. If the wind failed to blow, a horse-drawn treadmill was used to power the grinding wheel.

In 1914, Austin King and Lloyd Drayton built the Rex Theater. The beautiful structure held 250 to 300 patrons. Although it closed in 1970, the Orchard Historical Society restored the building, and it is available today for group meetings. The historical society also restored the District 57 schoolhouse, one of the first rural schools in northwestern Antelope County. By 1893, Orchard's population had reached 150, and in 1915 it peaked at 650. The 2010 census reported a population of 379.

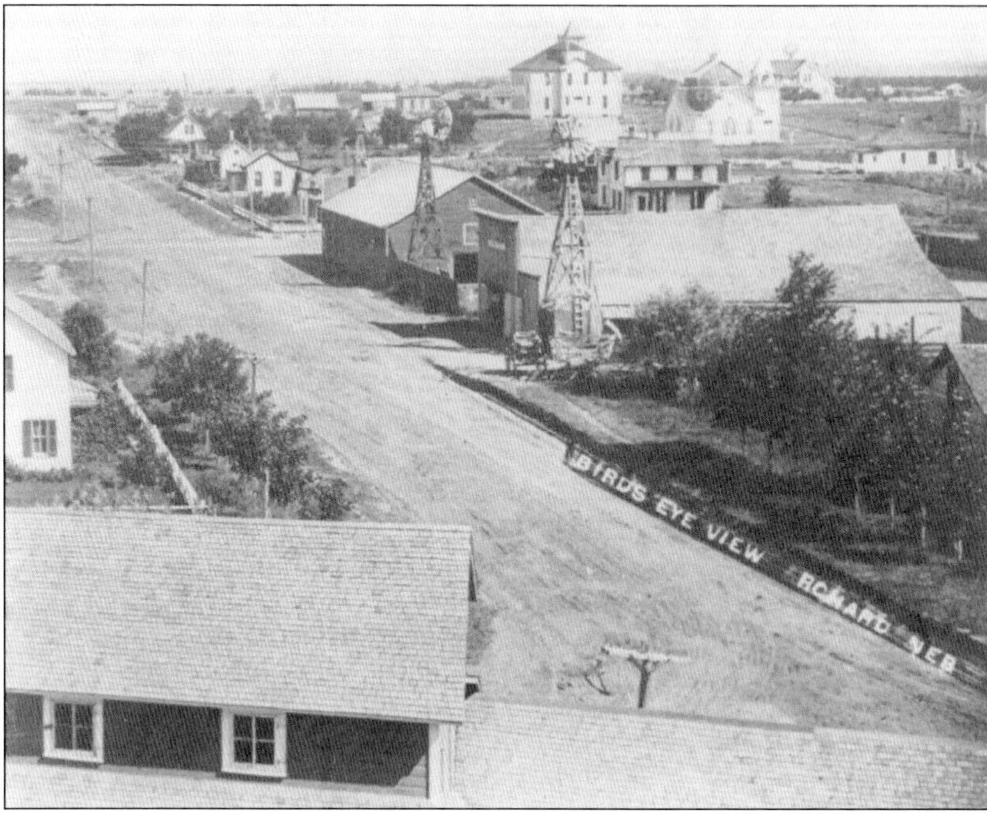

This photograph of Orchard, taken from the top of a grain elevator, looks northeast after 1905. Noble Street runs north and south, and Second Street extends east and west. The depot is in the left forefront, and the school and the Methodist church are prominent in the background. Two windmills are visible on Noble Street on either side of the stable. (Courtesy of Duard Dempster.)

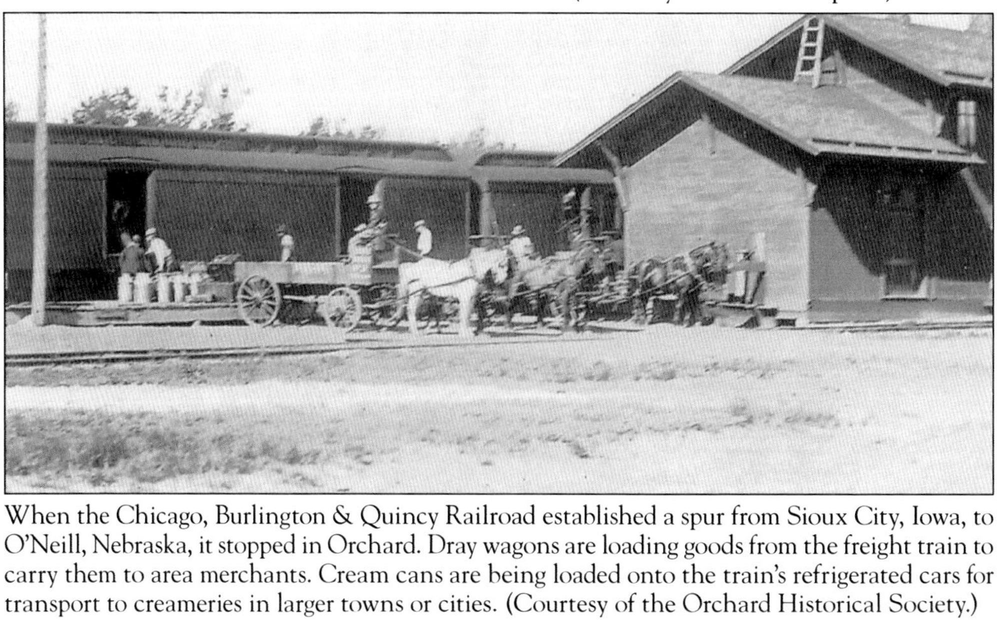

When the Chicago, Burlington & Quincy Railroad established a spur from Sioux City, Iowa, to O'Neill, Nebraska, it stopped in Orchard. Dray wagons are loading goods from the freight train to carry them to area merchants. Cream cans are being loaded onto the train's refrigerated cars for transport to creameries in larger towns or cities. (Courtesy of the Orchard Historical Society.)

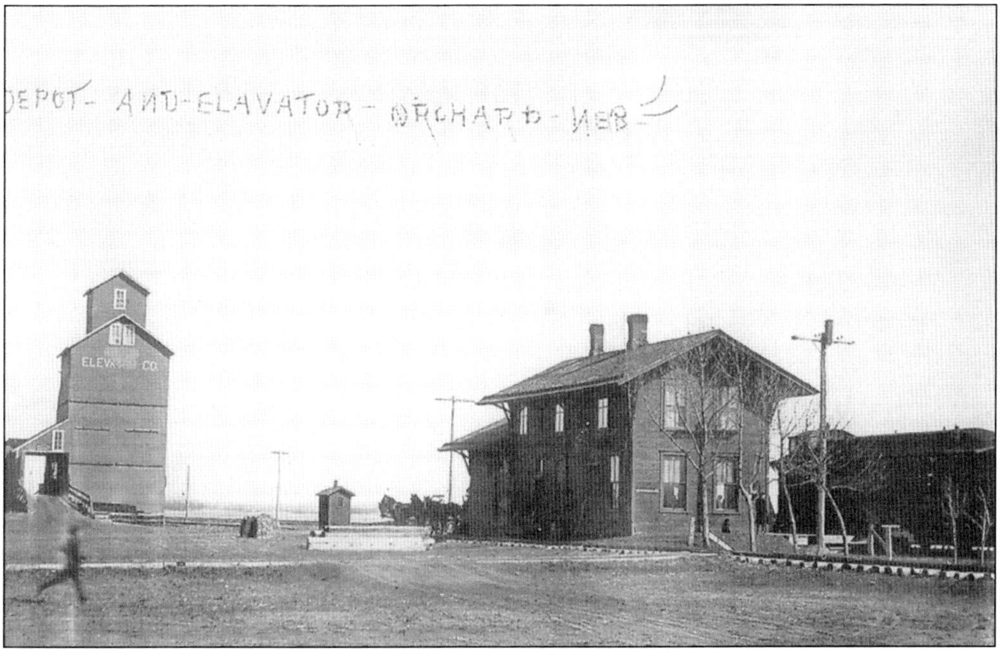

The Atlas elevator and lumberyard, built in 1903, had a capacity of 20,000 bushels. Modern equipment included Fairbanks scales and a gasoline lift engine. In 1920, the elevator was sold to Ed Rector. Joe Meuret managed the renamed Rector Company. Rector ended up selling his share to Meuret that same year. Meuret eventually sold the business to Gordon Drayton in 1937 or 1938. (Courtesy of the Orchard Historical Society.)

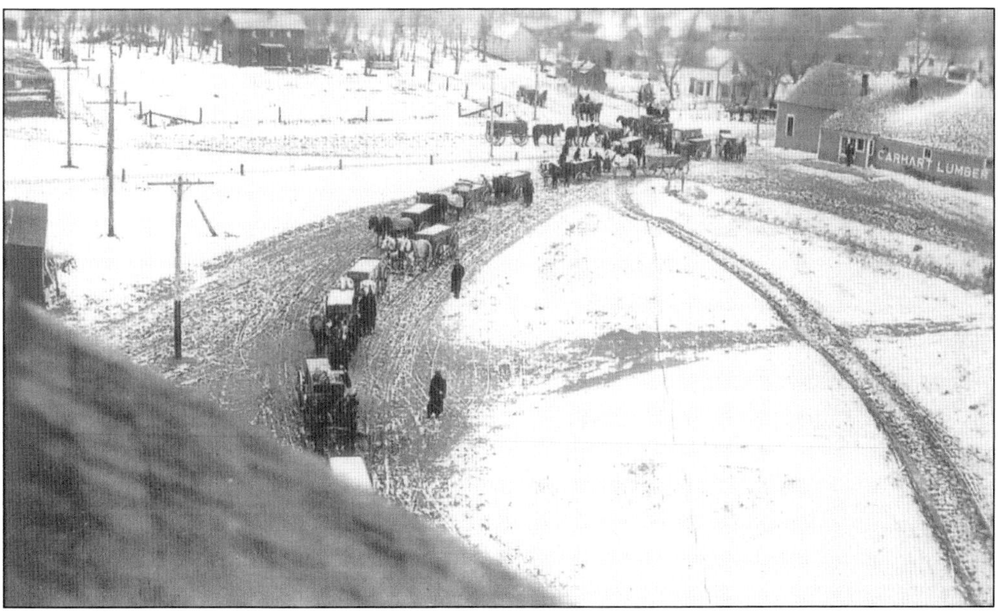

Wagons wait to deliver corn harvests to the Carhart lumberyard in Orchard. In the autumn of 1917, prices fell from $3.47 a bushel to $1.13. Rumors of World War I ending disturbed the commodity markets and raised the prospect of Argentine corn becoming available for 63¢ a bushel. (Courtesy of the Orchard Historical Society.)

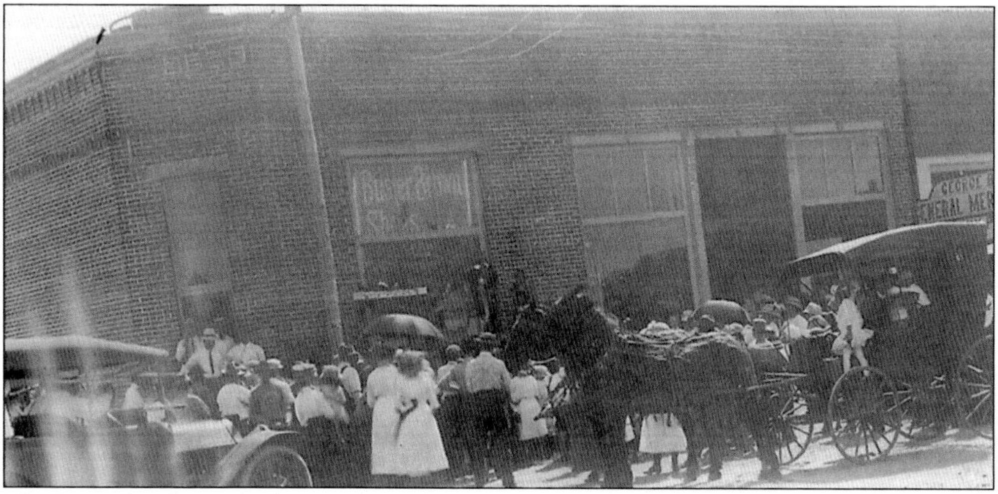

The George brothers, Abraham and Joseph, emigrants from Lebanon, took their father's first name when establishing their businesses. Abraham bought a mercantile store in Venus, and Joseph sold Venus merchandise from a cart until he opened a store in Royal. In 1906, he sold the Royal store to the Rundquists, and he and Abraham established an Orchard store, which they sold in 1938. (Courtesy of Duard Demptster.)

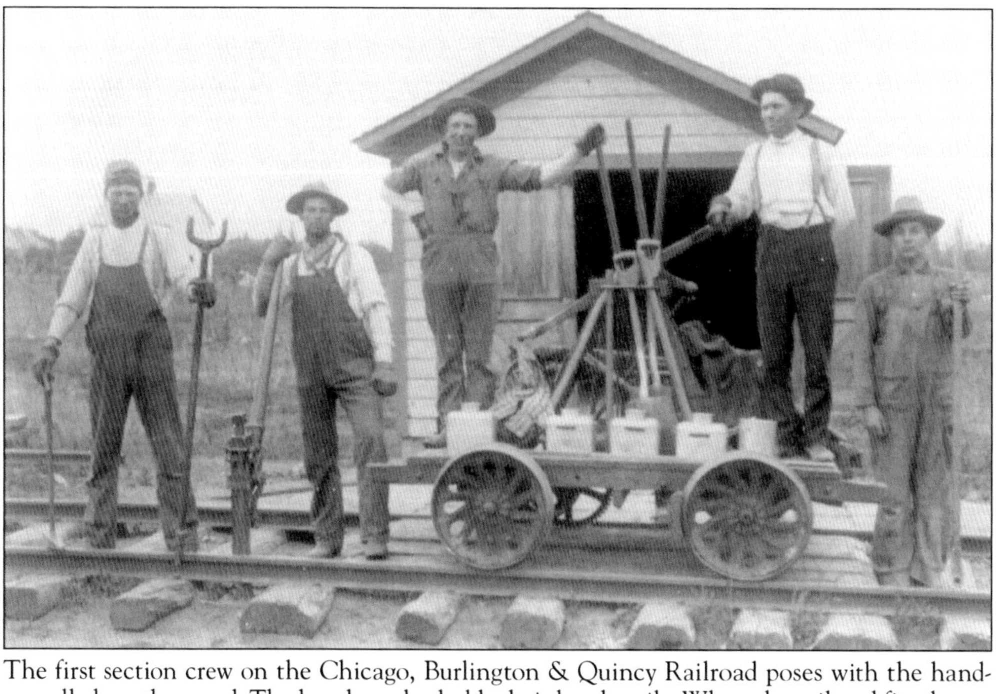

The first section crew on the Chicago, Burlington & Quincy Railroad poses with the hand-propelled car they used. The handcar also holds their lunch pails. When the railroad first began construction, every town had a section crew responsible for maintaining several miles of track. (Courtesy of George Strassler.)

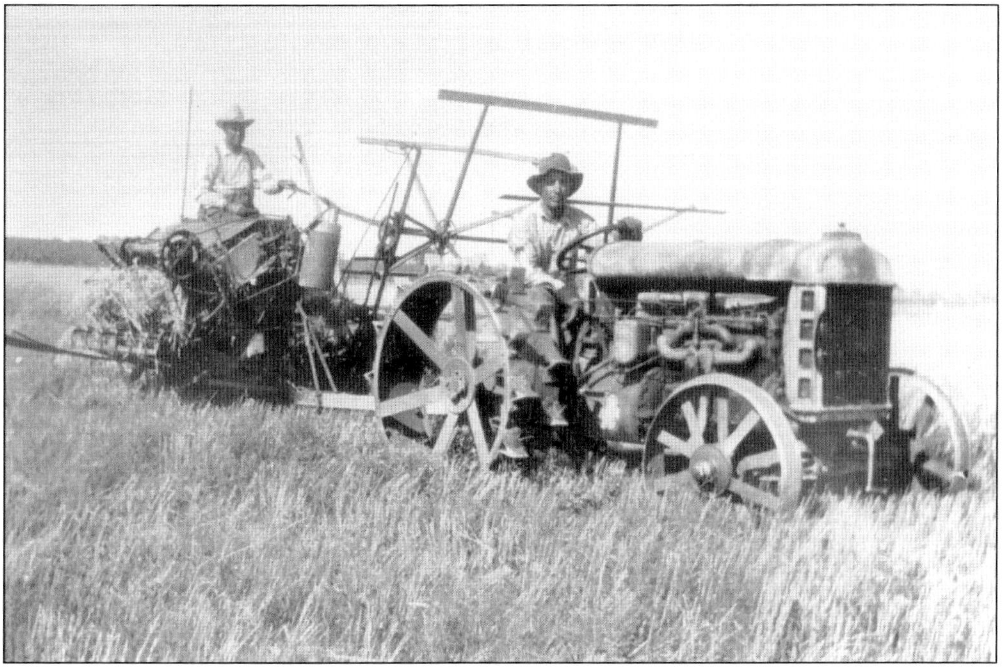

Pictured northeast of Orchard in 1928, oats are being harvested on the Oliver Dempster farm. A Fordson tractor pulls the binder. Dempster bought the tractor in Laurel, Nebraska, for $25 in 1927. He is seen driving the tractor, with Philo Grove operating the binder. (Courtesy of Duard Dempster.)

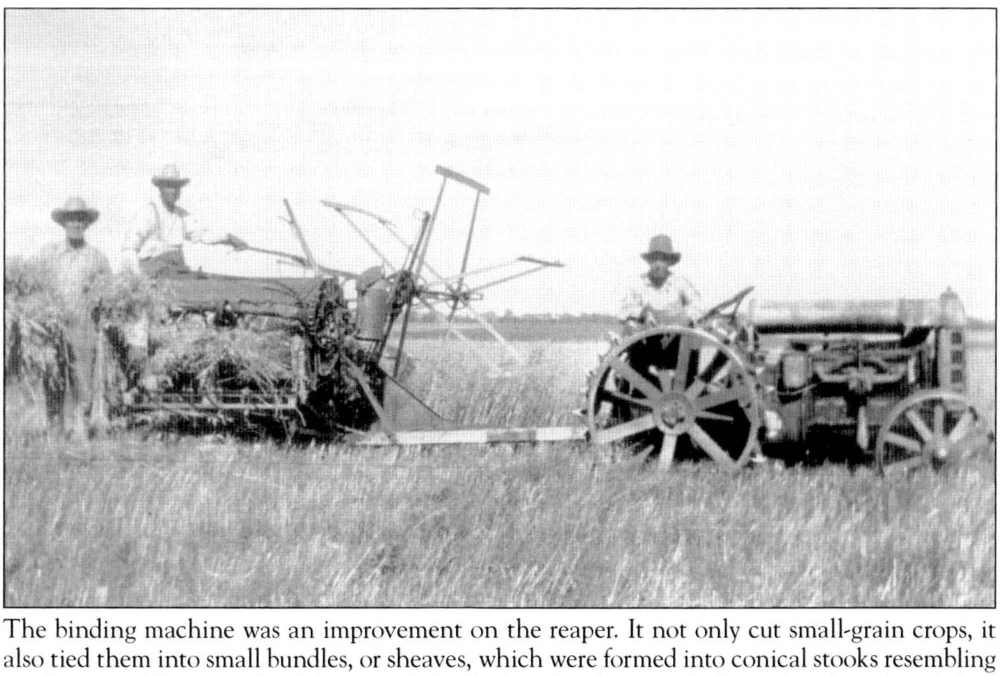

The binding machine was an improvement on the reaper. It not only cut small-grain crops, it also tied them into small bundles, or sheaves, which were formed into conical stooks resembling small tepees. The grain dried for several days before threshing took place. Seen here from left to right are James Grove, Philo Grove (on binder), and Oliver Dempster (on tractor). (Courtesy of Duard Dempster.)

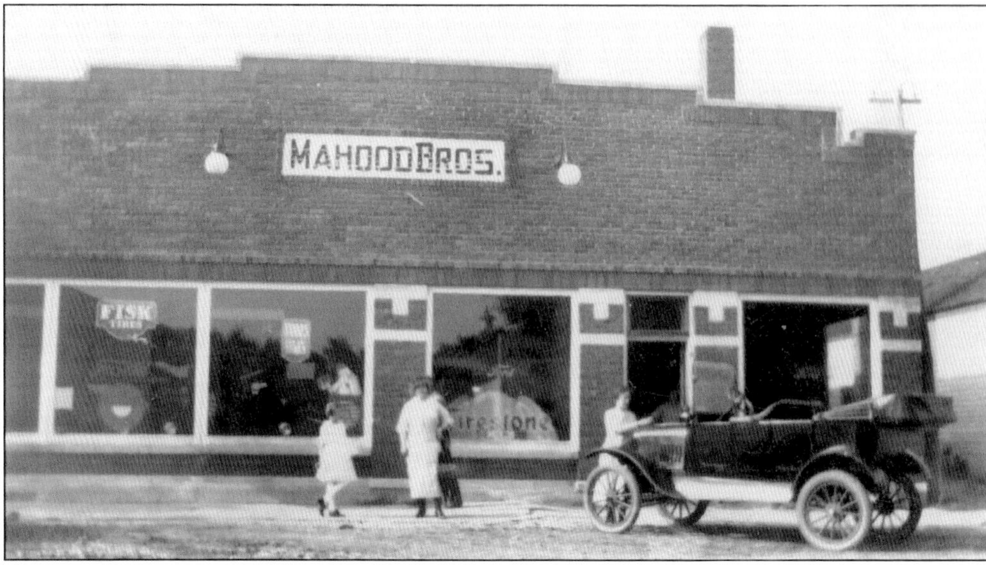

Albert, Wilbur, and Calvin Mahood opened the first garage in Orchard, where they sold Ford cars and gasoline. In 1912, they also established and operated the first electric-light plant in town. In 1926, they gave the electrical service to a company outside the community. (Courtesy of Duard Dempster.)

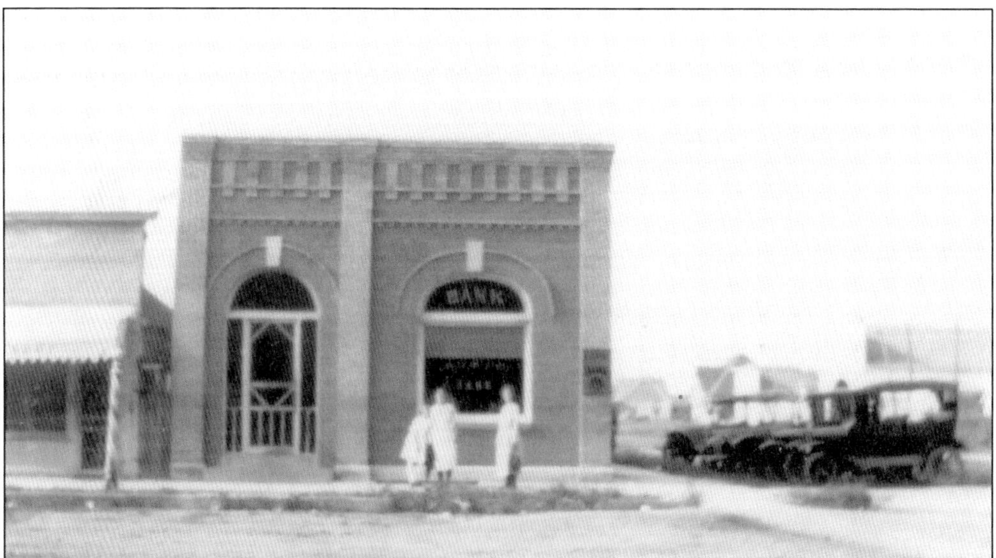

Established in 1905, the Citizens State Bank conducted business in the former Dart Bank building on the corner of Second and Windom Streets. In February 1907, T.A. Drayton accepted the position of cashier, and the bank moved to the Drayton block. The bank closed its doors in 1931, leaving the town without a bank for several years. (Courtesy of Duard Dempster.)

Alex Browning began constructing a three-story building in 1914 and completed it in 1915, although the top two floors never were finished. The main floor held the Kings Bank, along with offices and a large storeroom. In 1927, the top two floors were condemned and removed from the structure. (Courtesy of Duard Dempster.)

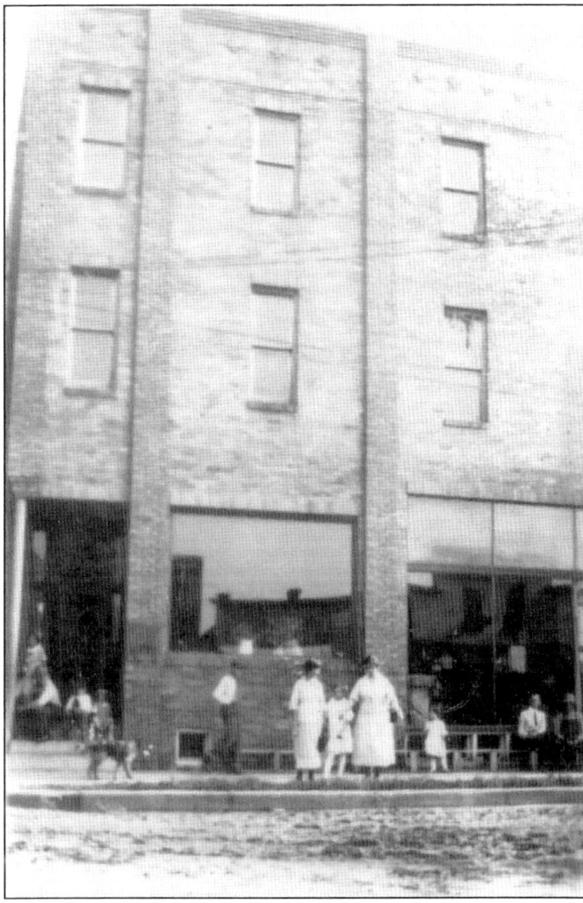

James Clifton Sr. arrived in Orchard with his family in a covered wagon. His son James Jr. married Tina George, and they farmed west of Orchard. When James Jr. became interested in the hardware business, they left the farm and moved to town. He took over the hardware store in the Drayton building, pictured here around 1920. (Courtesy of Duard Dempster.)

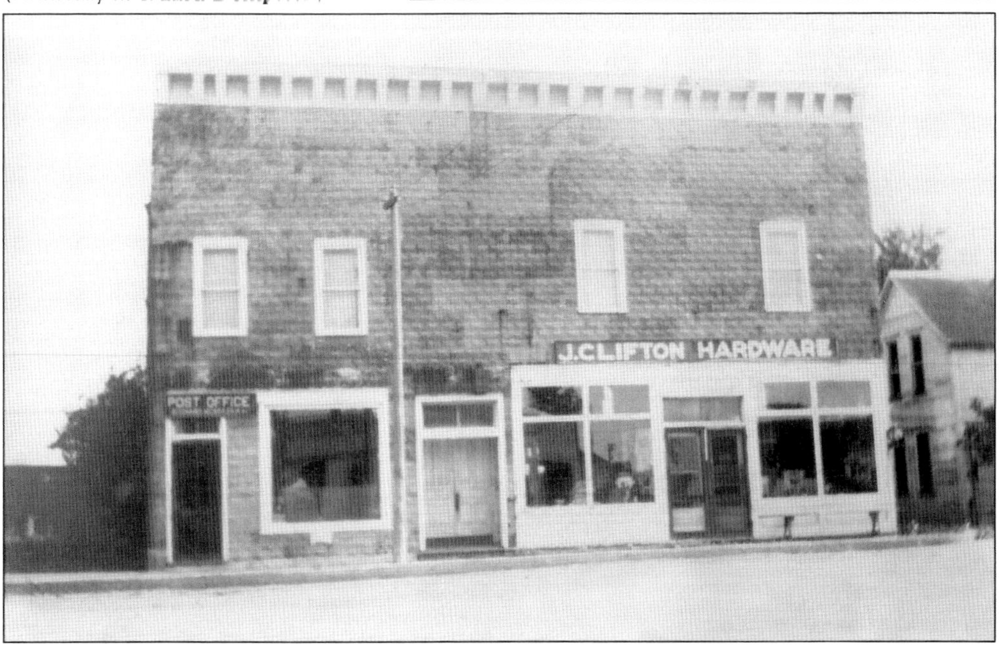

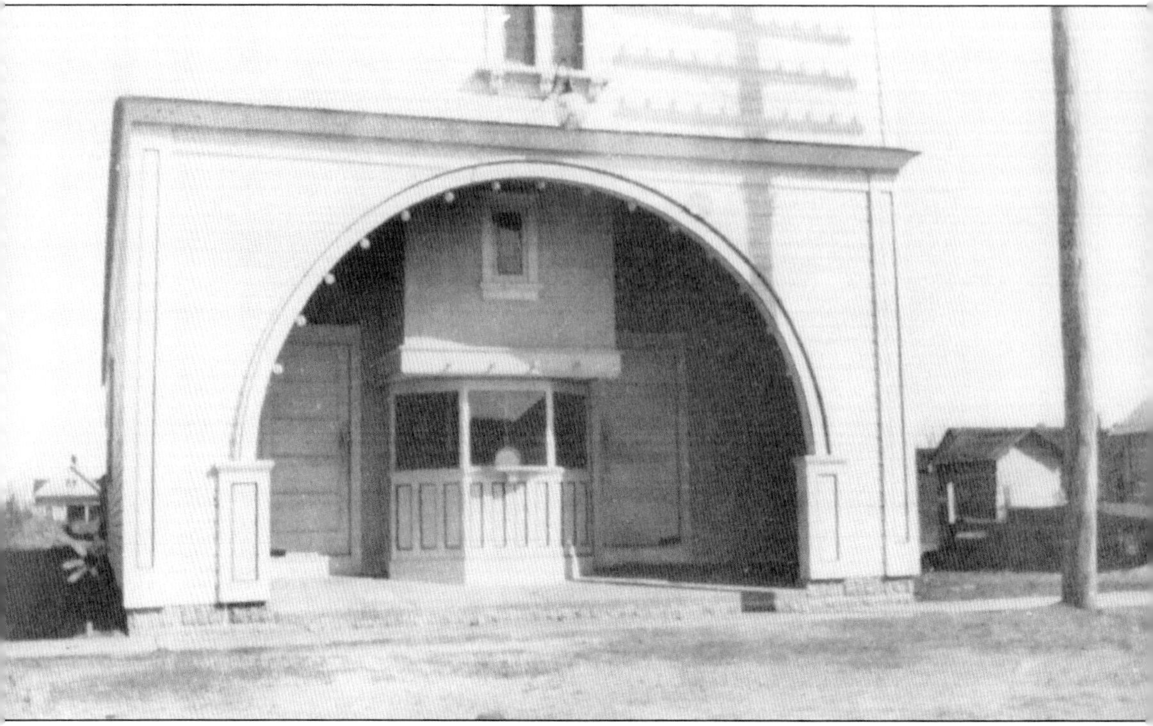

Austin King and Lloyd Drayton built the Rex Theater in 1914. Usually, one feature played on Tuesday and Wednesday and another played on Saturday and Sunday. In addition to the feature, a cartoon, a newsreel, and a serial also appeared on the screen. The building seated 250 to 300 people. The theater closed in 1970, but it has been restored and is now used for meetings and celebrations. (Courtesy of George Strassler.)

Eight

Brunswick
Keeping the Trains

In 1879, Charles Galloway and his wife and six children came from Illinois to Ellsworth Township. The parents and three eligible children filed homestead claims. They then built a house on the intersection of two roads, allowing the family to sleep on four adjacent land claims and meet the legal requirements for proving ownership. Charles Galloway applied for and received a grant for a post office at the family home in 1881. He called the settlement Little Chicago.

By 1888, the nearby hamlet of Clear Springs had taken over the Little Chicago post office. Another Illinois emigrant, Henry Nagel, had arrived in Little Chicago and married Kate Galloway in 1883. Nagel fulfilled his dream of founding a town when he donated land in the shape of a cross on which to establish a community. Because Nagel raised sugar beets with the same chemical makeup as those grown in Brunswick, Germany, he named the town Brunswick.

Around 1890, the railroad reached Brunswick. When the Burlington Northern threatened to abandon the line, concerned citizens arranged to upgrade the track. Brunswick remains on the Burlington Northern route because of the Meuret Grain Company. Established in 1934 by Joseph E. Meuret, the company is a major grain terminal for the area and has the storage capacity for several million bushels of grain along with modern load-out facilities. Brunswick's population has fluctuated since it was founded: in 1915, the town had 300 residents; the population peaked in 1920 with 800 inhabitants; and the 2010 census reported 138 residents.

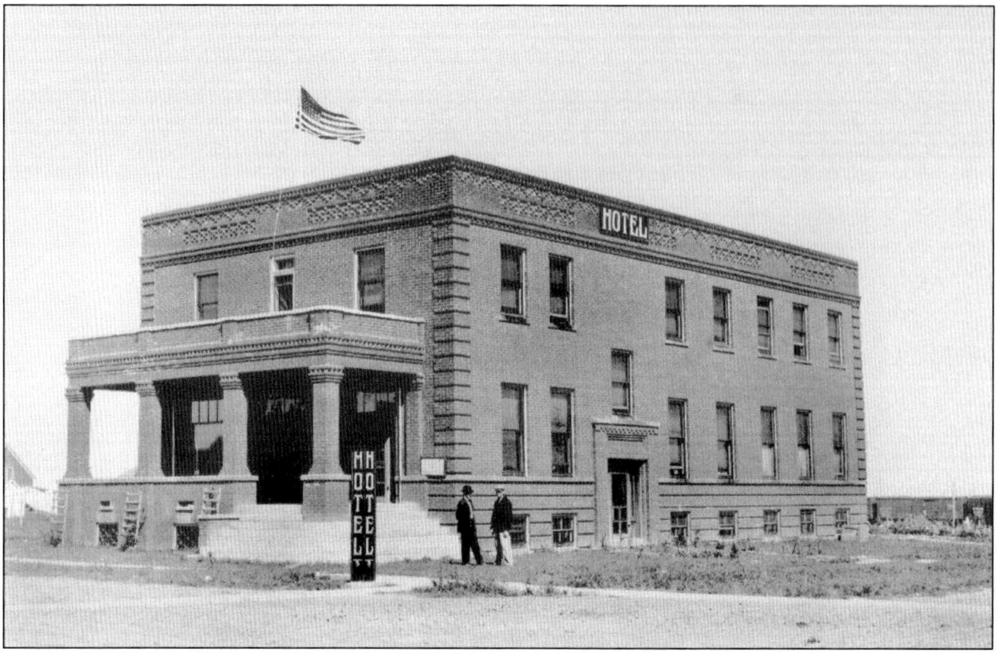

Located on Second and Proctor Streets, the Brunswick Hotel was owned and managed by Shane C. Omer. It is seen here in 1915. Small-town hotels catered to people passing through the area, usually on passenger trains. In 1985, the last year of its existence, the hotel was a rest home run by Lorena Heyers. The building was torn down in 1986. (ACHS.)

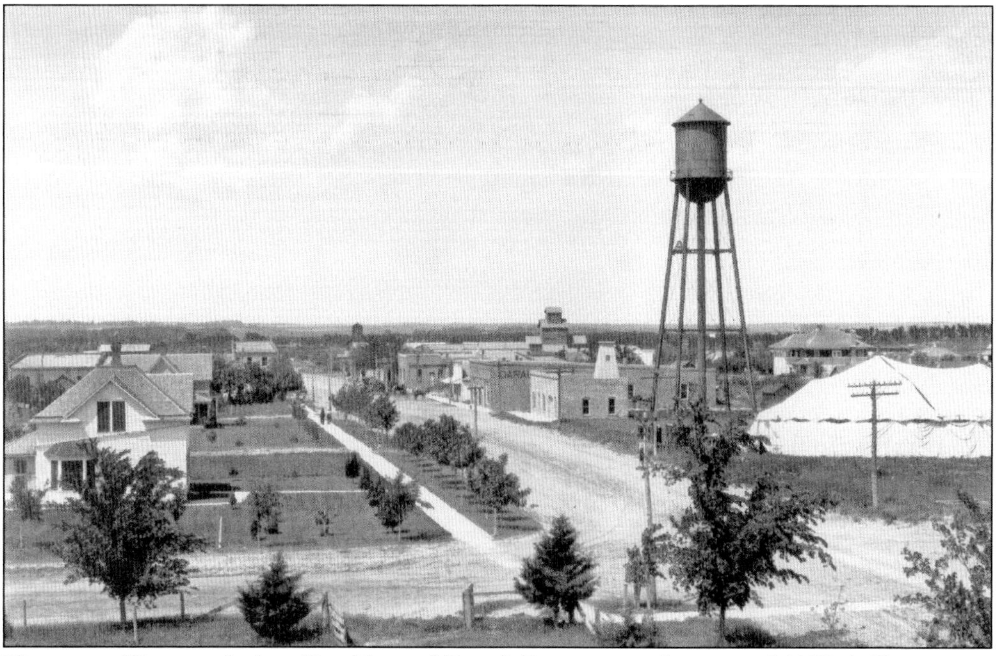

This view of Brunswick along Franklin and Fourth Streets was taken around 1915. A Chautauqua tent in the foreground was part of the circuit Chautauqua program, which provided entertainment and culture for communities all through the area. Nearly every town in the county welcomed Chautauqua companies for a week or two in the summer. (ACHS.)

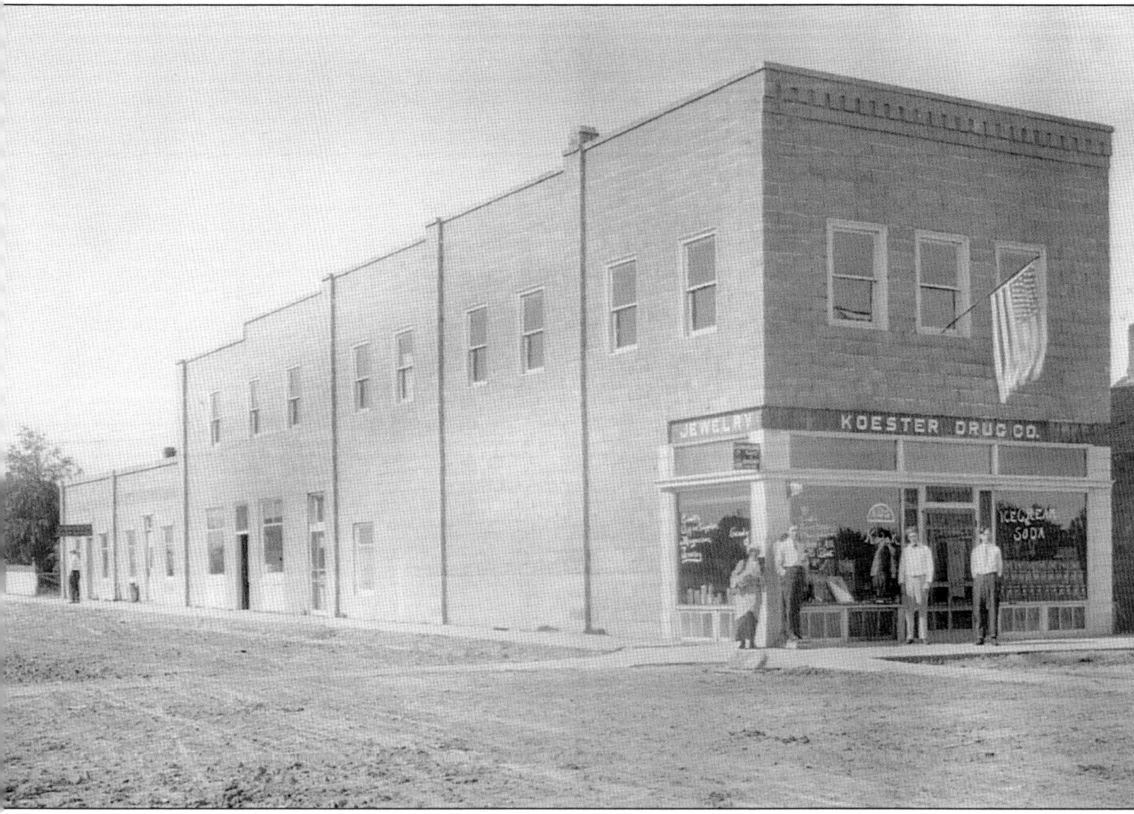

The American flag flies above the Koester Drug Company around 1915. The store was likely founded in 1912, surviving the fire that occurred that year. The small building in back is the post office. The first post office, established in 1881, was near Bazile Township and was named Clear Springs due to the many springs in the area. The first postmaster, J.A. Douglas, was followed by L. Murphy. It then moved to the home of Mr. and Mrs. C.H. Johnson in Crawford Township. Johnson served as postmaster until 1884, when the post office moved to the farm home of the new postmistress, Mrs. J.L. Renberg. In 1888, the Chicago post office merged with Clear Springs but remained in Mrs. Renberg's home. When Mrs. Renberg resigned in 1889, the Clear Springs post office relocated to the homestead of Willie Gunthorpe, the new postmaster. Ellsworth Township was later included in the town of Brunswick, and the post office name was officially changed to Brunswick in 1890. (ACHS.)

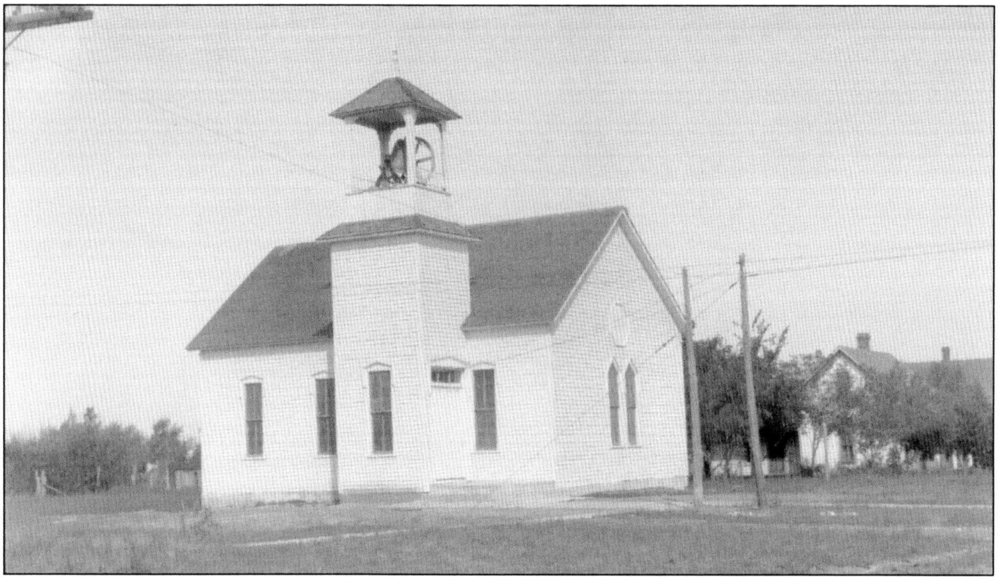

The Congregational Church was organized in 1891 with 19 members. Rev. H. Griffith served as pastor through 1892. The church building, seen above and below, was purchased from the Presbyterians and moved from the country into town in 1891. The Methodist Episcopal Church, organized in the late 1880s, functioned without an official pastor until Dr. William Gorst was appointed in 1900. By 1920, the Methodist Episcopal and Congregational Churches formed a federation known as the Community Church. In 1929, the Community Church was affiliated with the Christian and Missionary Alliance and received the official title Brunswick Community Church. Miss Aleda Peterson was appointed pastor, and the group met in the Methodist Church. When Peterson married Karl Zeiman in 1931, they shared the role of minister until 1942. In 1940, the Community Church purchased the church property from the Methodist Conference. (Both, ACHS.)

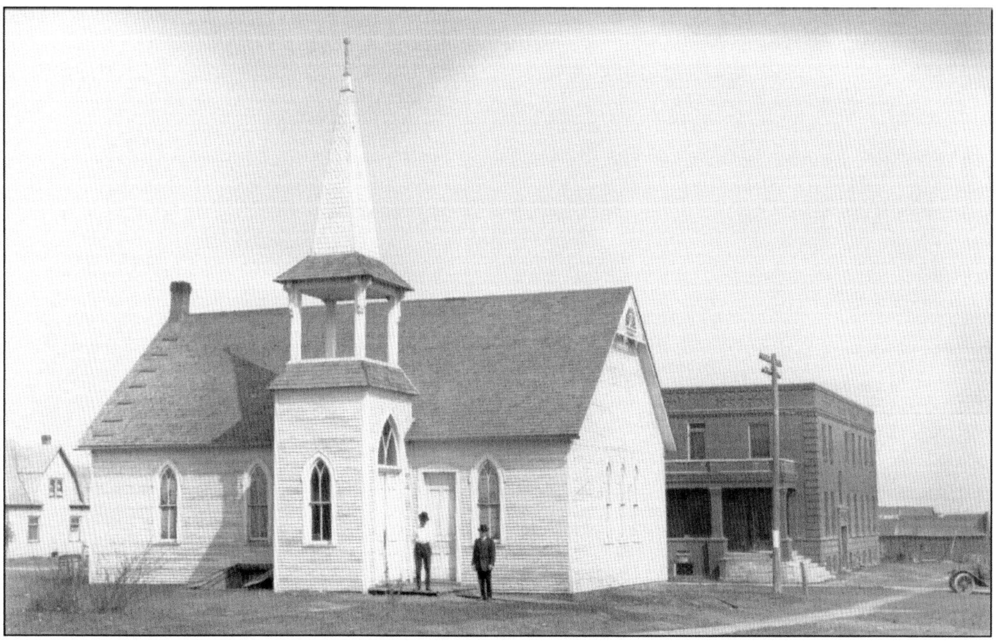

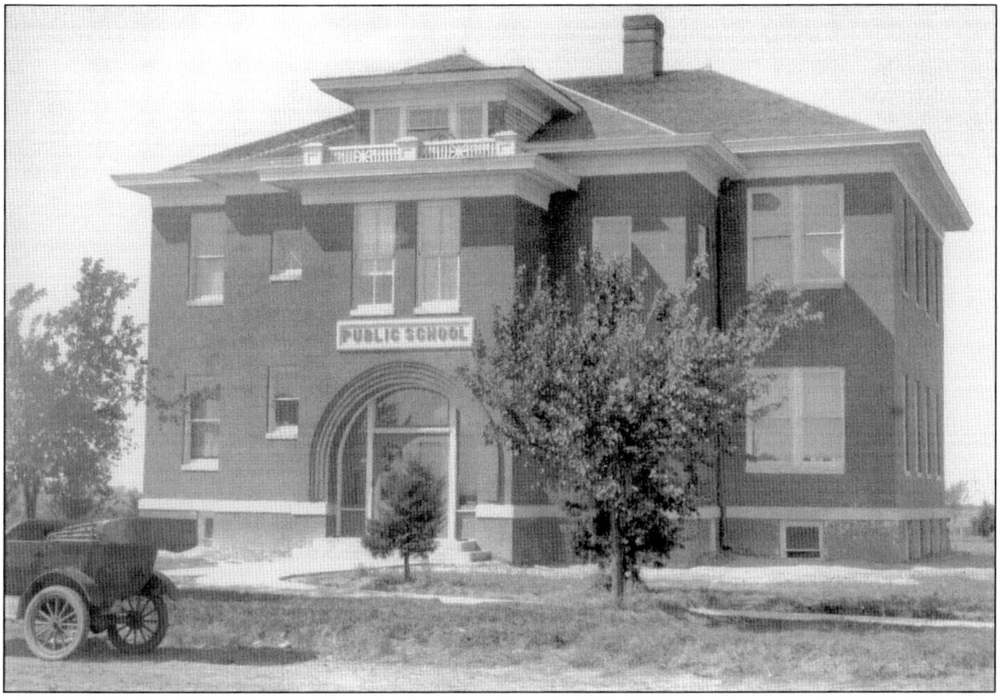

Built in 1910, the new school building had only 10 grades at first. A junior class was added in 1916, and in 1917 a senior class graduated. When the school population outgrew the 1910 structure, another building was erected to house grades one through four. The last class graduated from Brunswick High School in 1965, with 12 students. (ACHS.)

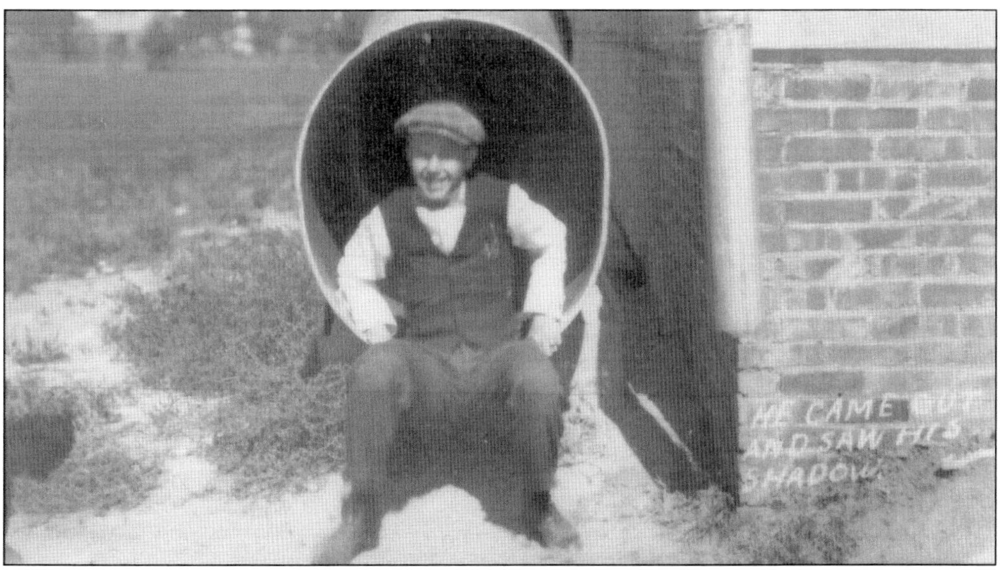

This large metal tube leading from the top floor of the Brunswick school provided entertainment as well as escape from the building during fire drills. After classes were dismissed, enterprising youngsters returned to school carrying pieces of wax paper. They crawled up the tube, sat on the wax paper, and slid down; if they lacked paper, they simply slid down. (ACHS.)

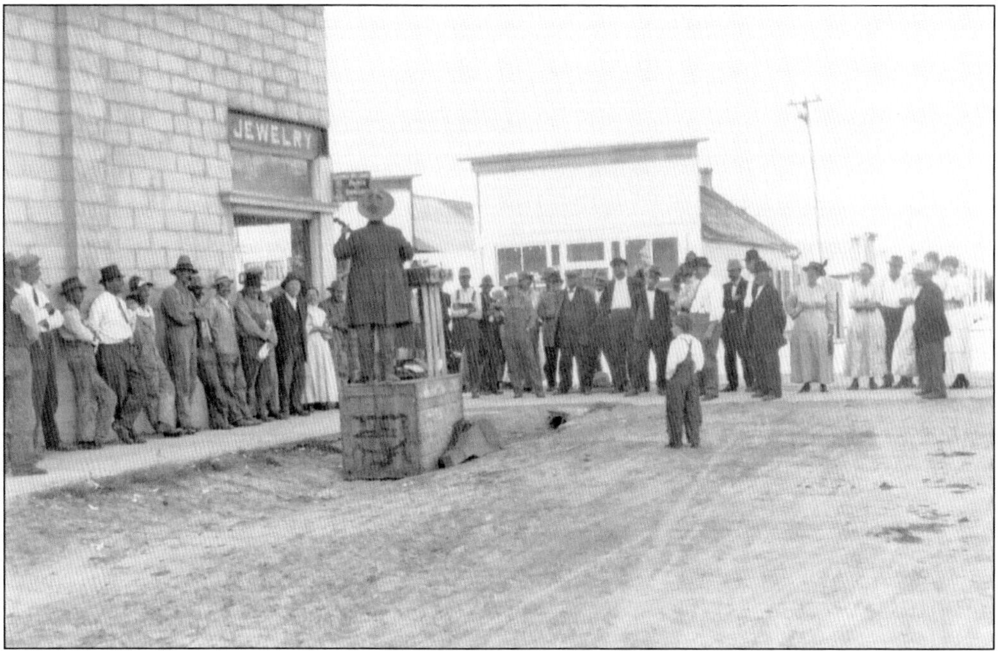

A banjo player stands on a wooden box around 1910, strumming a tune and luring people to downtown Brunswick. He attracted listeners at the intersection of Second and Franklin Streets, and townsfolk are lingering near the jewelry store. (ACHS.)

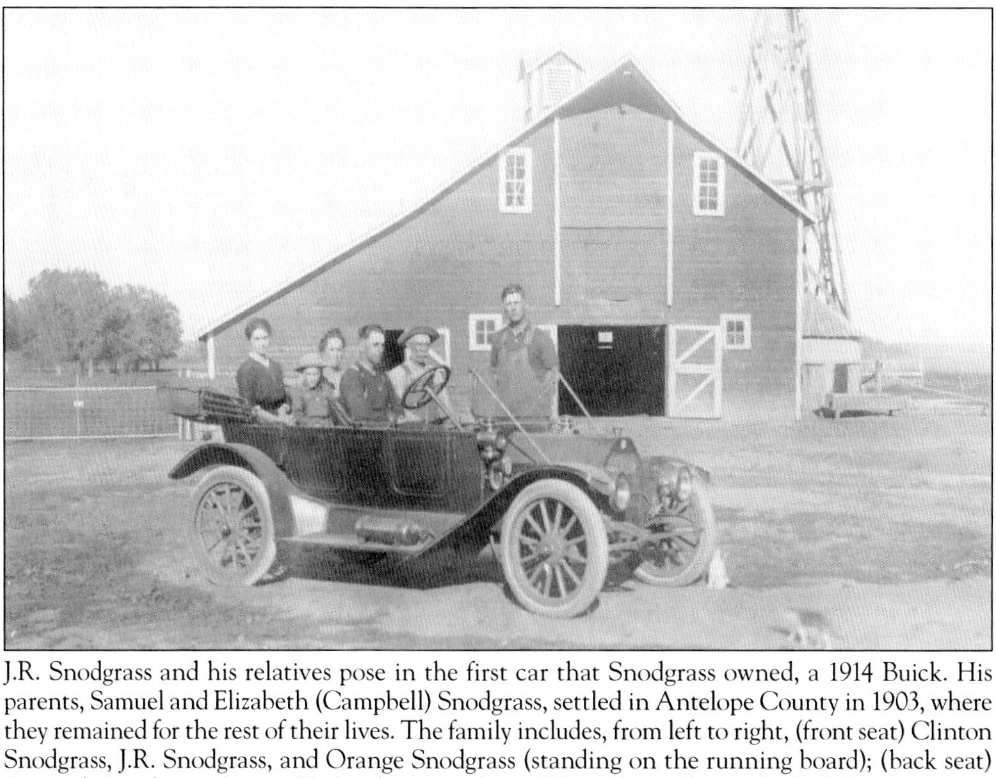

J.R. Snodgrass and his relatives pose in the first car that Snodgrass owned, a 1914 Buick. His parents, Samuel and Elizabeth (Campbell) Snodgrass, settled in Antelope County in 1903, where they remained for the rest of their lives. The family includes, from left to right, (front seat) Clinton Snodgrass, J.R. Snodgrass, and Orange Snodgrass (standing on the running board); (back seat) Gertrude Snodgrass, Lavern K. Snodgrass, and Mrs. Hannah Snodgrass. (ACHS.)

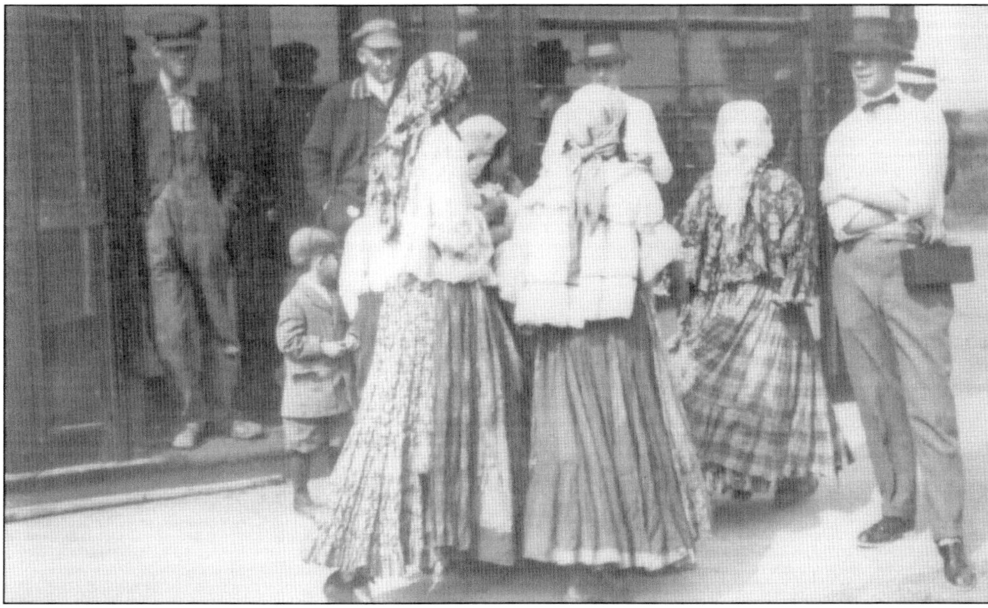

Gypsies visited Brunswick around 1910 and are seen here gathering on the southeast corner of Second Street. Horses pulled their brightly painted covered wagons as they traveled along rural roads, stopping to pick fruit from trees or bushes. They also visited farms and engaged in horse trading. People did not trust gypsies, and store owners would telephone merchants in nearby towns, warning them, "The gypsies are coming." (ACHS.)

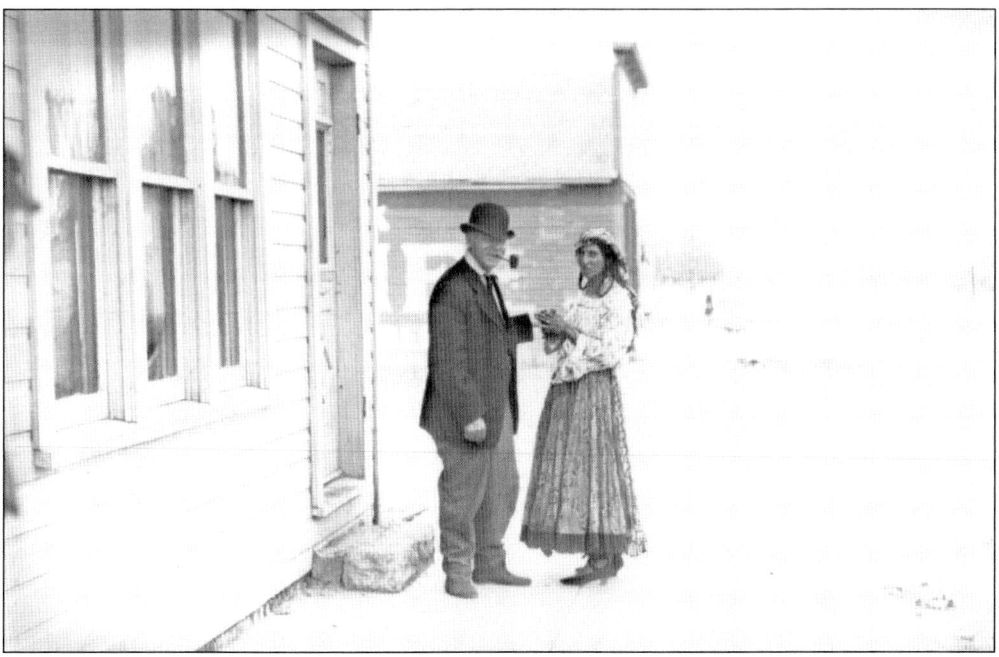

When gypsies came to town, the troop often included a fortune-teller. Here, Brunswick resident Albert Nagel appears to be enjoying having his picture taken while a gypsy predicts his future. This photograph was likely taken on the same day as the photograph at the top of the page. (ACHS.)

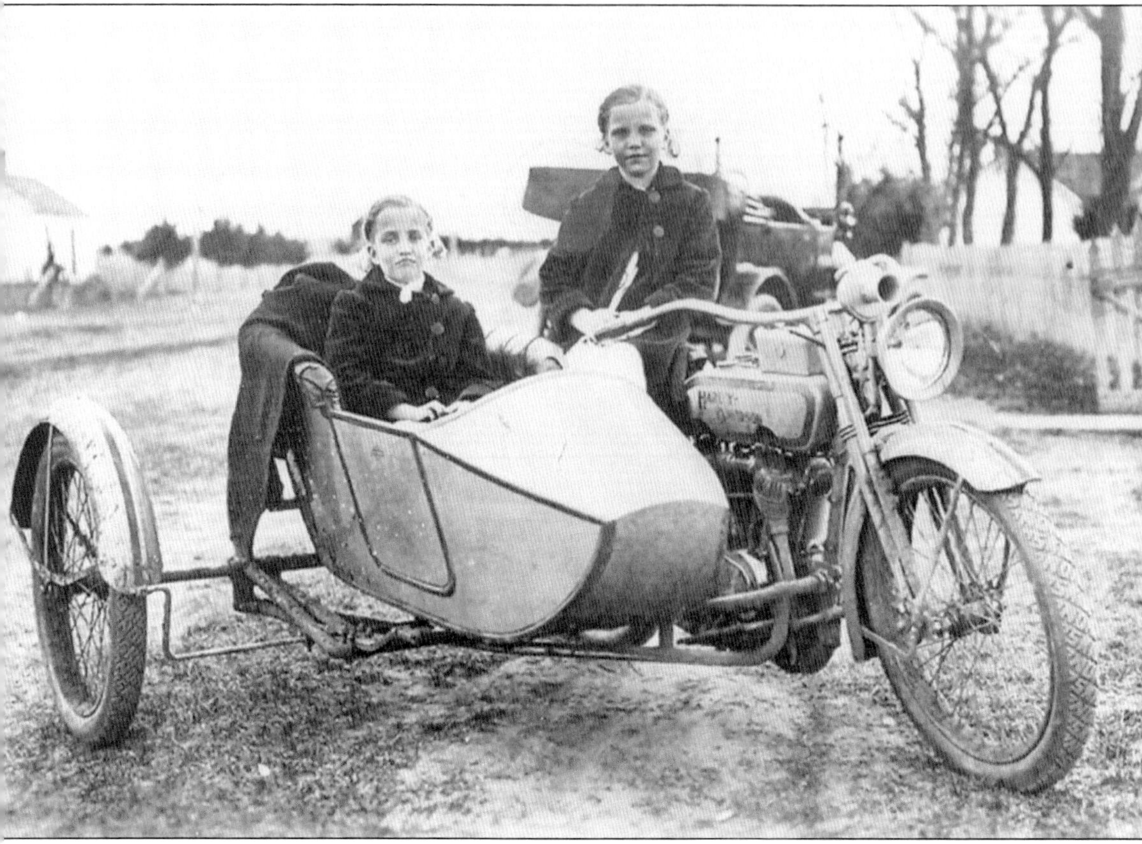

The Verle sisters pose in a Harley-Davidson motorcycle and sidecar. The sidecar was introduced in 1914, along with clutch and brake pedals. In 1914, motorcycles also began entering races, and by 1918 half of the motorcycles produced in America were used in World War I. Interestingly, after the armistice was signed in 1918, the first American entered Germany riding on a Harley-Davidson. (ACHS.)

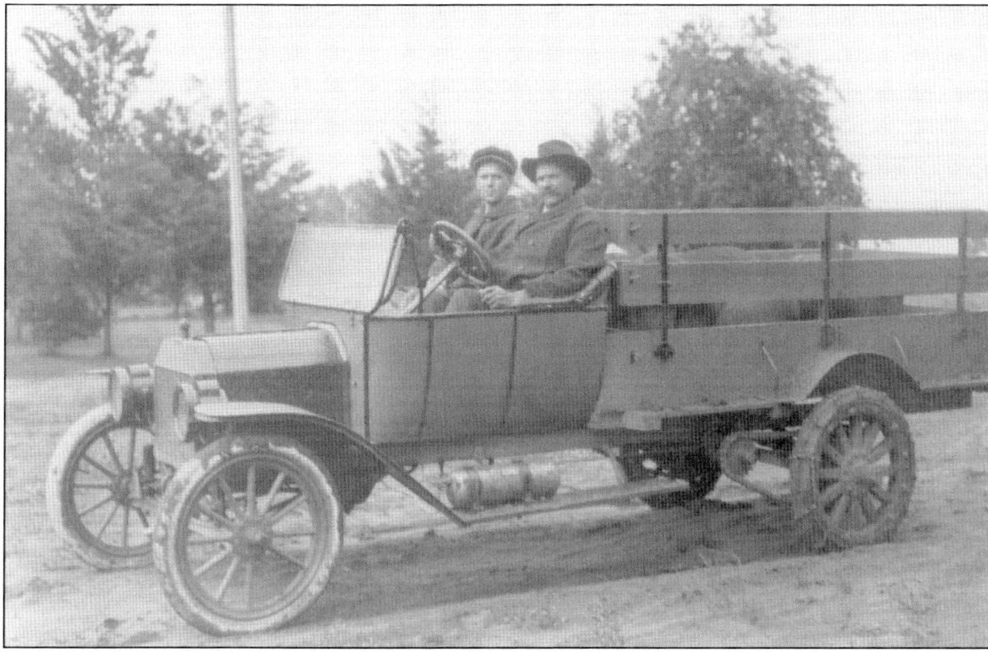

The first truck delivery of hogs to Brunswick occurred in 1915. The truck is a Ford car cut off behind the front wheelbase and lengthened to support a wagon box. The car is chain driven, and the chain is visible near the back wheel. Albert Hansen, driving the truck, owned and operated a garage. His father, N.P. Hansen, is in the passenger seat. (ACHS.)

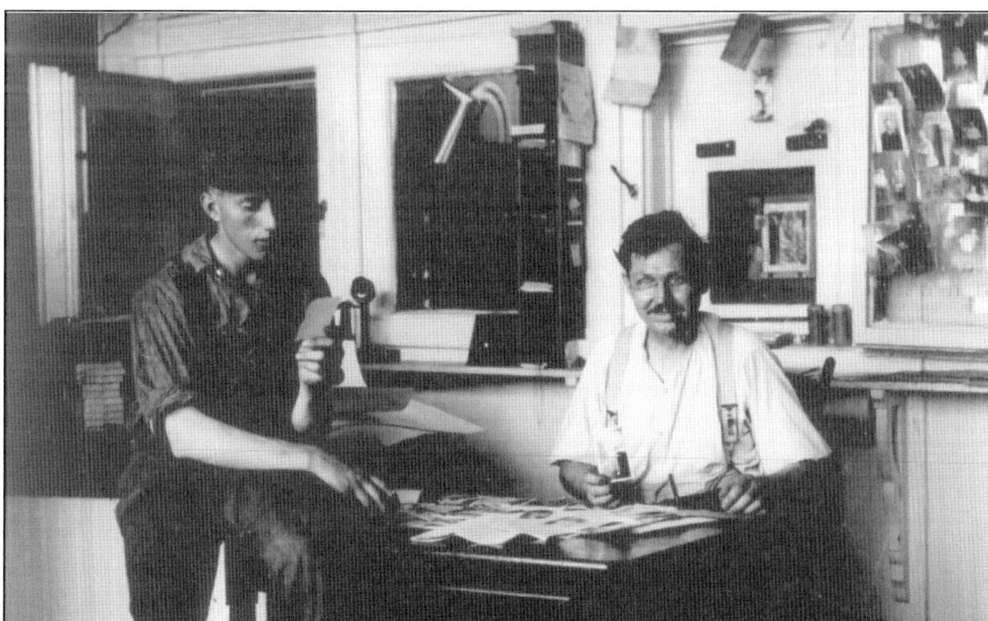

Surrounded by photographs, these unidentified gentlemen may be employees of an early Brunswick newspaper. The candlestick telephone and black-and-white photographs pinned on the wall indicate that this photograph was taken in the early 1900s. (ACHS.)

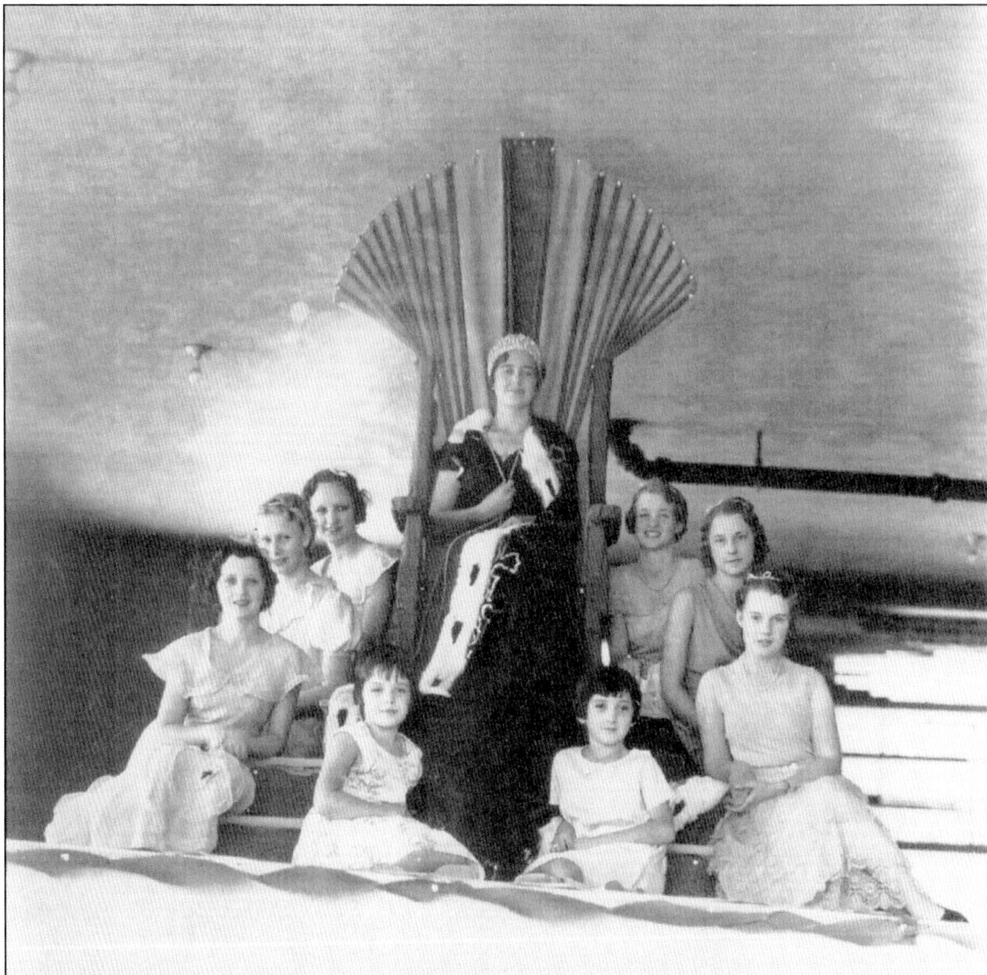

The queen of the 1931 Antelope County Fair and her attendants were Brunswick residents. On the last day of the fair, Mildred Rasmussen handed her crown to Leona Everheart of Orchard. The two young girls in front are Ruth Elaine Melleck (left) and Virginia Galloway, and the older girls are, clockwise from the bottom left, Helen Galloway, Lorene Martison, Josephene Hladavack, Mildred Rassmussen, Dorothy Frost, Helen Nagel, and Ruth Binning. (ACHS.)

Nine

Royal
Finding a Name

Settlement in the vicinity of present-day Royal began in 1879. Jules Hering, a native of Germany, built a gristmill 4.5 miles north of Royal. His mill served farmers within a 30-mile radius as well as those in three adjoining counties. Soon after the mill was established, the Burlington Northern Railroad planned a new line stretching from Niobrara, Nebraska, to the Gulf of Mexico. The possibility of a railroad passing near Herings Mill sparked business ventures in the area and prompted the Jessup Post Office to relocate near the mill site. Herings Mill was then renamed Jessup Roller Mills.

Abandoning its plan to run a line to the Gulf of Mexico, the Burlington built a short line from Sioux City, Iowa, to O'Neill, Nebraska, four miles south of the mill, and Jessup Township faded away. In 1890, the train to O'Neill ran through John Allen's farm, and he deeded part of his property to establish a town. At the same time, a Dr. Savage of Sioux City, Iowa, promised to build a school in any community along the railroad line that would adopt his name, and the town was named Savage.

A minister from Brunswick who conducted church services in Savage objected to calling his charge the Savage Sunday School and took steps to rename the village. He succeeded in renaming it Royal, which was the name of the post office that served the community. The small town thus endured three name changes, from Jessup to Savage to Royal. The 2010 census reported a population of 63 in Royal.

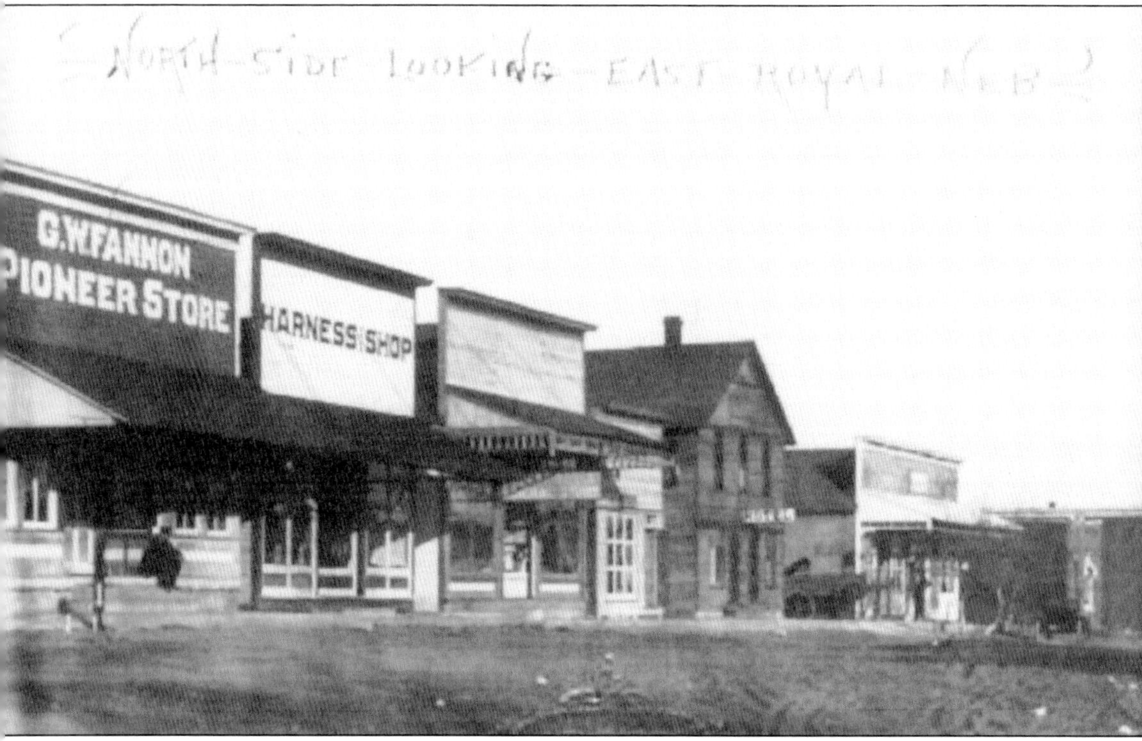

Main Street in Royal around 1900 features a Pioneer store, which likely served as a general store for area residents. The harness shop to the right of it thrived before the arrival of cars, trucks, and tractors. (Courtesy of Kenneth Krohn.)

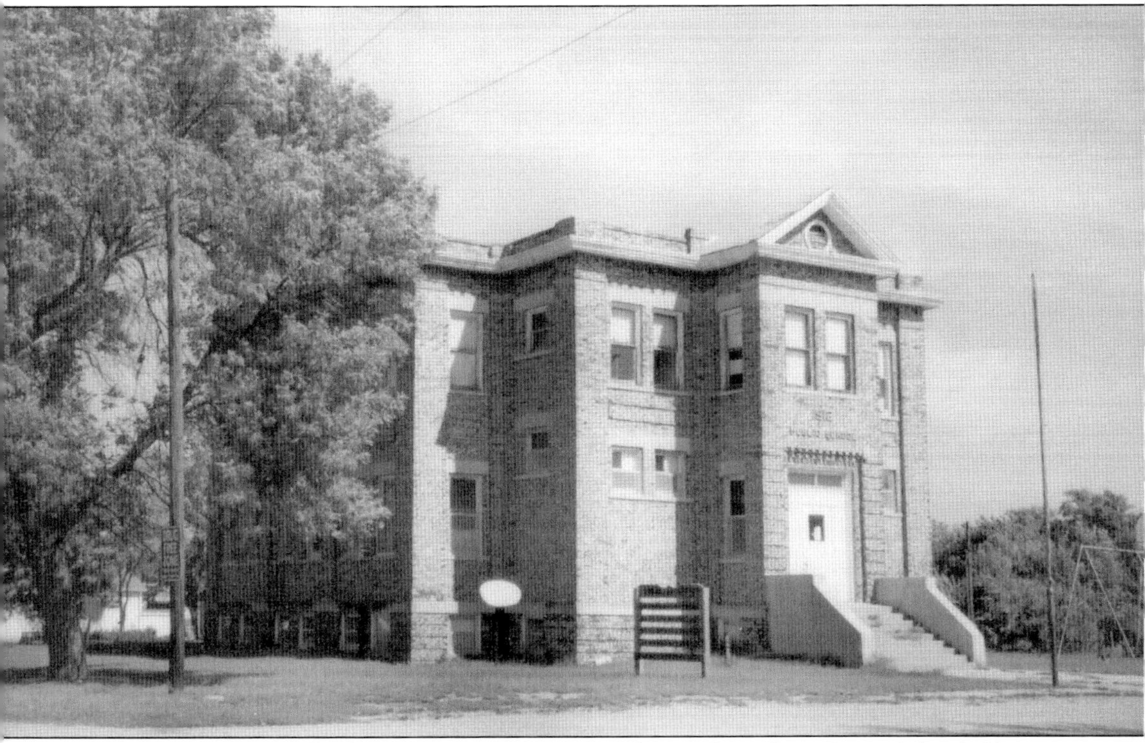

In March 1880, the first school opened in a log cabin northeast of Royal. It educated the children of five families. In the summer of that year, the school was moved to a sod house. Desks were built around the perimeter of the room and fastened to the walls. The stove, fueled with hay and wood, stood in the center of the room. School District 13 was formed in 1890, and in 1891 a wood-frame school was built. It educated students through the eighth grade, teaching children of the Holm, Dikeman, Allen, and Couch families. In 1913, a new school that went through the 10th grade was erected in town. By 1915, the 11th grade had been added, and in 1921 the school went through the 12th grade. The first graduates were Vera Allen, Charlotte Thomas Piersol, and Gerald Walker. The high school was closed in 1964, but elementary students attended school in Royal until 1987. (Courtesy of Patty Rader Eucker.)

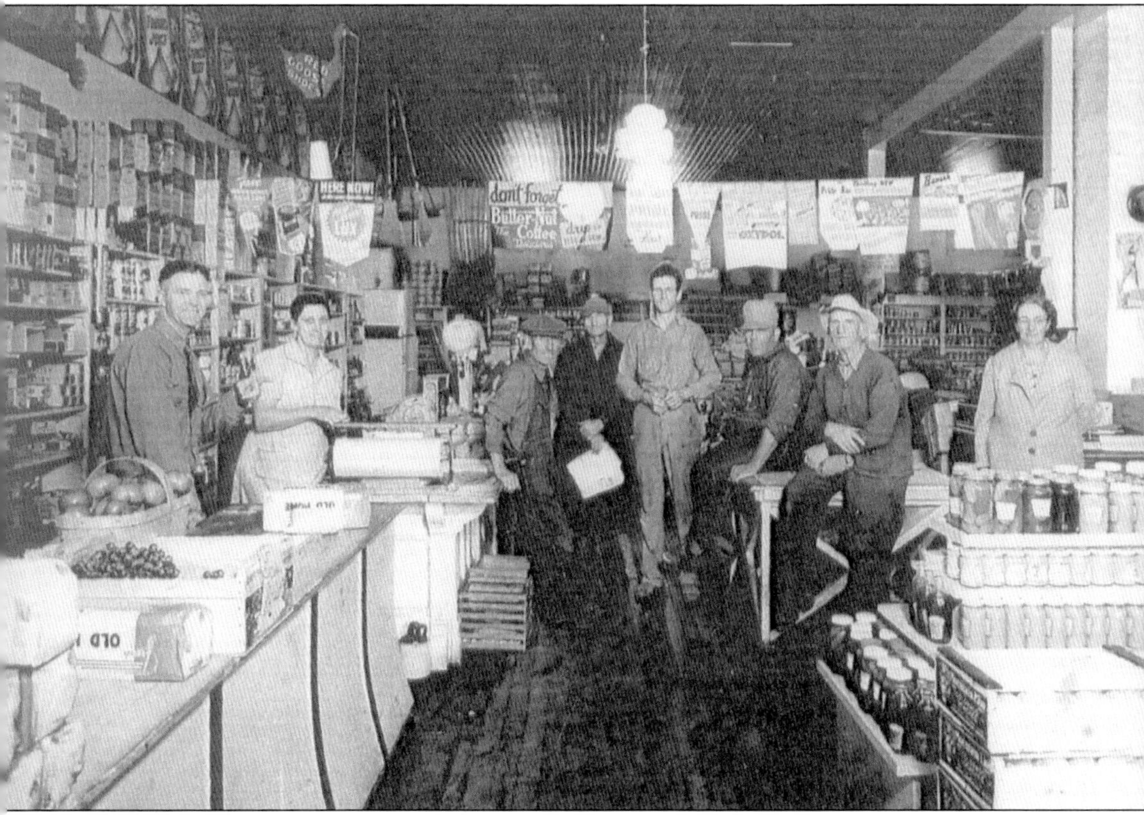

Matt Rundquist, a Royal pioneer, bought the Royal general store from Joe and Ed George in 1906. Rundquist had worked in Iowa's coal mines before staking a claim three miles southeast of Royal. In addition to buying the George brothers' store, Rundquist purchased a second store to eliminate competition. A few months later, his son Cliff took over the business, along with his brothers. They incorporated and bought another store in Clearwater and a ranch in Holt County before dissolving the corporation. When Cliff married his wife, Ollie, in 1911, she helped run the store. The couple was active in area organizations and maintained a diverse stock of goods by purchasing inventory from neighboring stores that went out of business. Ollie Rundquist kept the store open after her husband died in the 1970s. She operated it six days a week from 8:00 a.m. to 6:00 p.m. The store closed in the 1980s. Seen here from left to right are Cliff, Ollie, Fred Morsett, Fred Storm, Bob Hering, Jim Johnston, Elmer Lichty, and Saloma Hoddings. (Courtesy of Vanita M. Thomsen.)

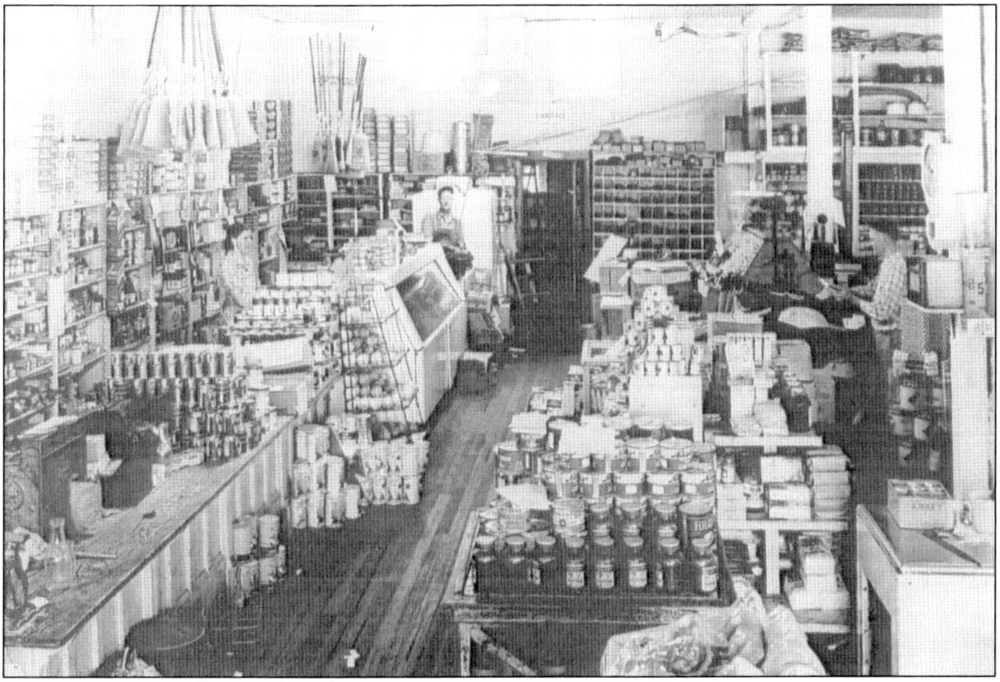

Through the years of its operation, the Rundquist Store carried a wide variety of products. The most difficult years were during the Great Depression. Foodstuffs were ordered by the barrel, and if they failed to sell in good time, mold destroyed them, causing profits to dwindle. (Courtesy of Vanita M. Thomsen.)

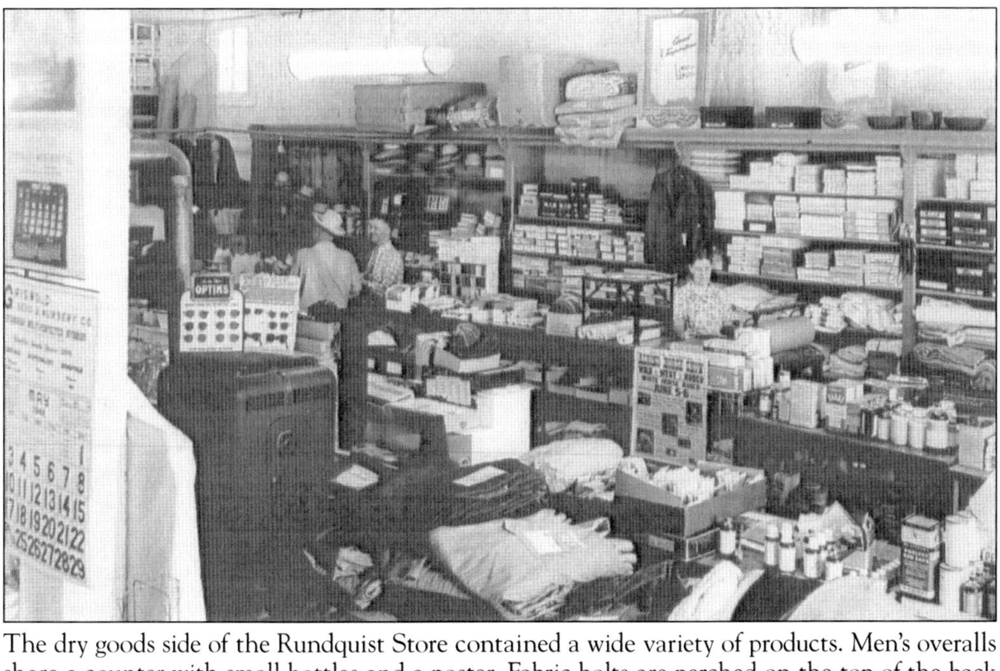

The dry goods side of the Rundquist Store contained a wide variety of products. Men's overalls share a counter with small bottles and a poster. Fabric bolts are perched on the top of the back shelves, and hats are displayed on a nearby shelf. Merchandise fills every available space. (Courtesy of Vanita M. Thomsen.)

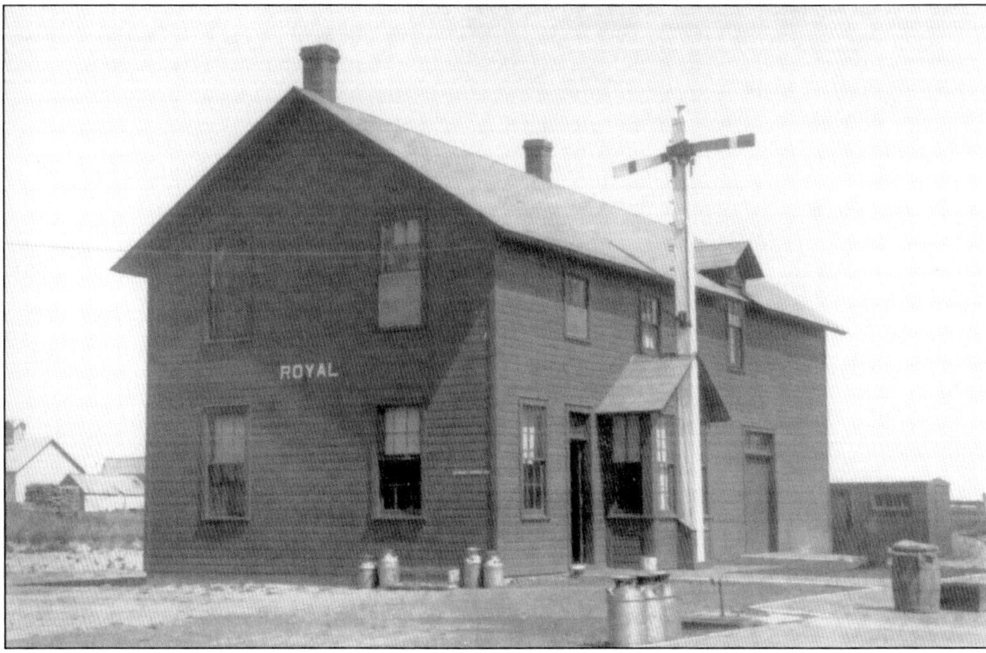

The 1890 Burlington depot, seen here, replaced the first depot built by the Pacific Short Line in Savage, which was renamed Royal in 1890. Cream cans stand outside the depot, waiting for the train to transport them to the city. (Courtesy of Patty Rader Eucker.)

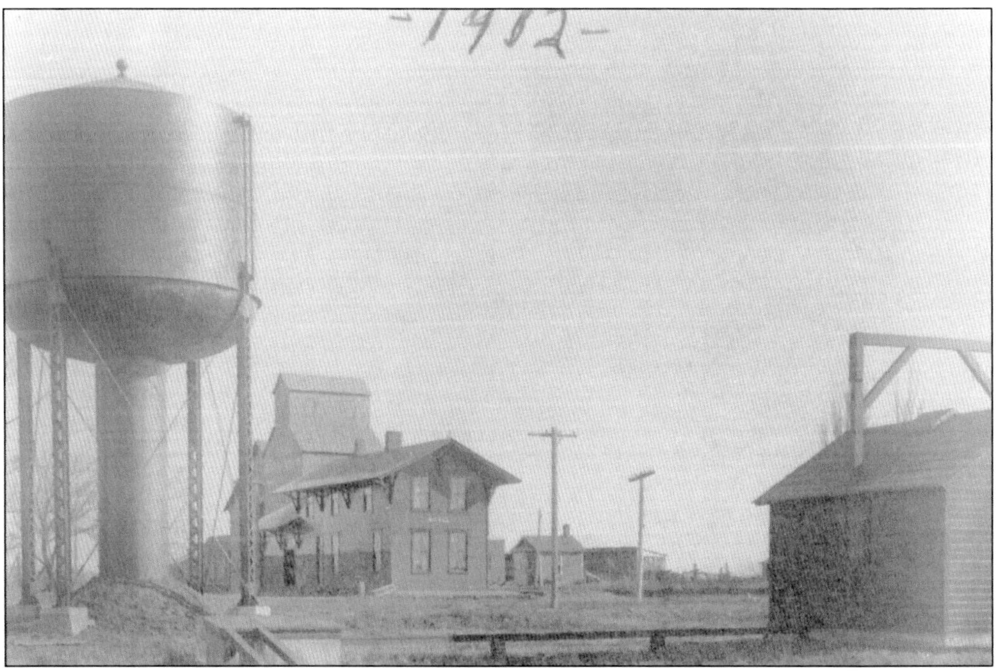

By 1912, the Royal depot area showed the improvements that had developed since 1890. An elevator has been erected for grain storage, and a water tank stands ready to fill the train engine. The telephone lines strung nearby indicate communication progress. (Courtesy of Patty Rader Eucker.)

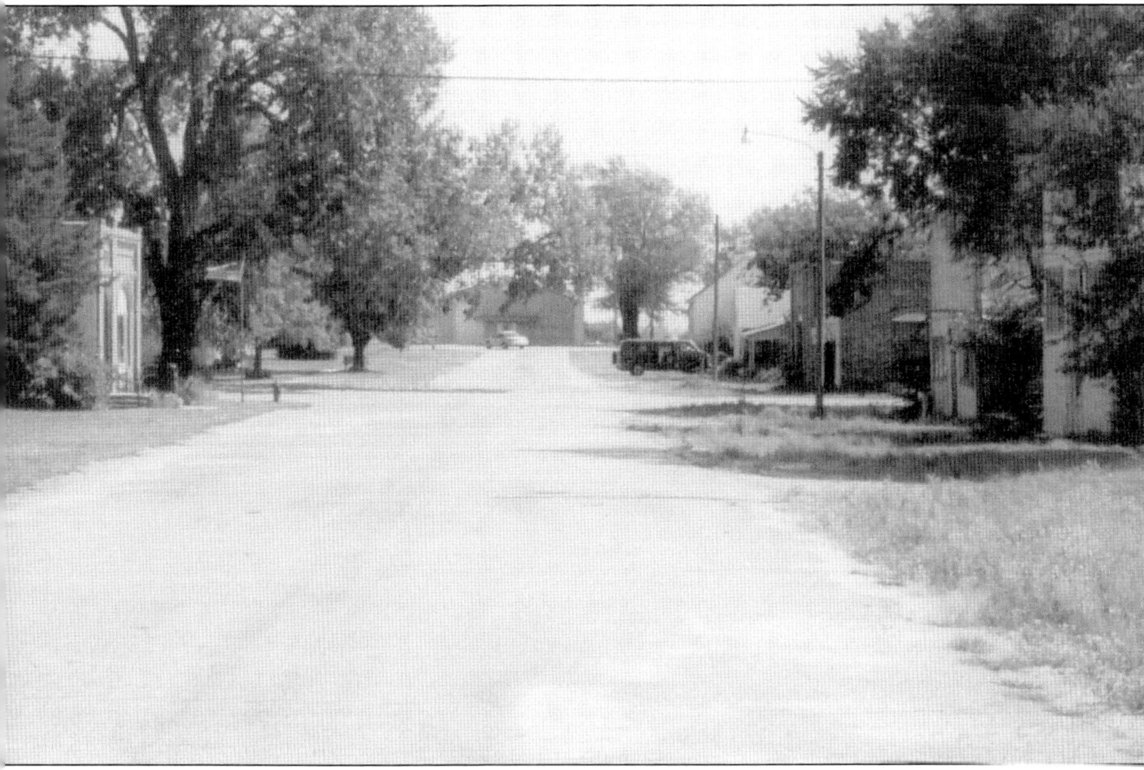

Seen here in the fall of 2006, Royal's Main Street is now a tree-shaded avenue. On the left is a former bank, which eventually became the post office. The former school auditorium is at the end of the street. Constructed in 1961, the building opened at Christmastime for a school band concert. The Methodist church, now closed, is to the right of the auditorium. (Courtesy of Patty Rader Eucker.)

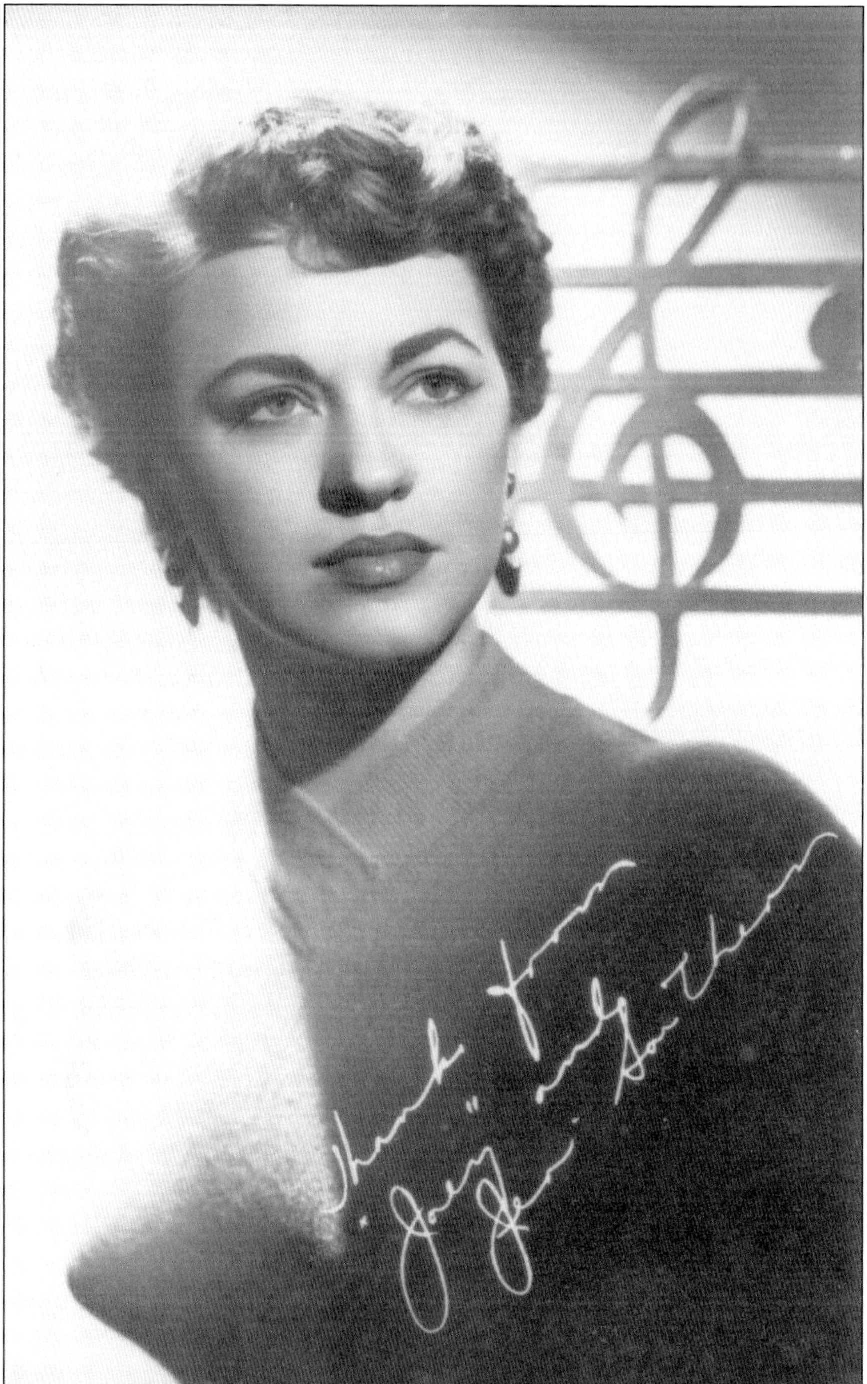

Jazz pianist and singer Jeri Southern was born in Royal. At age three, she began playing the piano, and at age six she began studying classical piano. During her musical studies, she became interested in jazz. After a successful singing and movie career, Southern taught music before moving to California to work on films. She died in 1991. (Courtesy of Patty Rader Eucker.)

Ten

Family Fun
Attractions and Recreation

With the founding of towns, recreation for many county residents moved beyond home-based activities to include public entertainment. Parks provided a venue for picnics, carnivals, fairs, horse races, and spectator sports. When Chautauqua companies pitched tents in parks for three- to seven-day stays, audiences experienced an enrichment of cultural knowledge. Many folks saw movies for the first time at a Chautauqua. Every town had a park, but Neligh's Riverside Park was the setting for the annual county fair, providing a carnival and horse racing for fairgoers to enjoy. The famous pacer horse Shade On trained on the park track and was stabled there.

By 1931, the Neligh American Legion post sponsored a baseball team that played in the park. Town bands were organized in nearly every community. The Clearwater Men's Cornet Band developed an outstanding reputation, playing in many areas of the state. A group of enterprising Clearwater women formed a second band, the Ladies X.L. Band.

Between 1920 and 1941, Clarence Dikeman's farm, in a valley along Verdigris Creek, developed into a park that attracted people from miles around. At first, they came to enjoy the shade of stately trees, providing relief from hot summer winds. Through the years, the park added a picnic area and a swimming pool as well as a golf course, and Verdigris Creek provided fishermen with trout. Today, the Ashfall Fossil Beds are the most popular attraction in the county.

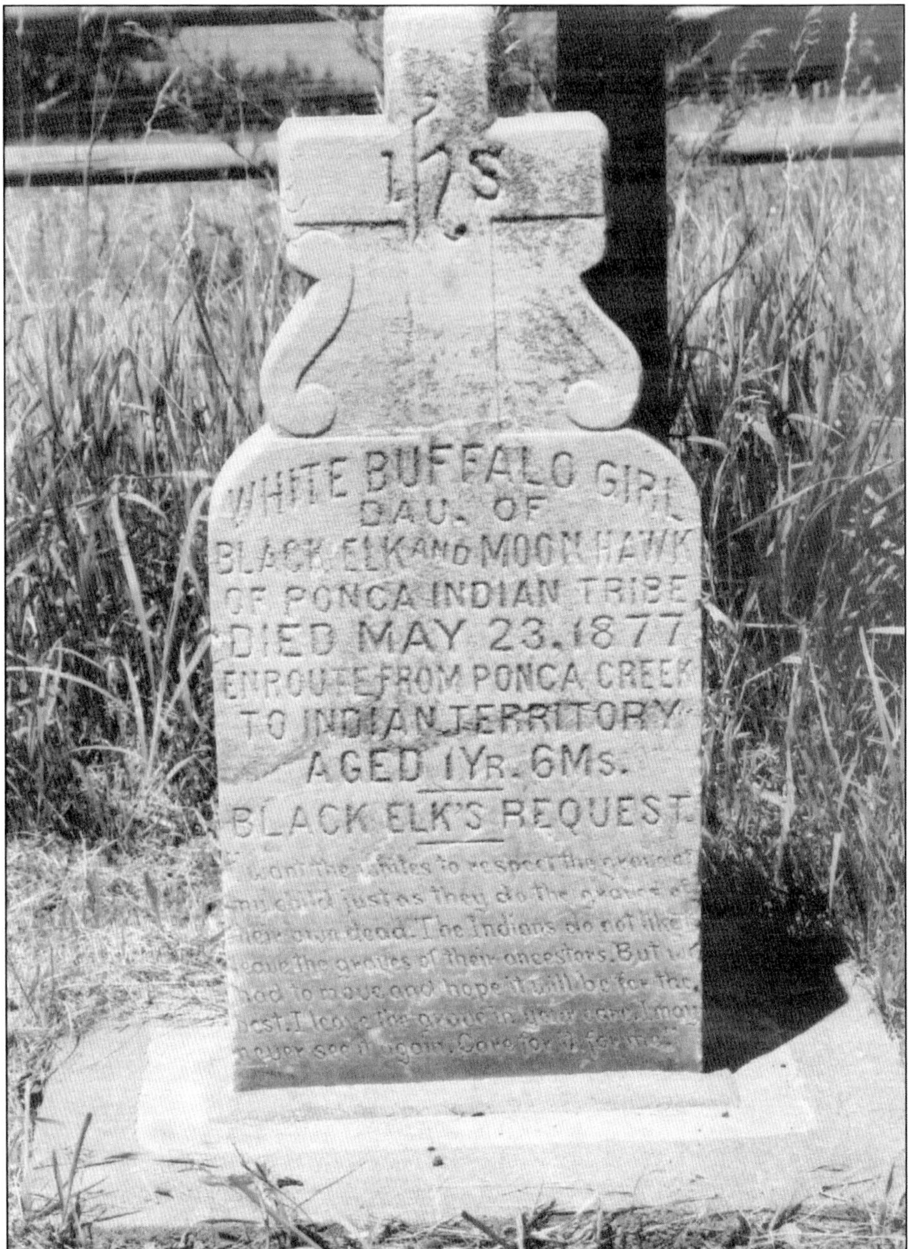

Under the leadership of Indian agents, the Ponca Indians were forced to leave their home on Ponca Creek in the spring of 1877 and begin their trek to Oklahoma Indian Territory, known as the Trail of Tears. Rainy weather forced the tribe to stop for several days near Neligh. During their stay, the 18-month-old daughter of Black Elk and Moon Hawk died. She was buried in the Neligh Cemetery, and Black Elk asked the people of the town to care for her grave. Through the years, necessary repairs have been made to the gravesite, and every Memorial Day children place flowers on the grave. Black Elk's words are engraved on the tombstone: "I want the whites to respect the grave of my child just as they do the graves of their own dead." In 1972, the Nebraska Historical Society placed a marker at the entrance to Laurel Hill Cemetery. (ACHS.)

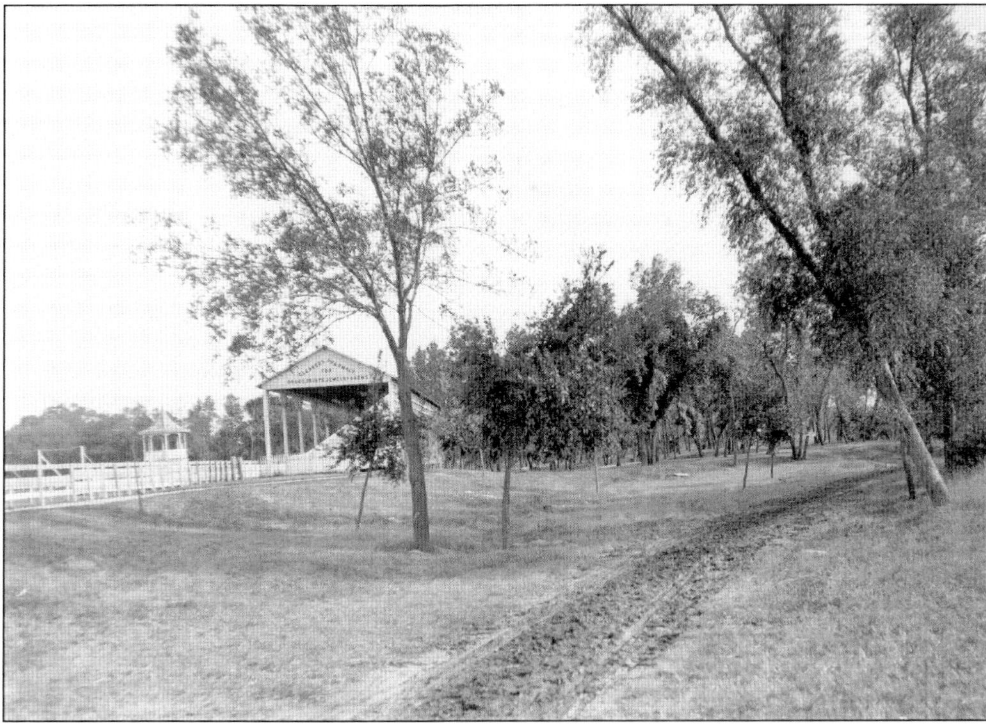

The desire for a town park inspired a group of Neligh businessmen to clear underbrush from a grove of trees at the fairgrounds in 1892. In 1903, the city passed an ordinance authorizing the purchase of 42 acres from the fair association for use as a park. (ACHS.)

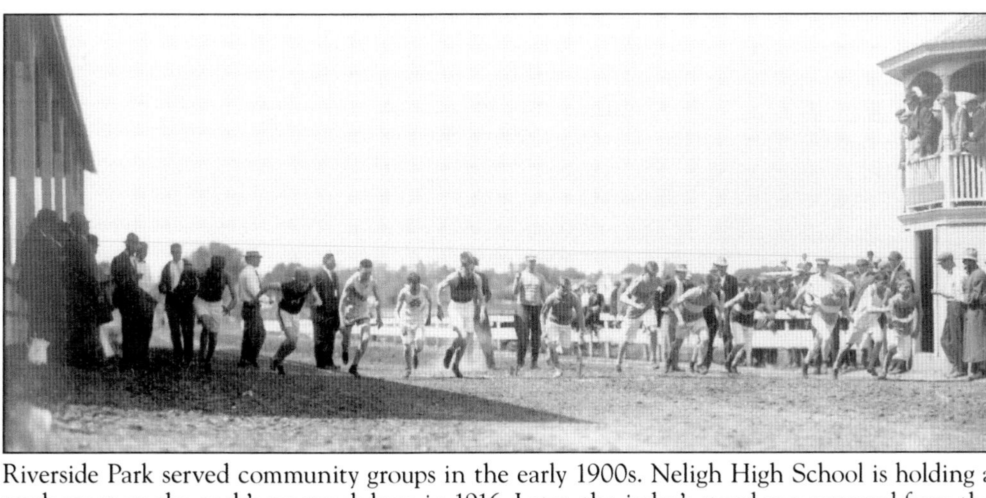

Riverside Park served community groups in the early 1900s. Neligh High School is holding a track meet on the park's racetrack here in 1916. Later, the judge's stand was removed from the sidelines. (ACHS.)

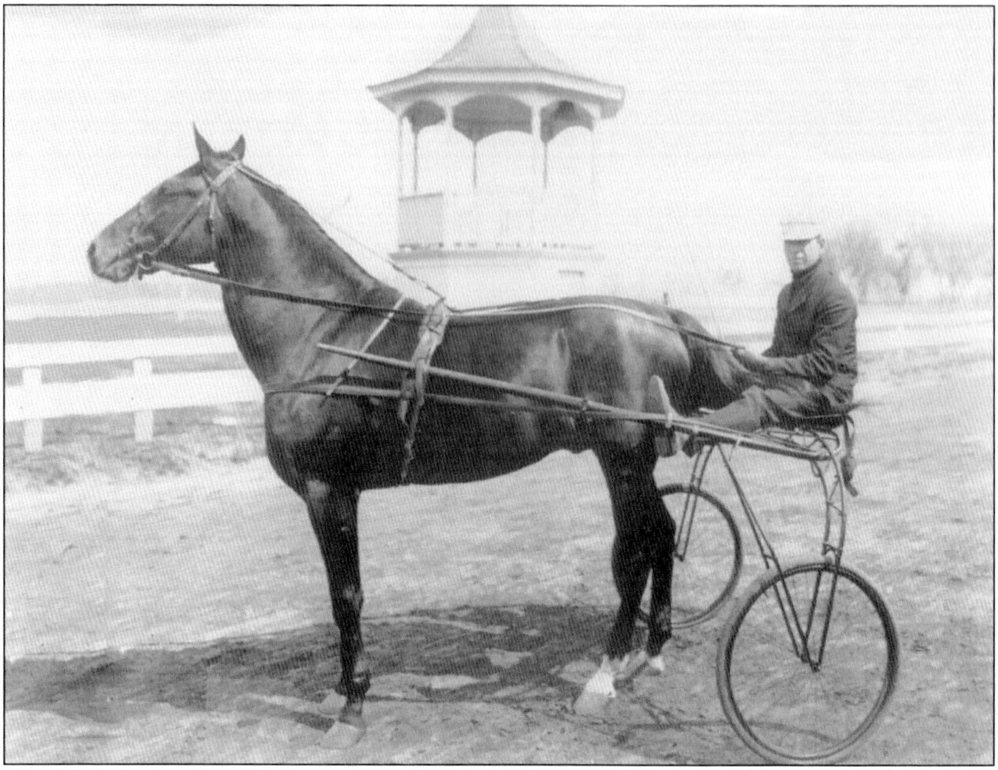

The pacer Shade On, owned by John Kay of Ewing, trained on the Riverside Park track and was stabled at the park after Kay and his family moved to Neligh in 1904. Shade On was a nationally known winner whose record time was 2:08.25. Kay is seen here behind the horse. (ACHS.)

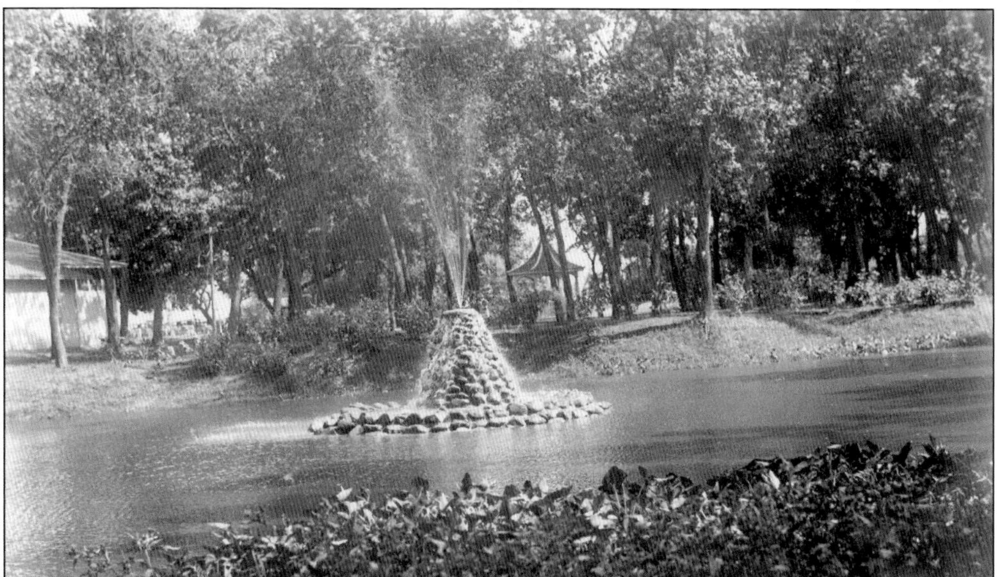

Now the site of the swimming pool, the Riverside Park lagoon was a popular feature, seen here around 1930. Built of local stone, the fountain spouted water into the air. The judge's stand from the racetrack was moved to an area behind the lagoon in 1928. (ACHS.)

In 1935, Byron Fuller designed and built a swinging bridge in Riverside Park. When officials asked him if the bridge would stand, he assured them that it would be in place 50 years later. The bridge remained a curiosity for park visitors for 75 years. It washed away in the flood of 2010. (Courtesy of George Strassler.)

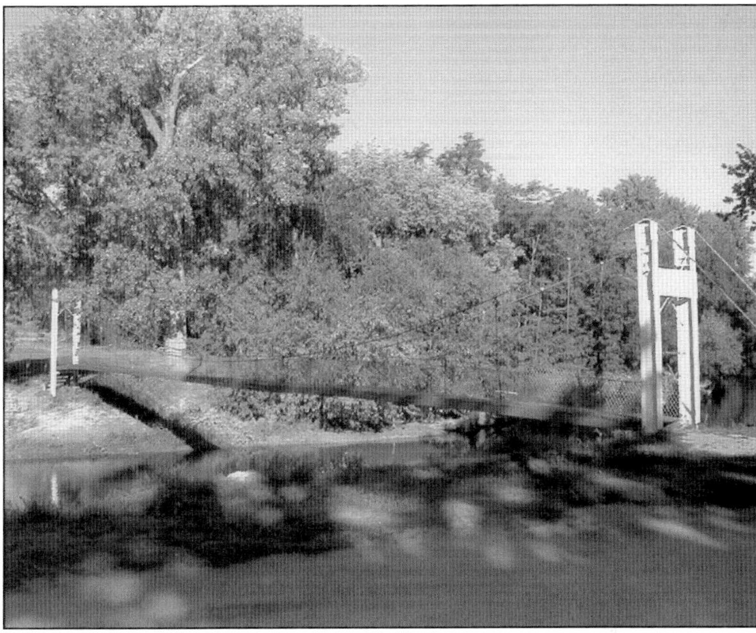

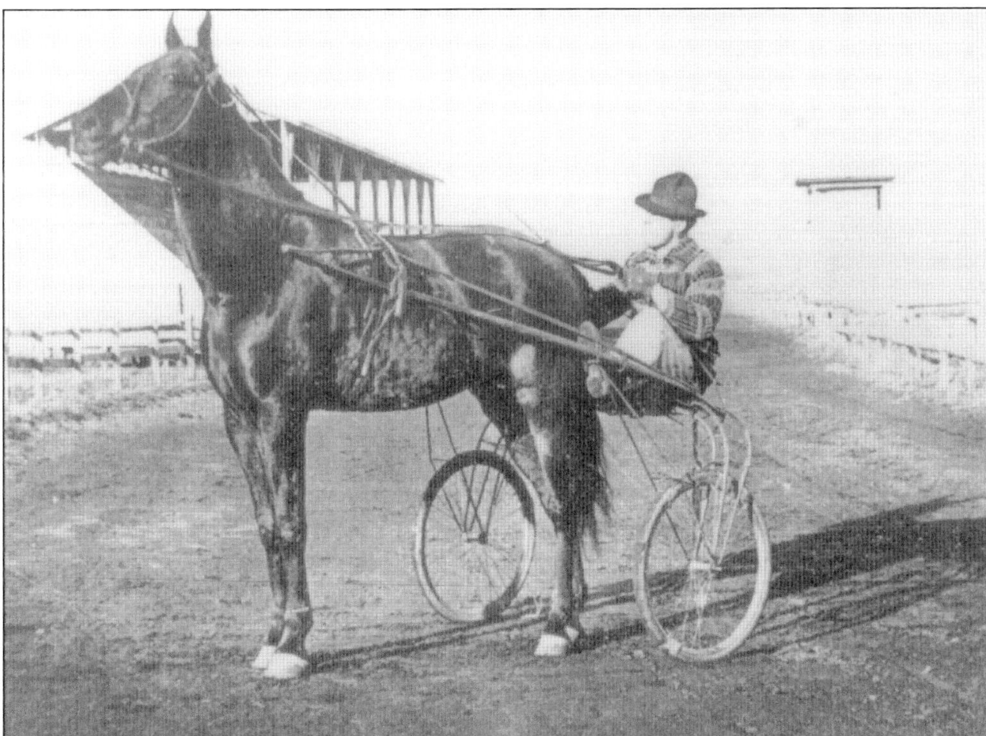

From the late 1880s through the 1890s, horse races took place on a track west of Tilden when the weather permitted. Many of the races were sulky races. Sulkies were light, two-wheeled carriages for a single person. This horse, Bessie Billion, participated in the Saturday races and is seen here with her owner, Herbert Osborn. (Courtesy of Arlene Hofmann.)

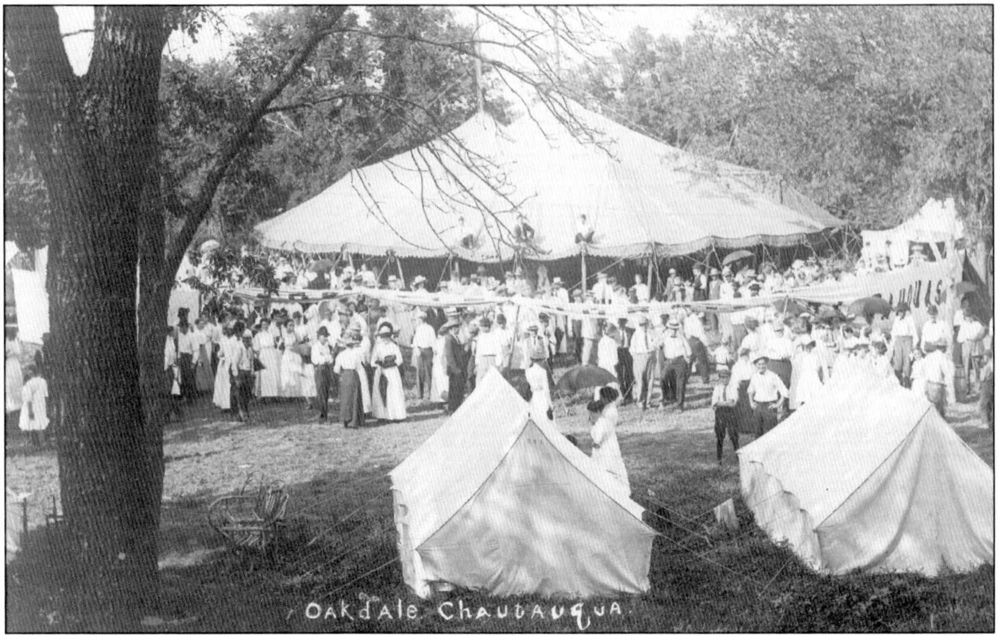

In the early 1900s, Chautauquas provided entertainment for Oakdale citizens and were a welcome diversion from everyday life. Inside the big tent, people listened to music and lectures on a variety of subjects. The traveling Chautauqua gave people an opportunity to expand their horizons and improve their minds. (Courtesy of Lois Johnson.)

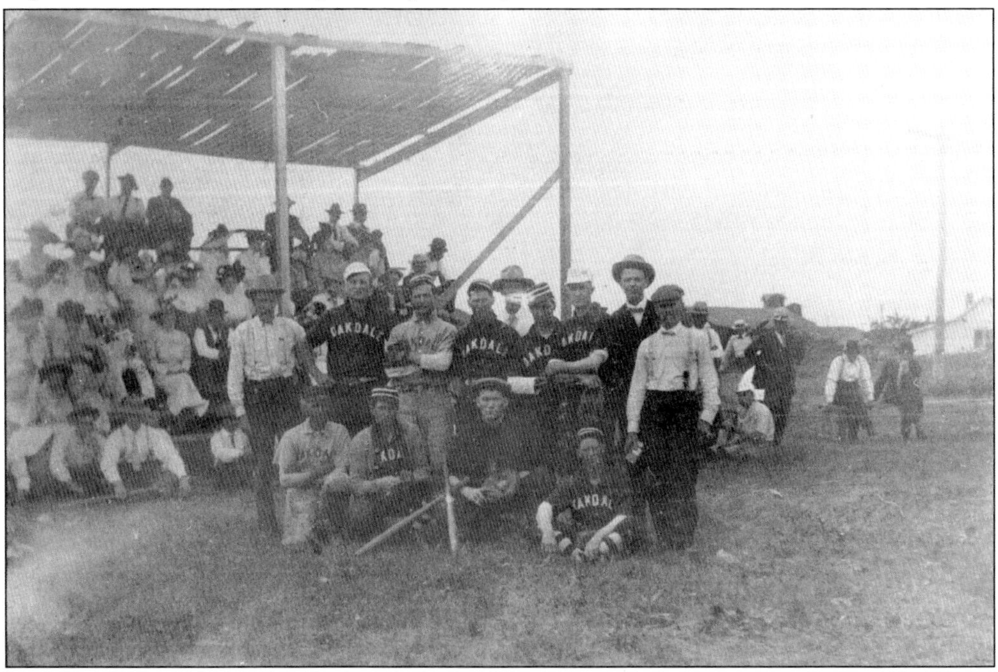

Oakdale's first baseball league started in 1874. The first teams were the Excelsiors of Oakdale and the Antelopes of Cedar Creek. This Oakdale team poses for a photograph before a game in 1909. Sitting beneath an open-air shelter with a roof of wooden slats, fans wait to cheer for their team. (Courtesy of Lois Johnson.)

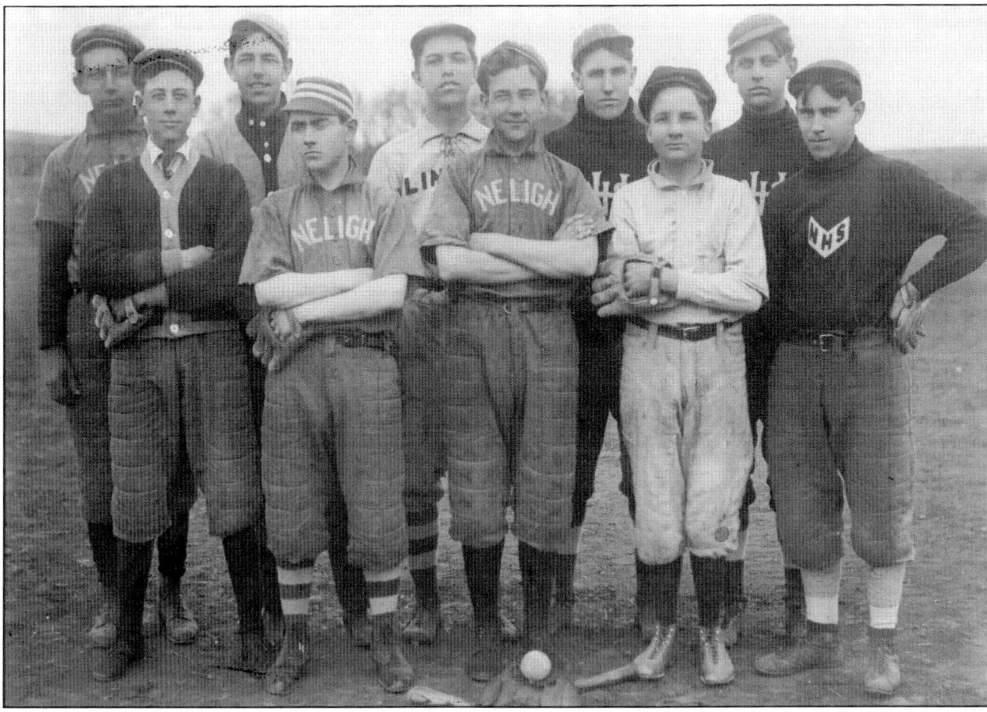

These Neligh boys formed a team around 1910, competing with teams from surrounding towns in the summer. The boys include, from left to right, (first row) Arch Sellery, Oliver Powell, Fred Sellery, unidentified, and Arthur Miller; (second row) unidentified, Charles Ryan, Leon Learnerd, Arch Fletcher, and George Harriman. (ACHS.)

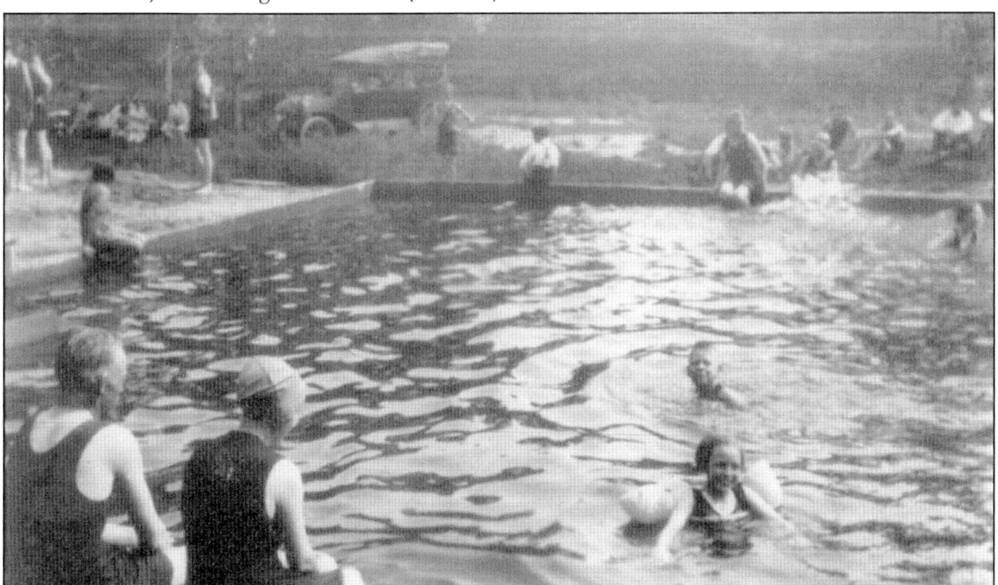

Dikeman's Park was 2.5 miles northeast of Royal. Established in 1920 on Clarence Dikeman's farm, the park attracted Sunday visitors from across the county. In 1923, the new swimming pool measured 50 feet by 90 feet. One end was eight feet deep, and it was the only cement swimming pool between Sioux City, Iowa, and Chadron, Nebraska. (Courtesy of Duard Demptster.)

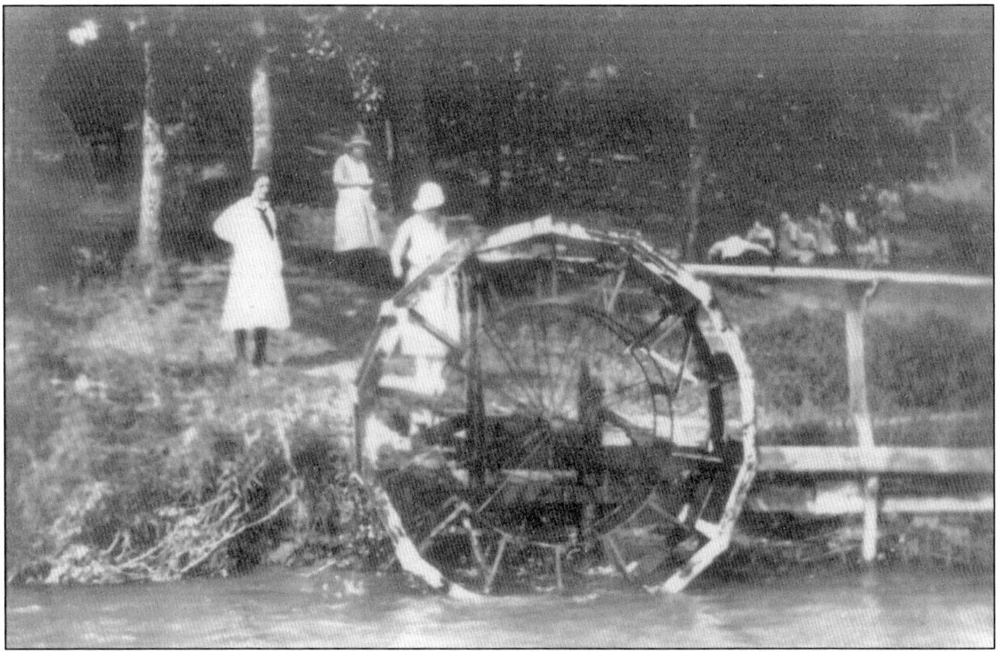

In 1923, Clarence Dikeman designed and built this waterwheel to supply water to a new, larger swimming pool. The waterwheel picked up freshwater from Verdigris Creek and dumped it in the sluice, which carried it to the swimming pool. Every Monday, the pool was drained and refilled with fresh creek water. Seen here from left to right are Esther Grove Demptser, Carrie Grove Wilson, and Bertha Grove. (Courtesy of Duard Demptster.)

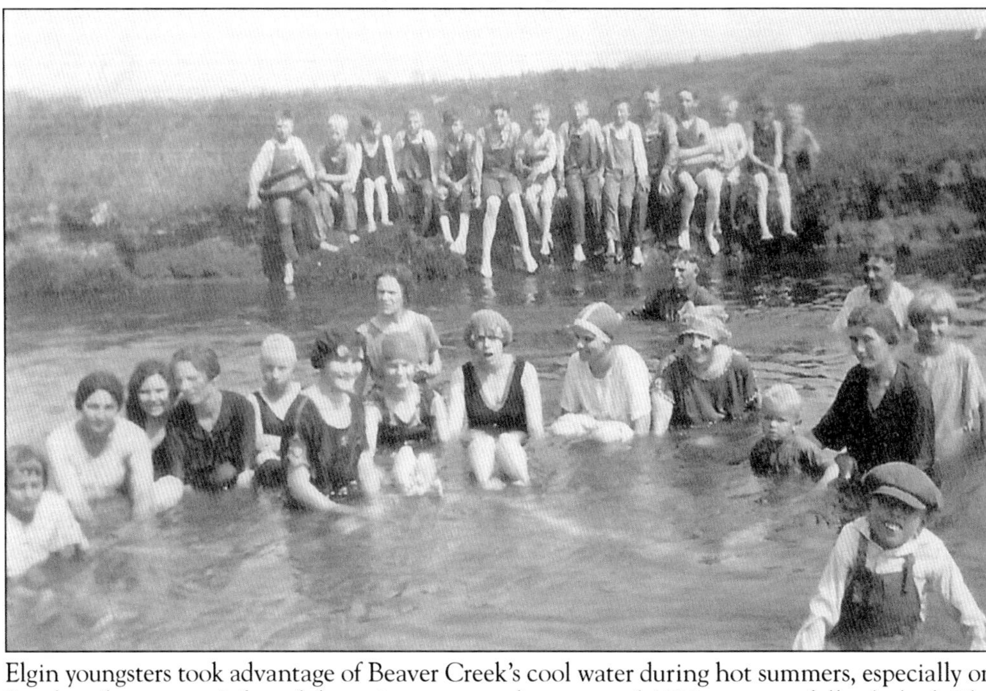

Elgin youngsters took advantage of Beaver Creek's cool water during hot summers, especially on Sunday afternoons. A few of the swimmers seen here around 1920 are even fully clothed. The boys perched on the bank wait for their turn in the water. (Courtesy of Robert Busteed.)

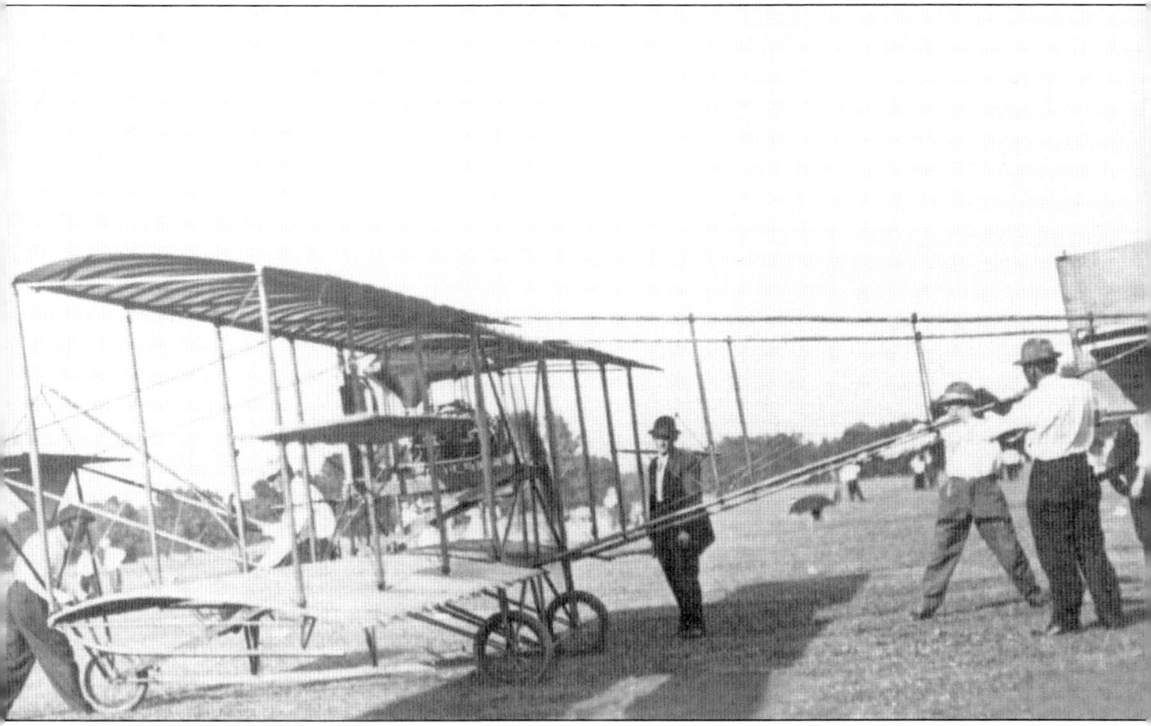

During a July 1912 Free Days celebration in Clearwater, John and Matt Savidge of Ewing, Nebraska, brought their biplane to town for a flying demonstration. After Ewing won a ball game with Elgin, the so-called "bird men" took to the air. Even though conditions were not right for flying, Matt flew over Clearwater Creek and Charley Nelson's farm. He then landed with the ease and grace of a bird. Later, John took the biplane up, but it dipped and rocked, forcing him to land. Dead air spaces made it too dangerous to fly that evening, so the brothers ended their demonstration. John and Matt were two of eight Savidge brothers who barnstormed over Antelope County until Matt died in a 1916 crash. The brothers designed their plane based on an idea George Savidge had contrived after accidentally sailing off a haystack while trying to take off his sheepskin coat in a high wind. (Courtesy of Walter Patras.)

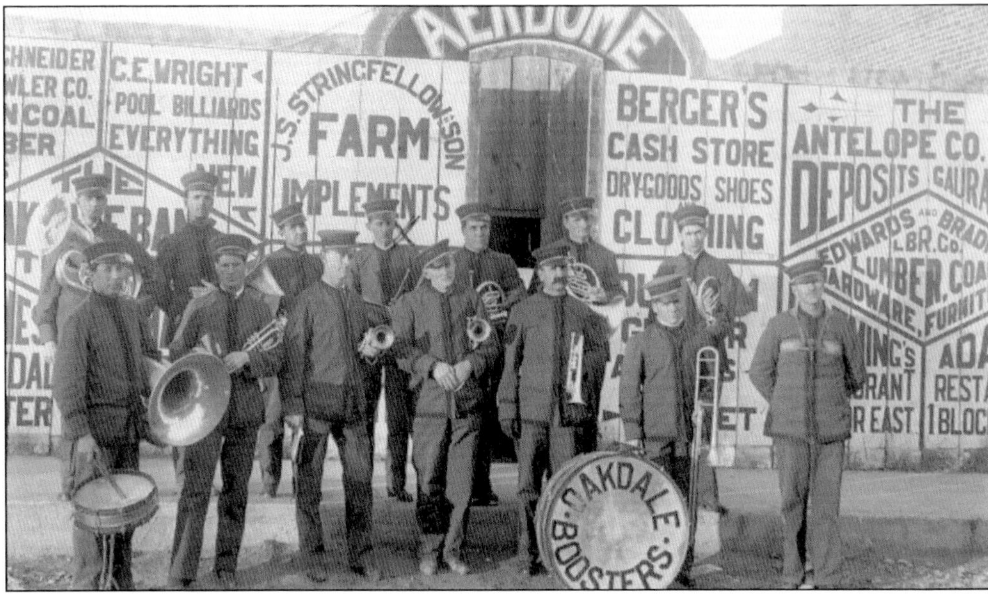

Oakdale organized a brass band in 1878. By 1887, it also had a cornet band. In 1911, this new band formed, becoming a popular attraction at area functions. Although it was a concert band, this photograph of the group taken in front of the Aerodrome Theater shows only brass instruments. Oakdale was the first town in the county to provide weekly band concerts. (Courtesy of Lois Johnson.)

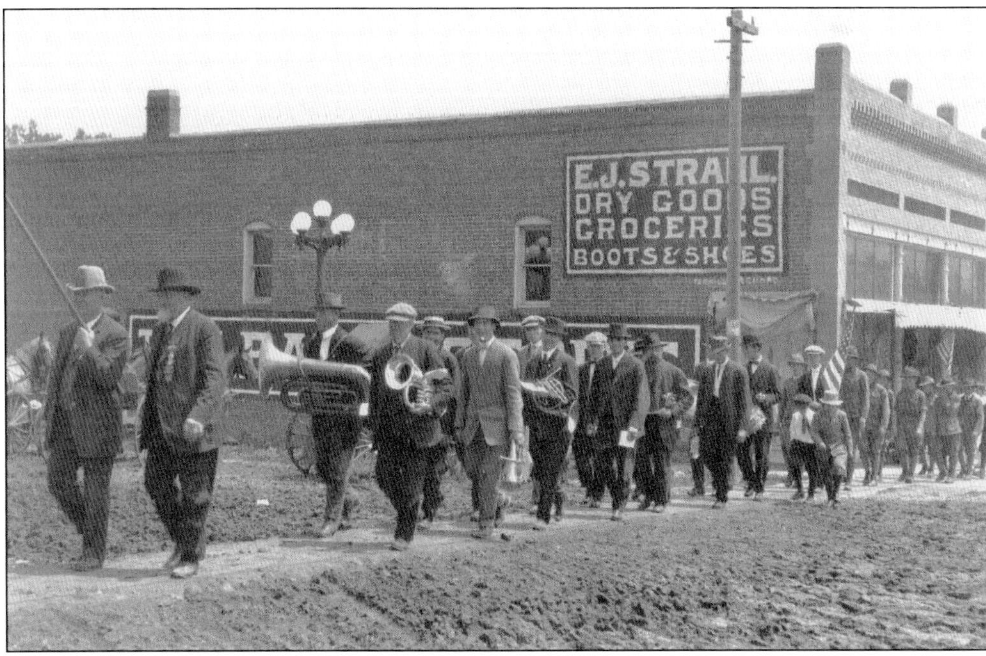

The Brunswick Band marches along Main Street with flag bearers bringing up the rear, reflecting the patriotism that dominated the early 1900s. "Old Glory," the American flag, was the subject of many compositions. (ACHS.)

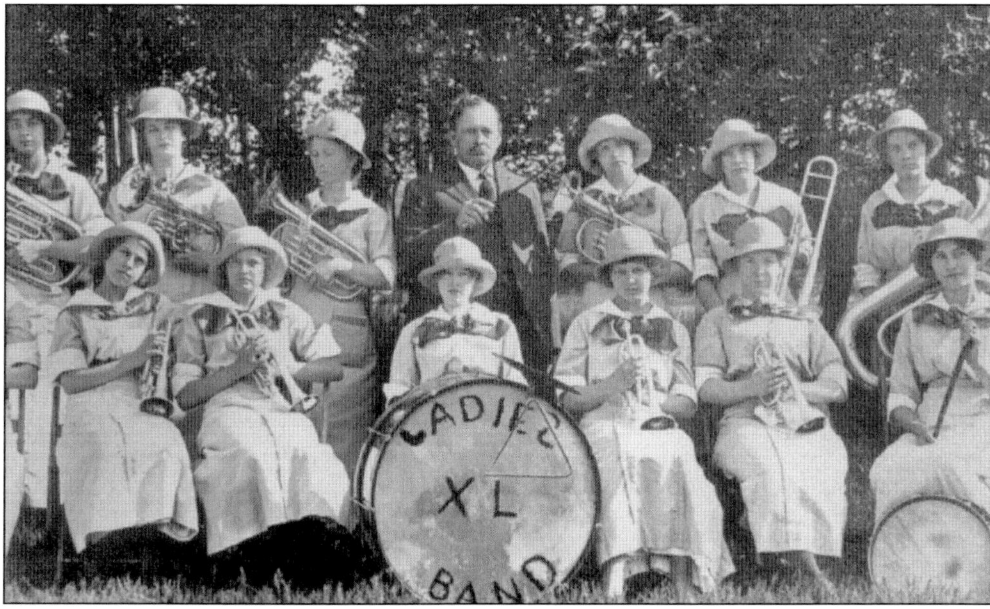

By 1916, every town in the county had a band, but only Clearwater had a ladies band. The Ladies X.L. Band performed concerts in surrounding communities and had a large following. The band members here include, from left to right, (first row) Dana Smith, Eunice Graham, Kit Mitchel, Maise Miller, Unice Edward, Esta Roth, and Emily Uridel; (second row) Cladys Walters, Verna Phillips, Mrs. Harrel, Professor Weber, Goldie Mitchel, Unice Hanson, and Gladys Hanson. (Courtesy of Walter Patras.)

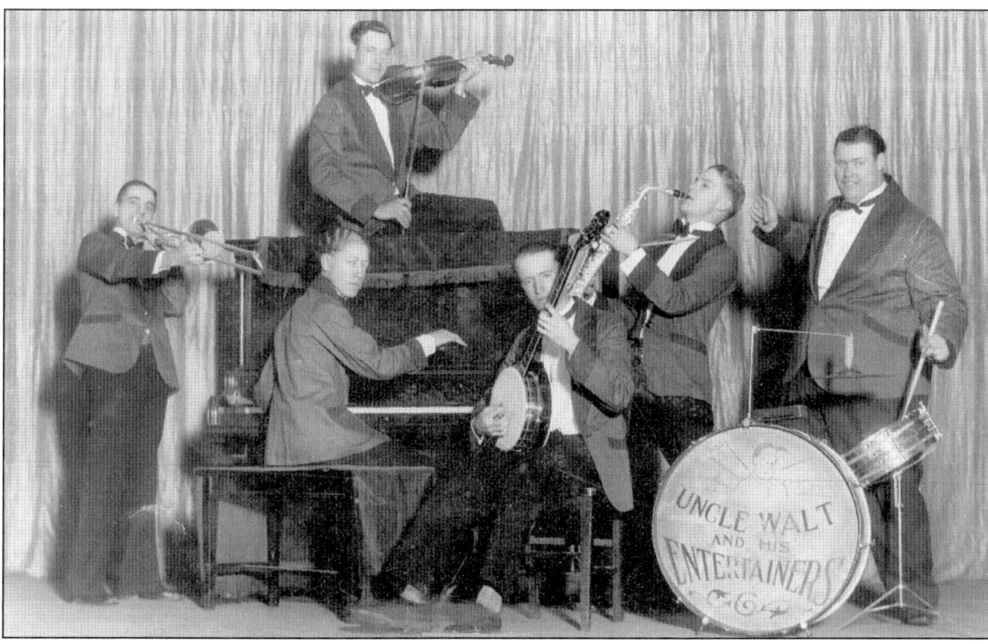

Eddie Bagley and his band were popular entertainers in the Oakdale area around 1925. With piano, trombone, fiddle, saxophone, banjo, and drums, the band provided music for dancing and listening. Note the bass drum displaying the name "Uncle Walt," which referred to the popular comic strip *Gasoline Alley*. (Courtesy of Lois Johnson.)

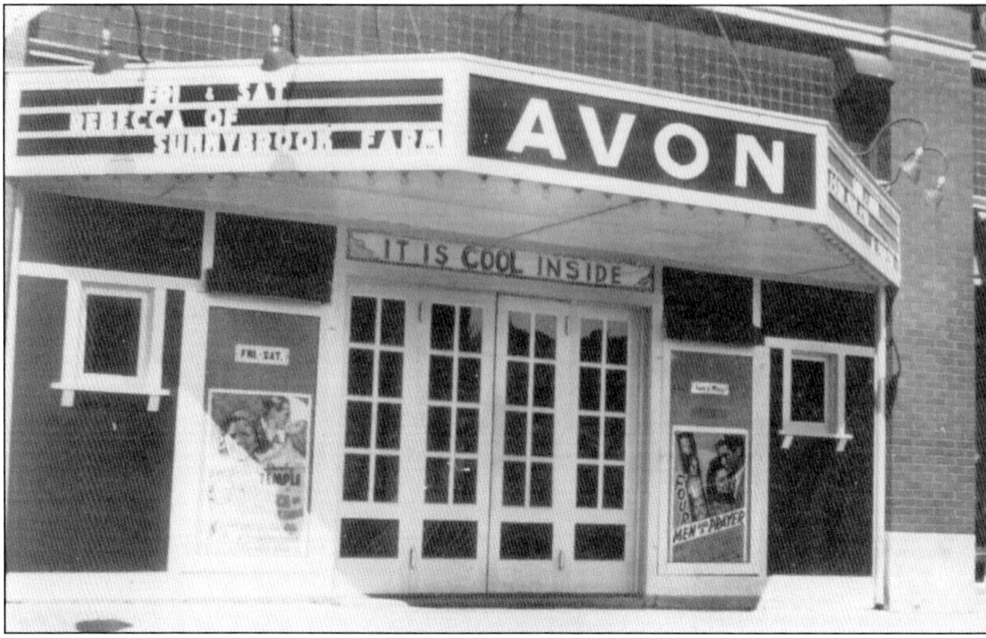

In 1910, silent movies were shown at the Elgin Opera House, which later became the Community Theater. Manager Frank Gross sponsored a contest to rename the theater in 1930, and it became the Avalon. In 1936, the theater moved to the south part of the Fair Store, and in 1938 it was renamed the Avon. The theater closed in 1971. (ACHS.)

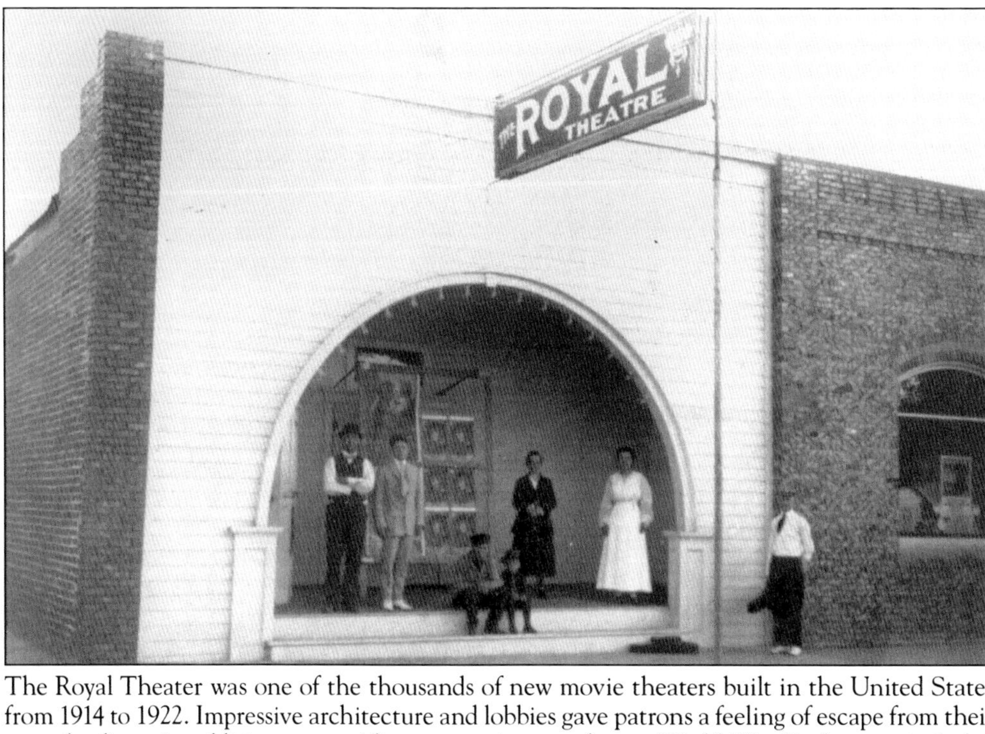

The Royal Theater was one of the thousands of new movie theaters built in the United States from 1914 to 1922. Impressive architecture and lobbies gave patrons a feeling of escape from their everyday lives. In addition to providing entertainment during World War II, theaters included newsreels about the war and information about bond drives. (Courtesy of Patty Rader Eucker.)

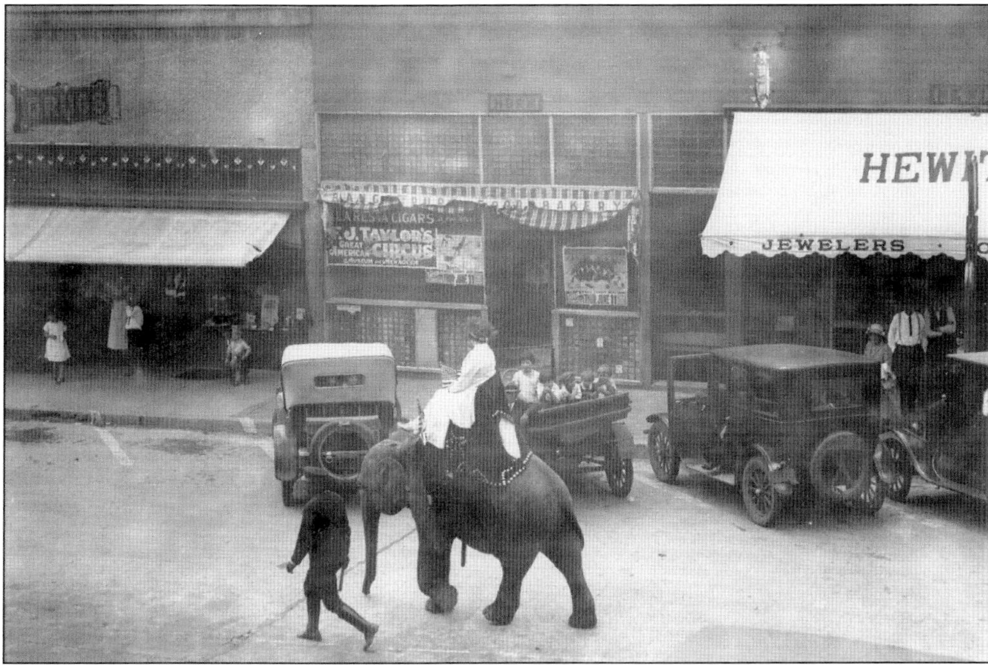

The woman riding atop a circus elephant in a c. 1930 parade fascinates onlookers. The sign in the window of the center store advertises it as F.J. Taylor's Great American Circus. Hewitt's Jewelry Store is on the right. (ACHS.)

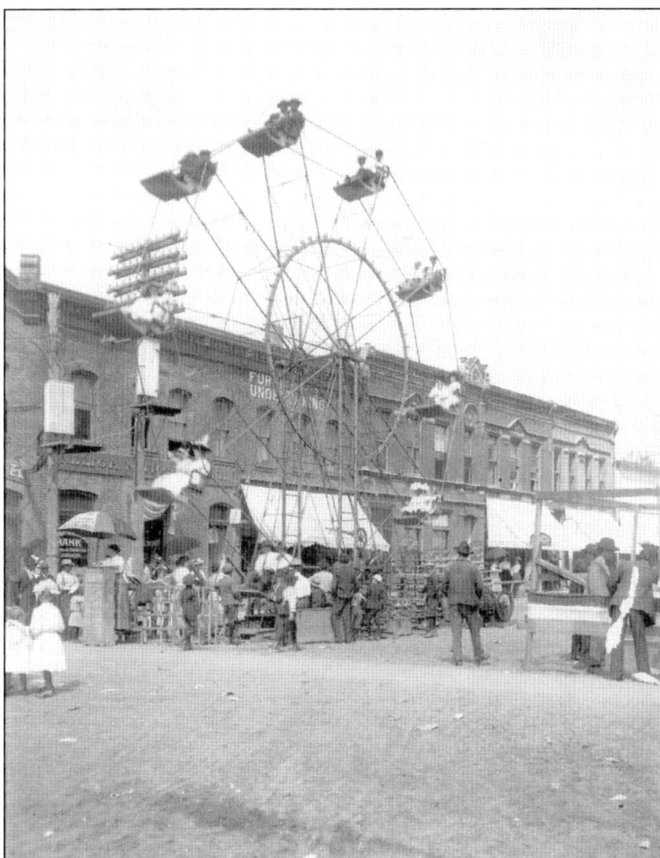

A Ferris wheel on Main Street in Neligh, seen here in 1910, attracts riders during a festival. It is positioned in front of the local furniture and undertaking business. The first Ferris wheel appeared at the 1893 World's Fair in Chicago. (ACHS.)

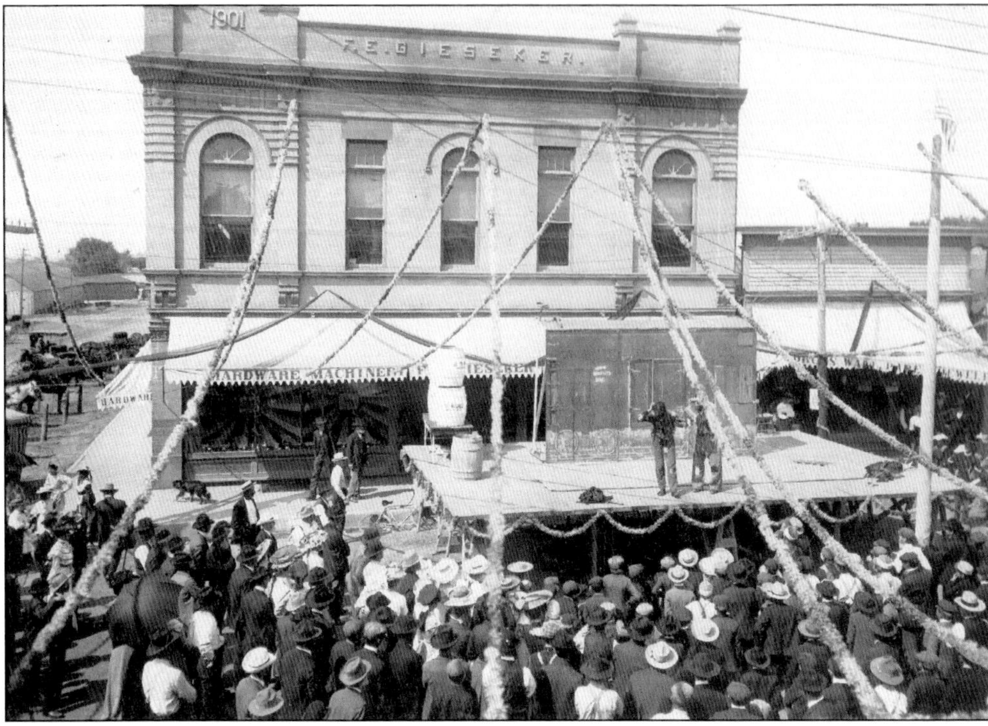

During the 1908 Fourth of July celebration in Neligh, Happy Hooligan and his sidekick Gloomy Gus entertain area residents. *Happy Hooligan* was a popular comic strip in the early 1900s about the explorations of a hobo who encountered misadventures and bad luck but always remained cheerful. (ACHS.)

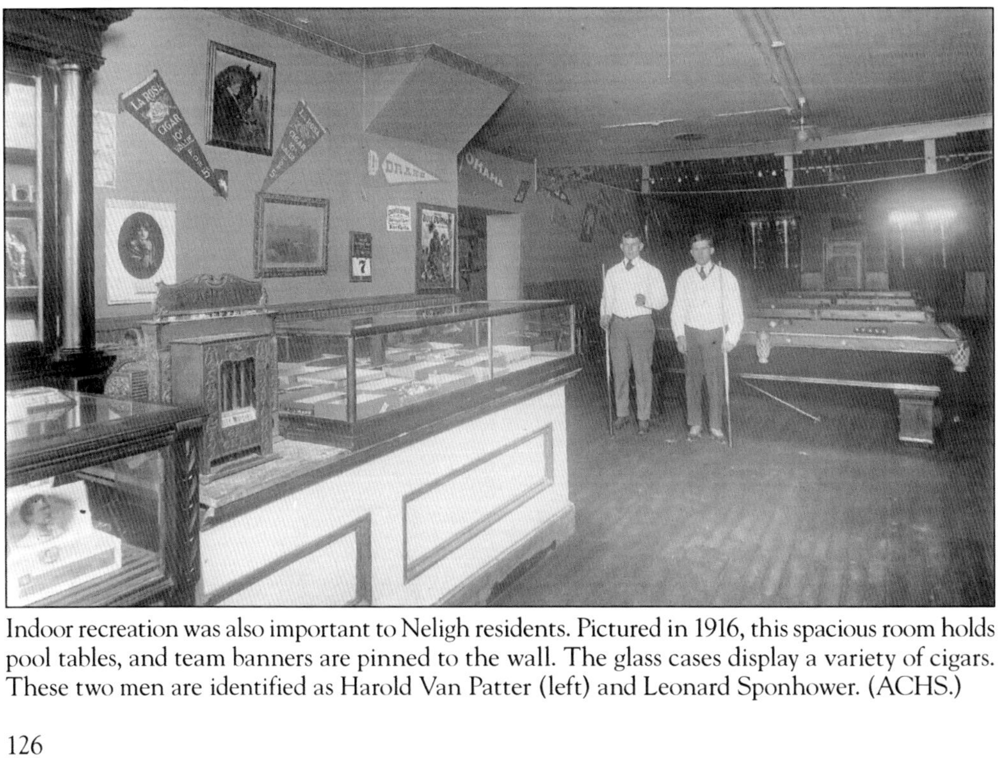

Indoor recreation was also important to Neligh residents. Pictured in 1916, this spacious room holds pool tables, and team banners are pinned to the wall. The glass cases display a variety of cigars. These two men are identified as Harold Van Patter (left) and Leonard Sponhower. (ACHS.)

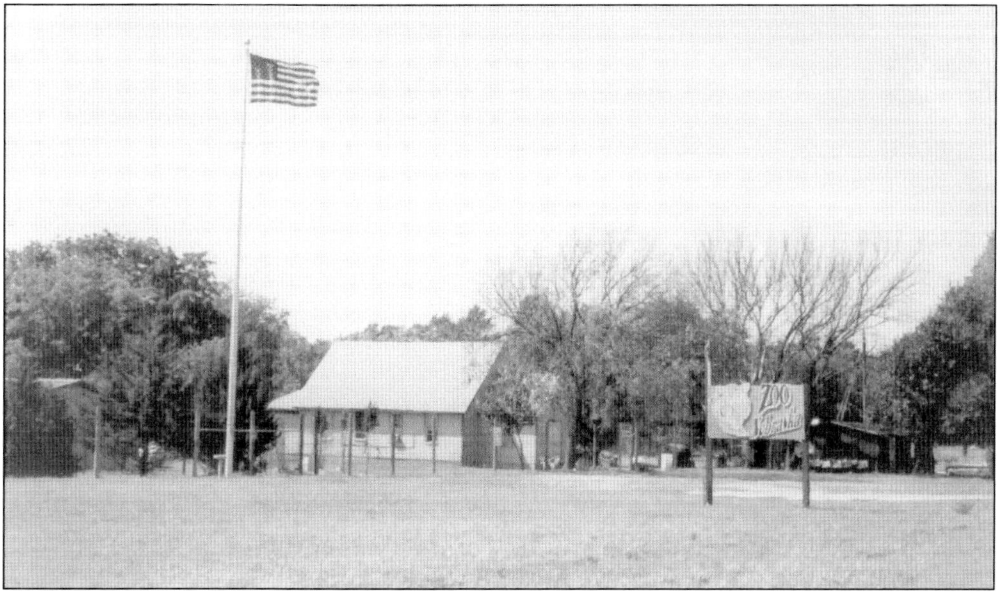

Zoo Nebraska was established first as a primate center in 1987, with one chimpanzee named Rueben. At its peak, the zoo had a wide variety of animals, including several chimpanzees. It closed in 2008 after three chimpanzees escaped and had to be killed. (Courtesy of Patty Rader Eucker.)

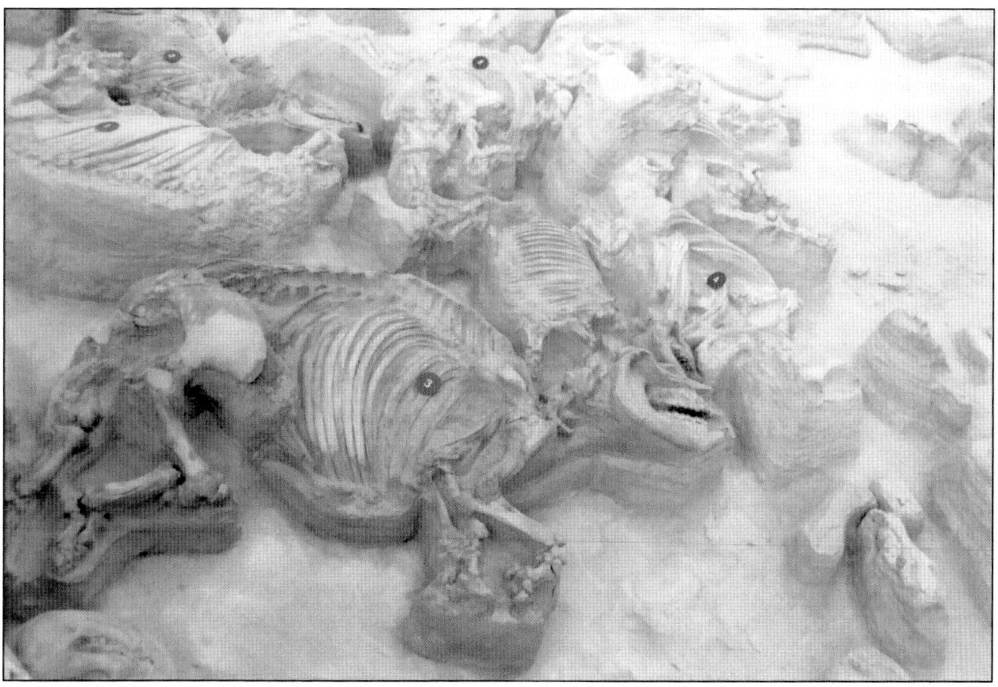

In the recently constructed Rhino Barn at the Ashfall Fossil Beds near Royal, the fully articulated fossil skeletons of a rhinoceros cow and calf have been left in place for the public to view. During the Miocene Age, a volcanic eruption in the Rocky Mountains blanketed the Royal area with ash to a depth of one foot. Today, Ashfall Fossil Beds is a Nebraska State Historical Park and a National Natural Landmark. (Courtesy of Kenneth Krohn.)